MEDIEVAL TRANSLATIONS
AND CULTURAL DISCOURSE

THE MOVEMENT OF TEXTS IN ENGLAND, FRANCE AND SCANDINAVIA

Medieval Translations and Cultural Discourse

The Movement of Texts in England, France and Scandinavia

Sif Rikhardsdottir

D. S. BREWER

© Sif Rikhardsdottir 2012

All Rights Reserved. Except as permitted under current legislation
no part of this work may be photocopied, stored in a retrieval system,
published, performed in public, adapted, broadcast,
transmitted, recorded or reproduced in any form or by any means,
without the prior permission of the copyright owner

The right of Sif Rikhardsdottir to be identified as
the author of this work has been asserted in accordance with
sections 77 and 78 of the Copyright, Designs and Patents Act 1988

First published 2012
D. S. Brewer, Cambridge
Paperback edition 2018

ISBN 978 1 84384 289 7 hardback
ISBN 978 1 84384 494 5 paperback

D. S. Brewer is an imprint of Boydell & Brewer Ltd
PO Box 9, Woodbridge, Suffolk IP12 3DF, UK
and of Boydell & Brewer Inc.
668 Mt Hope Avenue, Rochester, NY 14620–2731, USA
website: www.boydellandbrewer.com

A CIP catalogue record for this book is available
from the British Library

The publisher has no responsibility for the continued existence or accuracy
of URLs for external or third-party internet websites referred to in this book,
and does not guarantee that any content on such websites is,
or will remain, accurate or appropriate

Typeset in Warnock Pro by Word and Page, Chester

Contents

Acknowledgements   vii
A Note on Translations   viii
Timeline, 1100–1700   ix

Introduction   1

1. The Imperial Implications of Medieval Translations:
   Textual Transmission of Marie de France's *Lais*   24

2. Behavioural Transformations in the Old Norse
   Version of *La Chanson de Roland*   53

3. Narrative Transformations in the Old Norse and
   Middle English Versions of *Le Chevalier au Lion* (or *Yvain*)   76

4. Female Sovereignty and Male Authority in the Old Norse
   and Middle English Versions of *Partonopeu de Blois*   113
   Appendix: Summaries of the Versions of *Partonopeu de Blois*   152

Conclusion   164

Bibliography   169
Index   191

Acknowledgements

This work would not have come into being were it not for the support, encouragement and help of many people. First and foremost I must mention David Lawton, without whom this book would probably never have been written. His insightful and judicious reading has been invaluable in shaping it and deepening the argument. I must also thank Jessica Rosenfeld, who read an early draft of the book and offered valuable comments. Special thanks go to Robert Henke, Edward Donald Kennedy and the anonymous reader for Boydell & Brewer for their supportive suggestions, and to Caroline Palmer and Rohais Haughton, whose editorial assistance and enthusiastic encouragement have been invaluable.

I owe special thanks to the various archives and manuscript collections and staff that I have had the privilege to work with at the Bodleian Library in Oxford, the Cambridge University Library, the British Library in London, the Bibliothèque Nationale in Paris, Stofnun Árna Magnússonar í íslenskum fræðum and Landsbókasafn Íslands-Háskólabókasafn in Reykjavík, as well as Þjóðminjasafn Íslands (the National Museum of Iceland). I am indebted to the Institute of Historical Research at the University of London for the Mellon Fellowship which made the research with the manuscripts themselves possible and for their warm welcome in London during my stay there. A research fellowship from the Icelandic Research Fund (RANNÍS) was instrumental in providing the time and space to complete the manuscript. I am grateful for the publication subvention provided by the Institute of Research in Literature and Visual Arts at the University of Iceland for the publication of this book, which revealed their faith in this project at a time when funds were extremely limited. There are many others who have either directly or indirectly contributed – without their knowledge, perhaps – and I am also grateful to all of those friends and colleagues at Washington University and the University of Iceland and others I have encountered along the way.

Earlier versions of chapters one and two appeared in *Studies in Philology* 105.2 (2008) and in a special issue on translation of *Mediaevalia* 26.2 (2005) respectively and I am grateful to the editors of these journals and to the Center for Medieval and Renaissance Studies at Binghamton University for permission to use the material. I am obliged to my parents, whose lifelong passion for art, music and literature first introduced me to some of the greatest works of medieval literature and thus sparked my own interest in literature and cultures. Last, but not least, I must thank my husband for his unconditional support and understanding; and to my children, who in their few years have spent countless hours in libraries, travelled throughout Europe and the United States with me during research and played peacefully by my side as I wrote this book.

A Note on Translations

All medieval texts are quoted in the original followed (other than for those in Middle English) by a modern English translation. Where English translations exist I have generally used these, although in some cases they have been adjusted slightly for comparative purposes. In each case such amendments have been noted. The editions of the Old Norse texts used in this book range in varying degrees from unnormalised Old Norse to modern Icelandic orthography. Although the unnormalised versions may present some difficulties to the unaccustomed reader, I have opted for retaining the orthography of the editions since they are at all times followed by English translations. This is to prevent unnecessary confusion with respect to the quoted texts.

Following Icelandic convention, Icelandic authors without surnames are alphabetised by given name as opposed to patronymic in the bibliography.

Timeline, 1100–1700

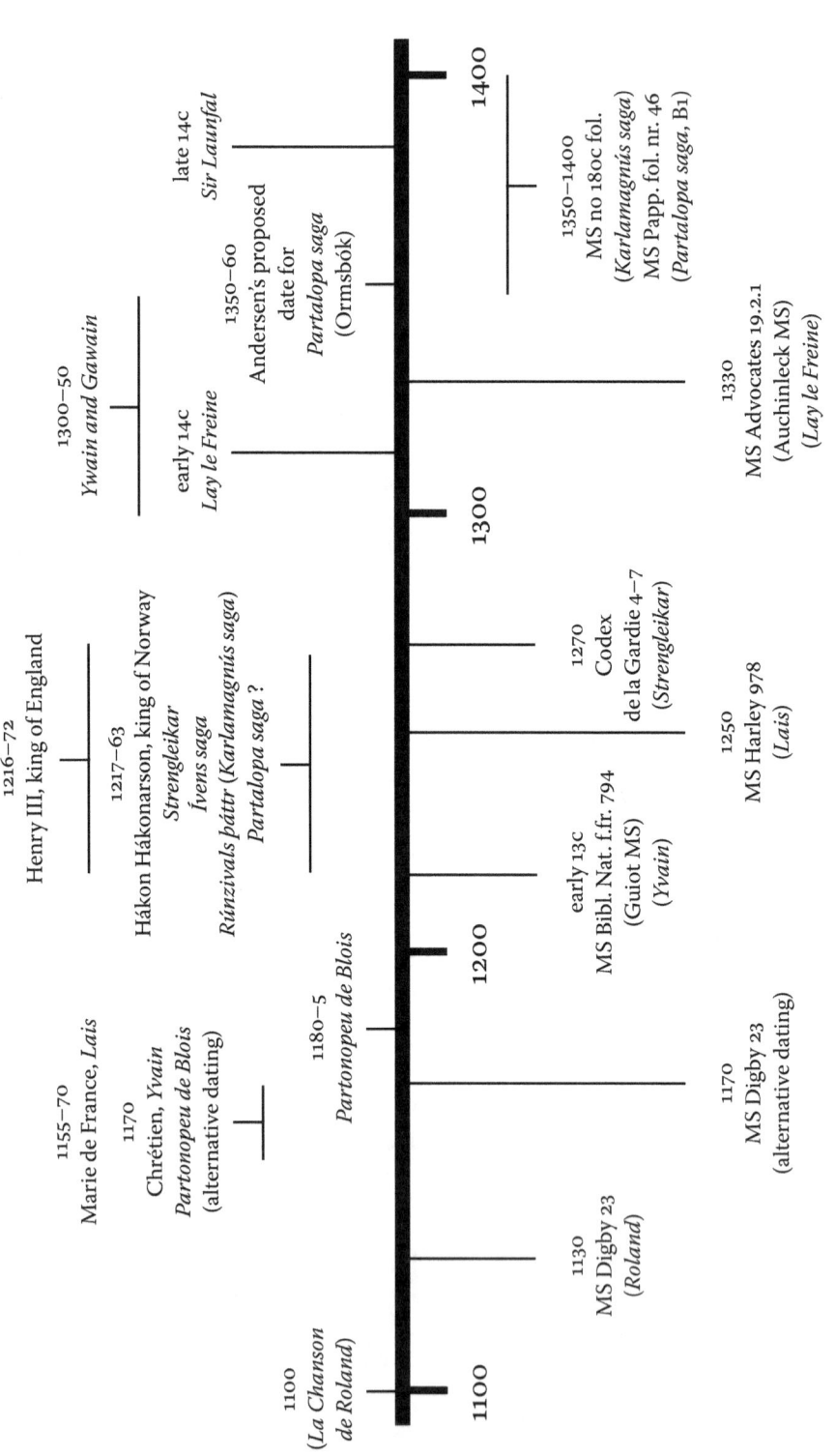

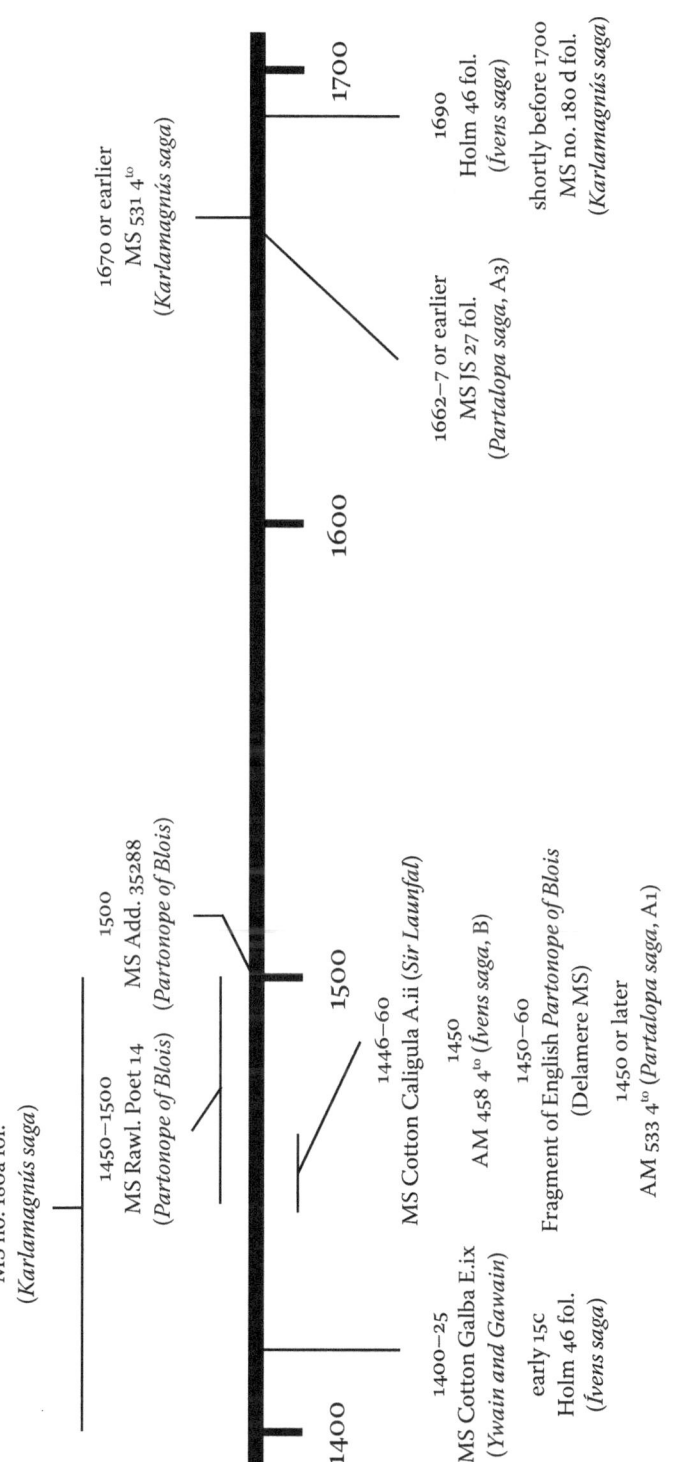

Introduction

THE HISTORY OF EUROPEAN LITERATURE is one of transformation, refashioning and intertextual relations. Narrative modes and ideas spread across the continent, influencing and enriching existing native literary forms. As old poetic traditions either stagnated or died out, new literary modes were fashioned from pre-existing forms, which were combined with novel narrative structures and ideas from imported materials. The foreign literary conventions did not replace existing forms, but rather served as the impetus for the enrichment of the native literary language and of its poetic and thematic representation. While medieval literary heritage reflects the ideological and social structures from which it originated, it also transcends the moment in history through this intertextual exchange. It both preserves traces of ideologies of that culture and foretells changes that lie ahead. In the literary legacy of any given community a modern reader can thus discern patterns of cultural movement and transformation as they have been preserved in time.

The role that translations play in this cultural exchange is often neglected. While modern scholarship on translation recognises the impact of culture as fundamental to the translation process, medieval translations have frequently been judged by their capacity (or failure) to reflect and capture the essence of the source text.[1] Recent criticism is, however, turning its focus increasingly towards reconceptualising the relationship of source and target texts in the Middle Ages in a manner that reflects the circumstances of medieval textual production.[2] In the last two decades, critics, particularly within English literary history and to a certain extent in Old Norse studies,

---

[1] For scholarship on translation in general see for instance Marilyn Gaddis Rose, ed., *Translation Horizons. Beyond the Boundaries of Translation Spectrum* (Binghampton: State University of New York, 1996); Mary Snell-Hornby, *Translation Studies. An Integrated Approach* (Amsterdam: John Benjamins Publishing Company, 1995); Susan Bassnet and André Lefevere, *Constructing Cultures* (Clevedon: Multilingual Matters, 1998); Dinda L. Gorlée, *On Translating Signs: Exploring Text and Semio-Translation* (Amsterdam: Rodopi, 2004); Susan Petrilli, ed., *Translation Translation* (Amsterdam: Rodopi, 2003); and Emily Apter, *The Translation Zone: A New Comparative Literature* (Princeton: Princeton University Press, 2006).

[2] See for instance Michelle R. Warren, 'Translation', in *Oxford Twenty-First Century Approaches to Literature: Middle English*, ed. Paul Strohm (Oxford: Oxford University Press, 2007), 51–67; Rita Copeland, *Rhetoric, Hermeneutics, and Translation in the Middle Ages. Academic Traditions and Vernacular Texts* (Cambridge: Cambridge University Press, 1991); Laura H. Hollengreen, ed. *Translatio or the Transmission of Culture in the Middle Ages and the Renaissance. Modes and Messages* (Turnhout: Brepols, 2008); several short deliberations by Jeanette Beer, Robert M. Stein, Michelle R. Warren, Sarah Kay, Marina Brownlee and David Townsend in *New Medieval Literatures* 9 (2007); and The Medieval Translator series.

have sought to reintroduce the social and cultural circumstances of textual creation and foreground the hermeneutic process involved in translation as an interpretative act. Marianne E. Kalinke's work with Icelandic romances, both indigenous and translated, has been instrumental in redirecting critical attention to the literary nuances of the texts themselves and their function within a larger European context.[3] Rita Copeland's volume on rhetoric has similarly sought to redefine translation as part of the system of rhetoric and hermenuetics in the Middle Ages. The recognition of vernacular translation as a 'primary vehicle for vernacular participation in, and ultimately appropriation of, the cultural privilege of Latin academic discourse' reconceptualises medieval translations as active agents in cultural formation, rather than passive transmitters of a perceived authority of an 'original' (in Copeland's case the classical *auctores*).[4] By reading vernacular translations in connection with and through the intellectual history that sustained them, they gain value as cultural and theoretical evidence of medieval reading practices. Translations not only provide evidence of the cultural conditions of their creators, but are the prime site for cultural encounter. They therefore reveal active engagement with the conceptualisation of linguistic and cultural identity, played out in the reconstruction of foreign or 'differing' literary material. The cross-cultural comparison presented in this study of vernacular translation, which takes into account both the relationship with the source text and the cultural conditions surrounding its refashioning, thus provides a model for the exploration of cultural formation and cohesion. This approach liberates the discussion of translations as secondary and hence inferior to native literary forms by considering their inherent dissimilarity as evidence of the impressions of the receiving culture, and hence as substantiation of the process of cultural transformation.

This book proposes a new way of considering medieval literary translations. It suggests a subtle modification in approach to the connections between translations and source texts on the one hand, and translations and native literary forms on the other that, however, alters the way they are perceived.

---

[3] *King Arthur North-by-Northwest. The 'matière de Bretagne' in Old Norse-Icelandic Romances*. Bibliotheca Arnamagnæana 37 (Copenhagen: C. A. Reitzels boghandel, 1981), and *Bridal-Quest Romance in Medieval Iceland*, Islandica 46 (Ithaca: Cornell University Press, 1990). See also Geraldine Barnes, 'Romance in Iceland', in *Old Icelandic Literature and Society*, ed. Margaret Clunies Ross (Cambridge: Cambridge University Press, 2000), 266–86, whose focus is on Icelandic romance, but the point of active engagement with continental forms is relevant; Jürg Glauser, 'Romance (Translated *Riddarasögur*)', in *A Companion to Old Norse-Icelandic Literatur and Culture*, ed. Rory McTurk (Oxford, Blackwell: 2005), 372–87; Regina Psaki, 'Women's Counsel in the Riddarasögur: The Case of *Parcevals saga*', in *Cold Counsel: Women in Old Norse Literature and Mythology*, ed. Sarah M. Anderson and Karen Swenson (New York: Routledge, 2002), 201–24; Carolyne Larrington, 'Queens and Bodies: The Norwegian Translated *lais* and Hákon IV's Kinswomen', *Journal of English and Germanic Philology* 108 (2009), 506–27, and her article 'The Translated *Lais*', in *King Arthur of the North*, ed. Marianne Kalinke (Cardiff: University of Wales Press, 2009), 77–97.

[4] *Rhetoric, Hermeneutics, and Translation in the Middle Ages*, 3. See also Jocelyn Wogan-Browne, Nicholas Watson, Andrew Taylor, and Ruth Evans, eds., *The Idea of the Vernacular. An Anthology of Middle English Literary Theory 1280–1520* (University Park: The Pennsylvania State University Press, 1999), and Warren, 'Translation'.

Introduction

By looking at the adaptations of the source text as evidence for the cultural predilection of reading communities that created and received those translations, one can discern patterns of literary, social and ideological preconceptions. In fact, translations are a unique medium for observing such cultural transformations as they capture in essence the encounter between the two distinct and separate cultural traditions and the subsequent effort at literary adaptation. This approach recognises that culture is in a state of continual transformation, and that any effort to encapsulate the ideological and ethical codes that constitute a society is thwarted by the fact that society itself is in a constant state of progress and reform. There are, nevertheless, definite and discernible differences between societies at any given time, and those differences can be observed and described, regardless of the inherent instability of the parts that make up the societal framework. Such divergences foreground the meaningful structures of those societies. These intrinsic structures then become perceptible through their incompatibility with those of the receiving society. This can often be best observed in translations as they must reconcile those differences in a manner that makes the text enjoyable and comprehensible to its new readers.

This work thus seeks to explore the cultural transformations that occur in the movement from one cultural context to another. These transformations in turn provide evidence of the inherent differences in cultural identity among members of separate linguistic and literary communities. They also draw attention to the correlations that exist between cultural identity and other aspects of community formation, such as linguistic expression, established codes of conduct and literary representation. This volume explores various texts transmitted from the Francophone domain to Middle English and Old Norse reading communities in order to foreground the manifold facets of such cultural transmission in the late Middle Ages.

The book encompasses a multitude of literatures composed at different times. They all, however, share a common origin in the French culture of the eleventh and twelfth centuries. The period covered spans the twelfth to the fifteenth centuries and reaches across northern France, England and Scandinavia. Texts originating from different locations as well as from different historical and social contexts, are addressed. Moving from the pinnacle of the *chanson de geste* tradition, *La Chanson de Roland*, through the compilation of *Lais*, customarily attributed to the enigmatic Marie de France, and Chrétien de Troyes's narrative masterpiece, *Le Chevalier au Lion* (or *Yvain*), the book explores the cultural transformations wrought upon those texts in translation, ending with the romance of *Partonopeu de Blois*. The breadth of the subject matter allows for the investigation of the English and Nordic renditions of the French literary material in a broader and more comprehensive context than the traditional direct comparison of, say, the Middle English versions with their French originals. Similarly, by reading those texts together certain patterns of transformations and cultural influences become apparent that would otherwise have remained obscure. These patterns reveal noteworthy affinities and divergences between translation practices in Britain and Scandinavia, which reveal the complex underlying cultural, political and social motivations behind literary production.

The linguistic qualifier 'English' generally refers to Middle English unless otherwise specified. French refers to any text written in a Francophone linguistic register, whether the French of the Île-de-France, or the numerous dialectical variants across the border regions. The complexities of terminology, particularly with respect to continental French and the French spoken in England in the Middle Ages (commonly referred to as Anglo-Norman) will be elaborated on where appropriate and to distinguish between cultural contingencies in linguistic conceptualisation, but will not be addressed beyond that.[5] Several recent volumes have appeared that consider the ramifications of the multilingual circumstances in medieval Britain for literary production, identity-formation and linguistic coherence, and these provide a critical framework for the discussion of French in England in this book.[6] The term 'Norse' similarly poses certain semantic problems. It is commonly used to designate the communal language spoken in Norway, Iceland and the Faroese islands in the medieval period and the common cultural heritage of those people, although at times the term incorporates the dialectical variants spoken in Denmark and Sweden as well.[7] Here it will be used to refer to the language and common cultural heritage of Norway and Iceland in the Middle Ages, while allowing for the fact that these begin diverging in the late-medieval period (as revealed in orthographic idiosyncrasies, for instance) and that there are distinct differences in the geographical, economical and societal structures of the respective communities that affect literary production despite the common origin and shared histories.[8]

The extent, both geographical and temporal, of the discussion necessarily

---

[5] The terminology used in this book, i.e. Anglo-Norman and Continental French, is intended to address the complexity of linguistic interaction in medieval England, rather than re-enforce notions of national divisions frequently associated with the terms. This approach recognises the inherent volatility of the terms, which draw arbitrary boundaries based on perceived national borders. Such distinctions are admittedly always problematic inasmuch as they contain within them a preconception of borders where there are none, or where such borders are inherently unstable. However, the use of 'Anglo-Norman' here is intended to denote the French being used in England in the thirteenth and fourteenth century, whereas the term 'French' is used to connote the vernacular 'romanz' and encompasses all its forms and variations (including Anglo-Norman). The intention is to accentuate the movement between the two languages, i.e. French (whether continental or any of its dialectic varieties) and English. Clearly neither French nor English were static and fixed entities at any given time, or within any given region, and moreover influenced each other through co-existence and exposure. Yet, despite inevitable influences the languages are, nevertheless, based on different grammatical, syntactical and phonetical structures and it is as such that they are addressed here.

[6] See for instance Jocelyn Wogan-Browne *et al.*, eds., *Language and Culture. The French of England c.1100–c.1500* (York: York Medieval Press, 2009), and Ardis Butterfield, *The Familiar Enemy: Chaucer, Language and Nation in the Hundred Years War* (Oxford: Oxford University Press, 2009).

[7] Old Norse has frequently been divided into West and East Norse to distinguish between the dialectical variation spoken in Norway, Iceland and the Faeroes on the one hand, and the form spoken in Denmark and Sweden on the other.

[8] Such differences may be noted in the discussion by referring to either 'Norwegian' or 'Icelandic' communities, or manuscript provenance, where it has been determined to be specifically one or the other.

makes it impossible to cover the details of all the intertextual relations existing between the French and the English texts on one hand, and the French and the Norse texts on the other. Such detailed comparative studies between translation and source text have been conducted by other critics and are cited where they are of relevance. The intention here is not to list such changes, but rather to interrogate the reasons behind them and what they may tell us about the translators and their audiences. The focus of the discussion will be on the reception of the French literary material and the possible reasons underlying the modifications evident in the Middle English and Old Norse works in an effort to understand what those texts may have meant to their medieval readers.

Medieval Textuality

By focusing on cultural exchange across multiple linguistic and temporal boundaries, some of the fallacies of a unilateral word-for-word comparison of a single source text and its translation can be avoided. The presumption of mistakes or misconceptions when the translated text deviates from the source precludes the recognition of the translator's creativity and active engagement with his material. E. F. Halvorsen's statement that the Norse version of *La Chanson de Roland* is clearly a translation (not an adaptation) – as it can be divided into lines corresponding to the verses of the French poem – underlies his assumption that failure to follow the source accurately reflects the translator's inability to correctly understand his source text.[9] The supposition that a translation, by virtue of its status as a translation (rather than an adaptation, for instance), requires a precise reconstruction of the source text in the target language negates the medieval conception of translation as well as the impact of cultural and historical context and linguistic differences in the creative process.[10] Many of the errors Halvorsen points out in fact reflect the translator's effort of adjusting his material to his new audience. This study proposes that those deviations do not denote the translator's lack of comprehension of his foreign material, but rather the recognition of and effort to bridge the cultural divide between the imported material and the literary tradition into which he is inserting his new text.

Similarly, negative judgements of the literary value of Middle English translations of French texts, based on their failure to transport the poetic quality of their sources, ignore the role played by the translator as active agent in the process of textual reconstruction. A. C. Spearing and Dieter Mehl base their criticism of the Middle English *Ywain and Gawain* and *Sir Launfal* on their authors' presumed inability to recapture the literary essence of their source

---

[9] *The Norse Version of the Chanson de Roland* (Copenhagen: Ejnar Munksgaard, 1959), 103.
[10] Susan Bassnett in fact rejects the differentiation between 'translation' and 'adaptation' altogether, arguing that it refutes the inherent complexity of the text and is based on a misconception of the reader as 'the passive receiver of the text in which its Truth is enshrined' (*Translation Studies*, London: Routledge, 1994, 79).

texts.[11] By focusing on what is missing in the translation, however, one may fail to notice the potential reasons behind those omissions and what they can tell us about English literary communities. The comparative approach adopted here not only highlights the distinctiveness of each receiving culture by virtue of the diverse textual presentations of those works, but it furthermore attempts to reposition the texts within their cultural context and hence cancel such qualitative judgements based solely on the perceived failure to recapture an essentially different literary quality. Instead, the text's function within various cultural contexts can be examined through the comparative reading of these texts and their respective patterns of alteration. The focus is not so much on what was taken from where, but rather how and why. This necessitates the examination of these texts as cultural evidence as well as linguistic and poetic entities. Their preservation history and manuscript context is thus of the utmost importance in understanding the role these texts played in their reading communities.

With respect to England this is often complicated by the fact that in many cases only a single manuscript has been preserved containing the Middle English version of the texts. Given the precarious preservation history of English vernacular literature it can be problematic to contextualise these versions, as any conclusions must be based on the single existing manuscript copies, which are not necessarily indicators of either the popularity or the distribution patterns of these texts. Recent studies in codicology and the work being done in linguistic analysis of texts with a view to localising English literary works is of help here in determining the potential reading communities that instigated and preserved these translations.[12] We must therefore take the manuscripts as evidence of the existence and circulation of these texts in that

---

[11] A. C. Spearing, 'Marie de France and her Middle English Adapters', *Studies in the Age of Chaucer* 12 (1990), 117–57, at 127 and 148–9, and Dieter Mehl, *The Middle English Romances of the Thirteenth and Fourteenth Centuries* (London: Routledge & Kegan Paul, 1968), 180–5. For a discussion of *Sir Launfal* see also Spearing's chapter on 'The Lanval Story', in his *The Medieval Poet as Voyeur* (Cambridge: Cambridge University Press, 1993), 97–120.

[12] For dialect studies and linguistic data of Middle English texts and communities see Angus McIntosh, M. L. Samuels, Michael Benskin, eds. (with assistance from Margaret Laing and Keith Williamson), *A Linguistic Atlas of Late Medieval English* (Aberdeen: Aberdeen University Press, 1986). For critical work in manuscript studies see for instance Linda L. Brownrigg, ed., *Medieval Book Production. Assessing the Evidence* (Los Altos Hills: Anderson-Lovelace, 1990); M. B. Parkes, *Scribes, Scripts and Readers. Studies in the Communication, Presentation and Dissemination of Medieval Texts* (London: The Hambledon Press, 1991); Murray J. Evans, *Rereading Middle English Romance. Manuscript Layout, Decoration, and the Rhetoric of Composite Structure* (Montreal: McGill-Queen's University Press, 1995); Ralph Hanna, *London Literature, 1300–1380* (Cambridge: Cambridge University Press, 2005); Richard Beadle, 'Middle English Texts and their Transmission, 1350–1500: Some Geographical Criteria', in *Speaking in Our Tongues. Proceedings of a Colloquium on Medieval Dialectology and Related Disciplines*, ed. Margaret Laing and Keith Williamson (Cambridge: D. S. Brewer, 1994), 69–92, and his 'Prolegomena to a Literary Geography of Later Medieval Norfolk', in *Regionalism in Late Medieval Manuscripts and Texts*, ed. Felicity Riddy (Cambridge: D. S. Brewer, 1991), 89–108. There is also a useful overview of the field in Ralph Hanna's article 'Analytical Survey 4: Middle English Manuscripts and the Study of Literature', *New Medieval Literatures* 4 (2001), 242–64.

Introduction

specific form, despite the fact that they may have existed in a different form at some point. This approach acknowledges the inherent instability of vernacular literature and the fact that the preserved text represents only an intermittent stage in the process of its own regeneration. The literary works discussed in the following chapters can be understood to epitomise a defined historical moment in the dynamic process of textual transformation by drawing on Paul Zumthor's conceptualisation of *mouvance*, or textual mobility.[13] Yet their very existence in a specific version, or in a particular manuscript copy, necessitates the acceptance of the text as it has come down as evidence of its deliberate fashioning and circulation in that form. Any assumptions about reading communities will therefore be based on the manuscript copies we have before us and any additional localising evidence available. The predicaments are of quite a different order when it comes to the Norse translations. Several of the texts discussed in this work in fact exist in multiple manuscript copies. Few, however, can be traced back to their original place or time of translation. Most of the translations exist only in Icelandic manuscripts, whereas the majority of them are believed to have been translated in Norway in the thirteenth century. Of the texts examined, only one has in fact been preserved in a thirteenth-century Norwegian manuscript. The remaining texts exist only in later Icelandic manuscripts, the earliest of which date back to the fourteenth century. This makes any discussion of the cultural context particularly difficult as it presumes such evidence reflects the text at the time of its composition. The complex manuscript transmission history of many of the Norse texts thus requires an awareness and recognition of multiple layers of cultural influence in the textual tradition. Yet these do not necessarily undermine such analysis. In fact, the existence of such discernible layers of culturally determined modifications foregrounds the impact the presumed public has had upon the formation of the text. Textual variants between the Nordic manuscripts thus provide evidence of cultural transformations that one can only assume with some of the Middle English translations.

This approach to the text as product as well as witness of the culture that created it originates in the recent declaration by the self-proclaimed New Medievalists of a 'return to the entire cultural circumstances of medieval

---

[13] Zumthor formulated the concept of *mouvance* in his *Essai de poétique médiévale*, published in 1972. He argued that any medieval work formed a complex unity that encompassed the original authorial conceptualisation of the text along with later rewritings or rearrangements by successive reciters or scribes. While his theory draws more on the epic conventions of the *chansons de geste* and the impact of oral performance on textual transmission than on the courtly tradition of the romances, it is nevertheless of relevance to the understanding of medieval textuality, particularly with respect to the notion of textual inviolability and manuscript preservation (*Toward a Medieval Poetics*, trans. Philip Bennett, Minneapolis: University of Minnesota Press, 1992, particularly 40–76). Bernard Cerquiglini applies this notion of textual multiplicity to manuscript studies by describing medieval texts as inherently variant, thereby rejecting the conception of textual stability. He proposes the term *variance* to describe medieval writing (*Éloge de la variante: histoire critique de la philologie*, Paris: Seuil, 1989, translated into English as *In Praise of the Variant: A Critical History of Philology*, trans. Betsy Wing, Baltimore: Johns Hopkins University Press, 1999).

textuality'.[14] The notion here of 'medieval textuality', which encompasses both the historical context, in terms of the cultural circumstances that brought forth the text, and the actual physical context of the text itself, the manuscript in which it has been preserved, is relevant to the current study. This methodology rejects any isolation of the text from its literary context which hinders the recognition of the text as a cultural monument. Yet it recognises the necessity of close reading and attention to textual detail that is often absent in historical approaches. In fact, Ralph Hanna proclaims that what was lacking before the 1980s was 'an articulated vision of medieval books as cultural phenomenon'.[15] Rather than viewing the text as an isolated and self-contained body of words unrelated to and disconnected from its surroundings, the text is understood as a product and symbol of its cultural context.

This shift in attention is particularly pertinent to medieval literature. For medieval readers the text was a dynamic corpus that was not restricted to the form or shape in which it was received, but was in constant flux, being refashioned and reshaped.[16] Nor was it synonymous with books.[17] In fact, texts were commonly stored by memory before, or even rather than, being written down.[18] The manuscript itself moreover demanded time-consuming and tedious labour by scribes, and was costly to produce. The resulting combination of text, the physical properties of the manuscript volume itself and the occasional illustration or commentary thus provided the medieval reader with an object that had a significant cultural value. This perception of text is reflected in medieval translation practices where translation can be perceived simply as another form of writing. The *translatio* (carrying across) of material that reproduces the continual movement of texts, ideas and objects reflects an

---

[14] Sarah Kay is here referring to the critical doctrine of New Philology, which encompasses the analysis of the text both in its manuscript context (whtether it was preserved in a collection, with what texts etc.) and the actual visual representation of the text within that manuscript copy (such has scribal hand, illuminations, notes in margins etc.) ('Analytical Survey 3: The New Philology', *New Medieval Literatures* 3 (1999), 295–326, at 311). The theoretical model of New Philology underlies the New Medievalists' objective of a reconstruction of our very notion of the 'medieval'. The New Medievalists therefore incorporate and expand on the ideas set forth by the originating New Philologists of a return to the cultural context and medieval conceptualisation of text. For critical works that align themselves with this new approach see, for instance, Marina S. Brownlee, Kevin Brownlee and Stephen G. Nichols, eds., *The New Medievalism* (Baltimore: The Johns Hopkins University Press, 1991), and Kevin Brownlee and Marina Scordilis Brownlee, eds., *Romance. Generic Transformation from Chrétien de Troyes to Cervantes* (Hanover: University Press of New England, 1985).

[15] 'Analytical Survey 4: Middle English Manuscripts and the Study of Literature', 244.

[16] There is an apparent shift in late-medieval England, with some authors becoming more aware of, or more concerned with, the preservation of their texts' coherence and accuracy. Chaucer's concern with scribal errors in the reproduction of his works reveals his awareness of this textual fluidity and the sense of authorial intent and the potential for textual corruption.

[17] This comment pertains only to secular literature, as sacred works, such as the Bible, were characterised by the inviolability of their content, stemming from the sacred character of the words contained there. Most other texts were not, however, defined by such rigid delineations.

[18] For information on the role of memory in the Middle Ages and the medieval perception of memory and the written words see Mary J. Carruthers, *The Book of Memory. A Study of Memory in Medieval Culture* (Cambridge: Cambridge University Press, 1990).

Introduction

aesthetic of literary production that is profoundly foreign to the modern conception of authorship and copyrights. Such an approach therefore perceives the translated text as a part of a whole, which is the textual process, rather than as a secondary derivative of a unique and fixed original.

Stephen G. Nichols notes that the critical effort of New Medievalism lies not so much in 'predicating a specific methodology', as in 'designating instead a predisposition to interrogate and reformulate assumptions about the discipline of medieval studies'.[19] It is therefore not a rejection of previous critical directions, but rather a questioning of the basic assumptions one has when approaching a text, particularly perhaps a medieval text. This is relevant here as the objective is to illuminate the process of textual adaptation by refuting the common dismissal of the English and Norse translations as secondary or inferior replicas of their source texts. By redirecting the focus away from the basic assumption of literary inferiority, these texts can be examined as evidence of the literary predilections, ideological values and behavioural preconceptions of their authors and audiences.

The discussion of the texts in the following chapters draws on a wide variety of critical discourses, ranging from post-colonial criticism to gender theories that serve, however, only as guides to provide a critical framework for the discussion of a particular concept. Theories traditionally applied to post-colonial studies are used to explore pre-colonial patterns of cultural dominance and subversion.[20] By analysing the ambivalent interconnections of Anglo-Norman, English and Norwegian literary communities in the thirteenth and fourteenth centuries, questions of linguistic integrity and cultural authority can be explored. Such a discussion proposes a new way of looking at the concept of imperialism, not on the level of national aggression, but rather in terms of *cultural* hegemony, where such intercultural relations can be examined.[21]

This understanding of imperialist tendencies is of particular relevance to the medieval period, and, more importantly, to medieval translations. In

---

[19] 'The New Medievalism: Tradition and Discontinuity in Medieval Culture', in *The New Medievalism*, ed. Marina S. Brownlee, Kevin Brownlee and Stephen G. Nichols, 1–26, at 1.

[20] For general information on post-colonial criticism see for instance Bill Ashcroft, Gareth Griffiths and Helen Tiffin, eds., *The Post-Colonial Studies Reader* (London: Routledge, 1995). For works that argue for the application of post-colonial theories to the medieval period see Ananya Jahanara Kabir and Deanne Williams, eds., *Postcolonial Approaches to the European Middle Ages. Translating Cultures* (Cambridge: Cambridge University Press, 2005); Patricia Clare Ingham and Michelle R. Warren, eds., *Postcolonial Moves: Medieval through Modern* (New York: Palgrave Macmillan, 2003); and Jeffrey Jerome Cohen, ed., *The Postcolonial Middle Ages* (New York: St Martin's Press, 2000).

[21] The classical interpretation of imperialism is political rather than cultural. The term evokes the (usually) forceful national and political expansion of the sovereignty of a powerful ruler to include marginal or 'foreign' territories (see for instance Wolfgang J. Mommsen, *Theories of Imperialism*, trans. P. S. Falla, New York: Random House, 1980, and Edward W. Said, *Culture and Imperialism*, New York: Alfred A. Knopf, 1993). This notion of power politics serves here as a metaphor for cultural expansionism that reflects the idea of national expansion inherent in the conception of imperialism. Post-colonial theory has incorporated this understanding of the interplay of politics and culture in analyses of post-colonial encounters of dominant and marginal discursive traditions, which is elaborated in Chapter 1 within a medieval historical context.

fact, Rita Copeland reminds us that 'the essential paradox of the enterprise of translation' lies in its effort to replicate its source 'through difference, through displacement [and] substitution'.[22] While Copeland is here referring to canonical appropriation, that is, translations from Latin into the vernacular, the fundamental idea behind her sense of the paradoxical quality of translations can be applied just as much to other literary relations of linguistic or cultural inequality. The apparently laudatory effort of reproducing foreign material in a native tongue is undermined by the fact that, by virtue of being refashioned in a different language, the translated text not only reshapes its source, but furthermore appropriates its intrinsic literary authority by replacing the source with its own linguistic version. While French is in this case also a vernacular, the relationship between a culturally or politically dominant language with that of a less politically potent native tongue re-enacts those binary relations of authority and subjugation, which are then played out in subtle forms of literary appropriation.

Narrative theories serve in a similar manner to highlight the formal alterations that occur in the transmission of literary material and what such changes in narrative structure mean in terms of literary reception.[23] The theories form the basis for the analysis of structural modifications that in turn highlight a shift in the thematic orientation of translated texts. Analyses of behavioural structures and gender delineation similarly assist in drawing out such patterns of cultural transformation.[24] Ultimately, the discussion is determined by the preconceived notion that the texts were translated for a targeted readership and hence adjusted to fit or apply to their tastes and expectations. Such a

---

[22] *Rhetoric, Hermeneutics, and Translation in the Middle Ages*, 36.

[23] Models of narrative grammar developed by critics such as A. J. Greimas derive from the narratological studies that followed in the wake of structuralism in the 1960s and 1970s. My use of the conceptualisation of narrative structure in this discussion is only indirectly indebted to such theories of narrative grammar, as it does not try to dissect the text's underlying narrative structure, but rather to draw attention to the formal aspects of the work's narrative unity and development. For information on narrative grammar see for instance A. J. Greimas, 'Narrative Grammar: Units and Levels', *Modern Language Notes* 86 (1971), 793–806, and Peter Haidu, 'The Episode as Semiotic Module in Twelfth-Century Romance', *Poetics Today* 4 (1983), 655–81. For narratological theories see for instance Gérard Genette, *Narrative Discourse. An Essay in Method*, trans. Jane E. Lewin (Ithaca: Cornell University Press, 1980), and *Narrative Discourse Revisited*, trans. Jane E. Lewin (Ithaca: Cornell University Press, 1988). A good overview of the theories of structuralism can be found in Jonathan Culler's *Structuralist Poetics. Structuralism, Linguistics, and the Study of Literature* (Ithaca: Cornell University Press, 1993).

[24] Very little work has been done within medieval studies on the portrayal of behaviour in literature. The most prominent critical approaches to the representation of emotion in the Middle Ages are Barbara H. Rosenwein, ed., *Anger's Past. The Social Uses of an Emotion in the Middle Ages* (Ithaca: Cornell University Press, 1998), and her *Emotional Communities in the Early Middle Ages* (Ithaca: Cornell University Press, 2007). The discussion of gender constructions in this work is based not so much on feminist or queer theories, but rather makes use of the conception of gender as a socially constructed category derived from historically and culturally determined attributes. The recognition of these attributes is vital to the conceptualisations of appropriate gendered behaviour. The deviations from these pre-existing structures of masculine and feminine behaviour patterns thus obfuscate such gendered distinctions.

Introduction

notion of the built-in reader draws on theories of readership stemming from the 1960s and 1970s.[25] My approach rests, however, more on the current ideas developed by critics such as Suzanne Reynolds and A. J. Minnis. Reynolds approaches 'the reader' from a textual and historical perspective by drawing attention to actual reading practices in the medieval period. Her analysis of interpretative glossing highlights the existence of both a presumed authorial intent and, more importantly, the underlying readerly goal that informs the reading itself.[26] Minnis, on the other hand, looks at the medieval conception of authorship as significant in establishing a contemporary shift in authority from Divinity to the writer himself.[27] Such a reorientation in authorial control is important with respect to vernacular writers as it indicates the conflicting conception of literary and linguistic authority and textual innovation by readers and writers in the medieval period. Underlying both those approaches is the notion that the inscription of the authors and their audiences can be found in the texts themselves and that the recognition of those literary and historical figures is fundamental to the understanding of medieval literary productivity.[28]

The editors of *The Idea of the Vernacular* note that 'audiences are born (and reborn) somewhere between authorial desire, the desires of actual historical audiences, and the cultural and linguistic possibilities that shape acts of reading'.[29] The intended reader of the translated text can thus provide some insight into the expected target audience of the translator. The manuscript copies themselves, which often date from considerably later periods than the 'original' translations, indicate on the other hand the literary predilections of their actual historical audiences, which have left their mark on those texts through their own scribal adjustments. These intended and actual readers thus form the 'reading community' of any given text. This term, as it is used

---

[25] Theories set forth by the North-American Reader-Response Criticism (see as above Culler's *Structuralist Poetics*) and the German advocates of the *Rezeptionsästhetik* (Reception Aesthetics) (see for instance Hans Robert Jauss, *Toward an Aesthetic of Reception*, trans. Timothy Bahti, Minneapolis: University of Minnesota Press, 1982) sought to reintroduce the reader as an active agent both in the creation and in the interpretation of the text.

[26] *Medieval Reading. Grammar, Rhetoric and the Classical Text* (Cambridge: Cambridge University Press, 1996).

[27] *Medieval Theory of Authorship. Scholastic Literary Attitudes in the Later Middle Ages* (Philadelphia: University of Pennsylvania Press, 1988). Theories of vernacular self-consciousness and the positioning of the audience are further developed in Alastair Minnis and Ian Johnson, eds., *The Cambridge History of Literary Criticism: The Middle Ages*, vol. 2 (Cambridge: Cambridge University Press, 2005). See especially Kevin Brownlee, Tony Hunt, Ian Johnson, Alastair Minnis and Nigel F. Palmer, 'Vernacular Literary Consciousness c.1100–c.1500: French, German and English Evidence', 422–71.

[28] This notion of the text as object, and moreover as cultural object, can be found in Cannon's work on English literary history, which conceives, however, of texts as existing in isolation from each other in a Marxist reading of early Middle English vernacular writing (Christopher Cannon, *The Grounds of English Literature*, Oxford: Oxford University Press, 2004). While arriving at the value of the text through its singularity, rather than its connectivity to a broader cultural context, Cannon foregrounds the cultural material deposited within any given work through the act of creative articulation.

[29] Wogan-Browne *et al.*, *The Idea of the Vernacular*, 111.

here, can best be defined as a community of readers that is made up of the patrons who commissioned the writings of those texts, the scribes who copied them and, ultimately, the audiences that received them. These as a group have in common the shared knowledge and interest (although those might of course differ considerably between each member) that shaped their reading and understanding of the text.[30]

My notion of reading communities draws on theories of readership developed by Brian Stock. He proposes the idiom 'textual community' to describe a group composed of one or more persons able to read a text to a group of possibly 'unlettered or semilettered members'.[31] His notion is thus limited to the literal reader and audience, that is, the group that received the text (either visually or aurally) at a specific moment. My use of the term 'reading community' here goes beyond Stock's model in incorporating a somewhat more extended notion of the readership, which would have included the person (or persons) instigating the translation and subsequent copying of the text as well as those for whom the text was translated (or copied) and ultimately the groups of audiences who actually read and preserved those texts. It similarly comprises the translators and scribes (as they also form the readership of the texts) and hence their imagined as well as actual audiences. Anne Middleton's distinction between 'audience' and 'public' is useful in this context.[32] She proposes the term 'audience' for the actual historical audience of a work, which in turn is determined by such factors as ownership, dating and location of manuscript copies. The 'public', on the other hand, is the 'readership imagined and posited by the composer as a necessary postulate in the practical process of bringing the work into being.'[33] The public of any given work can be discerned in the rhetorical and formal characteristics of a text. It is therefore possible that the figures behind those two concepts differ significantly, both theoretically and in actuality.

Many of the texts discussed here have been preserved in manuscripts of considerably later date than their original compositions. This discrepancy between the date of composition and the date of the manuscripts is particularly notable in the case of the Norse translations. Moreover, the question of public and audience is complicated by the fact that the translations contain within them multiple levels of conceived public as well as actual audiences by virtue of their nature as *translations*. The translated text encompasses both

---

[30] Jocelyn Wogan-Browne's criticism of the word 'community' to describe medieval society is noted here in recognition of the inherent instability of the medieval and the modern tendency of imposing structures and boundaries upon what can best be defined as an organic and fluid cultural body ('Analytical Survey 5: "Reading is Good Prayer": Recent Research on Female Reading Communities', *New Medieval Literatures* 5 (2002), 229–97, at 231). For a lack of a better way of describing such collections of writers and their readers the designation 'reading community' will be used to incorporate the conception of such audience groups, which assumes a degree of inherent lack of constancy and permanence in its construction.

[31] *Listening for the Text. On the Uses of the Past* (Baltimore: The Johns Hopkins University Press, 1990), 23.

[32] 'The Audience and Public of *Piers Plowman*', in *Middle English Alliterative Poetry and its Literary Background*, ed. David Lawton (Cambridge: D. S. Brewer, 1982), 101–23.

[33] Ibid. 102.

Introduction

traces of the readership the French author envisaged as well as that of the English or Norse translator (and later scribes). The aim here is to differentiate between the original and the target public of a text as evidence of the shift in authorial objective between source text and translation. Such evidence is of value in detecting the potential reading communities for which the texts were intended. Similarly, recognising the disparity between the envisioned public and the actual audience is valuable for mapping the possible interests and cultural preferences of the communities in which the texts circled. The discussion in the following chapters will thus make use of the texts as they have come down to us as the evidence of the literary desires of the reading communities that created these texts and preserved them, while making allowance for the fact that the texts themselves represent simply a moment in their textual progression that has been captured in a manuscript copy and thus preserved in that form for future generations. They embody the spirit of a specific time and culture and can therefore bear witness to the traditions that formed them.

Cultural Discourse

The underlying assumption behind the entire discussion here is that culture as such can be defined as a semiotic system that in turn can be described, deciphered and portrayed by examining and interpreting the cultural and linguistic artefacts it produces. While this approach acknowledges David Lawton's warnings of the inherent danger of 'cultural construction', where we, as modern readers, necessarily bring 'our modernity into dialogue with our understanding of the medieval', it seeks to approach the medieval from the perspective of the texts that both produced and depicted the cultural environment that sustained them.[34] By looking at behavioural codes, gender conventions and socially prescribed actions as the articulation of the ideological system of a given culture, one can discern the basic semiotic components that govern those ideological structures.[35] These in turn find their expression in literary works, which preserve the semiotic codes that dictated their ideological construction and the moral and ethical values presented there within. None are of course intrinsically representative, or inherently subjected to the semiotic systems that informed their writings, but they do nevertheless reveal those systems by virtue of their acceptance (or rejection) by the reading communities.

Inherent to this conceptualisation of texts is the perception of literary genres and works as discourse, and moreover as cultural discourse. Eugene

---

[34] 'Analytical Survey 1: Literary History and Cultural Study', *New Medieval Literatures* 1 (1997), 237–69, at 240.
[35] For information on the notion of culture as a semiotic system that is expressed through behaviour or linguistic act see for instance Robin P. Fawcett, M. A. K. Halliday, Sydney M. Lamb and Adam Makkai, eds., *The Semiotics of Culture and Language*, 2 vols (London: Frances Pinter, 1984), and Clifford Geertz, *The Interpretation of Cultures* (New York: Basic Books, 2000).

Vance claims that the essence of the French courtly romance lies not so much in its formal attributes as in the semiotic signification of its language.[36] The understanding of romance genre as discourse is of relevance here, both with respect to notions of imperial tendencies, discussed in the first chapter, and to the analysis of the reception and modifications of those intrinsic semiotic patterns by the English and Norse translators of the French romance. By looking at the translated texts as cultural discourse – not only as diverse linguistic constructions, but also as a matrix of semiotic codes whose signification and connotations differ from that of the original audience – one can discern the defining values that guided the reconstruction of those texts within the new semiotic system. Simon Gaunt notes that not only texts are ideological constructions, but so are genres: 'The formal and structural features of a text do not produce aesthetic effects that can be divorced from content and thereby from ideology, but on the contrary they signal participation in a discursive framework that implies a world-view with a heavy ideological investment.'[37] This is of course particularly applicable to courtly romance, which heralded the introduction of courtly ethics in France and later in England and Norway. It is, however, also relevant to other genres, such as the *lais*, or the *chansons de geste*, which intimate a particular cultural motivation and inference.

The complex history of the relations between the English and French languages and culture in England in the late Middle Ages makes the reading of the Middle English translations and their French counterparts particularly intriguing. The seemingly peaceful co-existence of the two vernaculars in England in the centuries following the Conquest raises questions on the function of the English translations within the reading communities. While the descendants of the earlier Norman invaders were being assimilated into English culture in the first half of the twelfth century, the marriage of Henry II and Eleanor of Aquitaine in 1152 led to a renewed immigration of Norman courtiers to the English court.[38] Eleanor's patronage of the French courtly romance and lyrical poetry of the troubadours similarly reinforced the dominance of French (or Anglo-Norman) as a literary language.[39] The marriage therefore both consolidated Norman influence and encouraged the use of Anglo-Norman as a literary language. The prestige of French continued throughout the thirteenth century and its most extensive spread and use

---

[36] *Mervelous Signals. Poetics and Sign Theory in the Middle Ages* (Lincoln: University of Nebraska Press, 1986), 120.

[37] 'Romance and Other Genres', in *The Cambridge Companion to Medieval Romance*, ed. Roberta L. Krueger (Cambridge: Cambridge University Press, 2000), 45–59, at 46.

[38] The court of Henry II was decisively international and there was a current of intellectual and artistic exchange between England and the continent. The patronage of French literature was, however, particularly prevalent due to the cultural dominance of the courtly romance and troubadour poetry. For information on literary practices and the relations between England and the continent during the reign of Henry II, see Elizabeth Salter, *English and International: Studies in the Literature, Art and Patronage of Medieval England*, ed. Derek Pearsall and Nicolette Zeeman (Cambridge: Cambridge University Press, 1988), 1–74.

[39] Douglas A. Kibbee, *For to Speke Frenche Trewely. The French Language in England, 1000–1600: Its Status, Description and Instruction* (Amsterdam: John Benjamins Publishing Company, 1991), particularly 14–26.

Introduction

coincides surprisingly with the advent of anti-French sentiment in England.[40]

There is, however, a discernable shift in the literary culture in fourteenth-century England. Around the turn of the fourteenth century French was still 'the accepted medium of high literary expression'.[41] In the 1360s this seems, however, to alter, with English taking an increasingly dominating role, both politically and in secular literature. By the end of the century English had all but replaced French as the literary medium. The decline in the use of Anglo-Norman in the fourteenth century, both in literature and in the legal system, was hastened by the social and political consequences of the Hundred Years War (1337–1453), resulting in English almost completely replacing French in the literary (and public) realm by the end of the century.[42] None of the Middle English texts discussed here dates from further back than the fourteenth century, indicating the prior dominance of Anglo-Norman both in political and literary circles. While texts were being written in Middle English in the thirteenth century, the escalation in Middle English translations of Anglo-Norman and French texts early in the fourteenth century points to a shift in balance between the two vernaculars and the growing need for English translations for readers unable or unwilling to read French any more.

While French courtly literature was intimately linked with the civilising movement of the courtly ideology, it seems to have served a different purpose in England. Both English translations of French romances and original native works were written significantly later than their French counterparts – indicating both a temporal and cultural disparity between the reading communities of the French and English romances. It is often suggested that the English translations were intended for a lower-class audience, which would explain the alterations in form and matter of the texts as well as the need for the rendition into the English language.[43] The problem with this assumption

---

[40] Ibid. 4, 27–57. While it is difficult to ascertain how many were indeed capable of speaking or writing French (or Anglo-Norman) in the centuries following the Conquest, the royal court remained very significantly French-oriented. Serge Lusignan notes that 'every king from Henry III until Henry VI had a wife in their first or second marriage whose first language was French'. ('French Language in Contact with English: Social Context and Linguistic Change (mid-13th–14th centuries)', in *Language and Culture. The French of England c.1100–c.1500*, ed. Jocelyn Wogan-Browne *et al.*, York: York Medieval Press, 2009, 19–30, at 20.) The court thus remained a centre with a significant French presence from the Conquest until the end of the fourteenth century at the least.

[41] Michael Bennett, 'France in England: Anglo-French Culture in the Reign of Edward III', in Wogan-Browne *et al.*, *Language and Culture*, 320–33, at 320.

[42] Kibbee, *For to Speke Frenche Trewely*, 58–62. Michael Bennett suggests that the political conditions of the Hundred Years War may initially have increased the literary contact between England and France through campaigns and diplomatic interaction. The habit of taking nobles as prisoners to obtain ransom for their release may have lead to increased interchange, particularly in the middle of the century (Bennett, 'France in England'). For an in-depth analysis of how the Hundred Year War affected literary production in England see Butterfield, *The Familiar Enemy*.

[43] The preservation of the Middle English romances in manuscripts of lesser quality and with less decoration and illumination than, for instance, contemporary manuscripts containing religious texts would seem to support this shift in social hierarchy of the audience (Karl Brunner, 'Middle English Metrical Romances and their Audience', in *Studies in Medieval Literature. In*

is that the evidence of the social status of the audiences of these texts is commonly based on the texts themselves. The perceived inferiority of the texts in comparison with their more distinctly courtly originals is rationalised by the slide in social status of its readership. The presumption of a lower-class audience is then subsequently used to explain the modifications in the texts. This circular argument is a hermeneutic blunder that can happen all too easily. Of necessity, any scholar approaching the medieval period must make certain assumptions based on the scarce evidence available to him. We can presume, for instance, that the extant manuscript copies do not necessarily give an accurate view of the number and circulation patterns of those manuscripts. They do, nevertheless, indicate that the texts existed in that specific form, in a particular region, and within a certain reading community. The text can thus provide information about the reading habits and scribal practices of that community, whereas its spread and origination can only be inferred, with greater or lesser conviction, from the available material.

Referring to the Middle English courtly translations, Dieter Mehl notes that 'most of the social occasions on which minstrels performed and, possibly, romances were read, appear to have differed considerably from the exclusive aristocratic festivities on the continent.'[44] While this shift in interest is not necessarily indicative of social status, there appears nevertheless to have been a difference in the makeup of the audience groups of the courtly material in twelfth-century France and in England in the later centuries. While courtly compositions seem to have been limited to the aristocratic courts on the continent, later Middle English texts were being translated and copied independently of the courtly centres and frequently in the more rural areas of the north. Evidence of manuscript copying and translation activity substantiates the formation of certain reading communities. The presumption of a particular reading community must, however, often merely be surmised from the available evidence of manuscript production and the likely historical locations for preservation.

Rather than simply proclaiming the Middle English texts to be the result of ignorance and incompetence arising from the social status of their creators and recipients, the following chapters will explore other possibilities to

---

Honor of Professor Albert Croll Baugh, ed. MacEdward Leach, Philadelphia: University of Pennsylvania Press, 1961, 219–27, at 220. For a discussion of manuscripts containing Middle English romances see also Murray J. Evans, *Rereading Middle English Romance. Manuscript Layout, Decoration, and the Rhetoric of Composite Structure*, Montreal: McGill-Queen's University Press, 1995). The religious manuscripts served, however, additionally as visual symbolic artefacts that required the elaborate and ornamental representation of the text. Moreover, they contained sacred words that would have demanded appropriate execution of the outward form. The romances and the courtly literature, on the other hand, served the purpose of secular entertainment that would as such not have required any elaborate presentation. Rather, the focus would have been on preserving the cost of illumination, or expensive vellum, by focusing on the material contained within and thereby, perhaps, make the acquisition of multiple texts possible instead. If they were intended to be read to an audience, such elaborate visual depiction would additionally have been less relevant than with a sacred text intended for display, whether in church or in a home.

[44] *The Middle English Romances of the Thirteenth and Fourteenth Centuries*, 4.

explain the shift in language and the apparent pattern of alterations as reflections of a cultural agenda. The increased frequency and number of textual modifications apparent in the translations from the latter part of the fourteenth century seem to allude to the social consequences of the political friction with the French court and the emergence of Middle English as a viable literary language at the expense of Anglo-Norman. They similarly point to a more direct engagement with the French material in an apparent effort to reorient the political or social subtext of their originals.

Historical circumstances were radically different in Norway. Since the eighth century, the story of Anglo-Saxons, Danes, and Norsemen had been intertwined through conquest and territorial battles. English rule was, however, lost to the descendants of Canute (Knútr) (994/5–1035) with the defeat of the Norwegian Haraldr harðráði (r. 1047–66) at Stamford Bridge and the Norman invasion – although given the Norse origin of the Normans themselves, this in fact completed a covert dominion begun several centuries earlier.[45] Previously King Magnús the Good (r. 1035–47) had claimed the throne of Norway and later succeeded to Denmark as well at the death of Harðacnut in 1042.[46] What followed were intermittent periods of civil discord with efforts at reclaiming lost territories and uniting the kingdom.[47] It was not until the late twelfth century, when the Norwegian throne was claimed by Sverrir Sigurðsson (1145/51–1202), that the previous civil strife was brought to an end, preparing the way for the reign of his grandson, King Hákon Hákonarson (1204–63), who united the kingdom of Norway.

The relationship that was established by the Norwegians with the new Norman rule in England was one of peaceful diplomatic and mercantile exchange. The tradition of diplomatic correspondence and trading with England that had begun during the rule of Sverrir was strengthened by the

---

[45] Knútr, or Canute, ruled over England from 1016 to his death, over Denmark from 1018 and Norway from 1028. He was succeeded by his illegitimate son, Harold Harefoot, and later by Harðacnut. For information on royal history in Norway see for instance Knut Helle, ed., *The Cambridge History of Scandinavia*, vol. 1, *Prehistory to 1520* (Cambridge: Cambridge University Press, 2003). For information on the battle at Stamford Bridge see Kelly DeVries, *The Norwegian Invasion of England in 1066* (Woodbridge: The Boydell Press, 2003).

[46] The royal history of Scandinavia in the late Middle Ages is one of changing territorial boundaries and intermittent conquests and disputes. While Knútr held England, Denmark and Norway under his rule, his sons were unable to maintain control. With Harðacnut's death the English returned to their own royal bloodline and the throne of Denmark passed to Magnús, later to be claimed by Sweyn II. Haraldr harðráði (the Ruthless) shared the throne with his nephew, Magnús, and became sole ruler of Norway at his death in 1047. He was defeated in 1066 at Stamford Bridge in the last Norse attempt to reconquer England, only days before William's landing in Sussex and the Battle of Hastings, which practically guaranteed the Norman victory.

[47] King Óláfr the Peaceful (r. 1066/7–93) was on friendly terms with William the Conqueror (r. 1066–87). His successor, Magnús berfœti (Barelegs) (r. 1093–1103), was more aggressive and brought the Orkneys, Hebrides and Western Isles under his control. The joint rule of his sons, Eysteinn, Sigurðr and Óláfr (1103–30), re-established and reinforced the friendships with England. At the death of Sigurðr the country was torn by rival fractions and civil strife for over a century (Henry Goddard Leach, *Angevin Britain and Scandinavia*, Cambridge: Harvard University Press, 1921, 45–7).

friendly relationship that developed between King Hákon and the young ruler of England, King Henry III (r. 1216–72).[48] It was during this time that much of the French courtly material was introduced to Norway. Given the close and affable connections between the two monarchs, it is not unlikely that the manuscripts containing the French and Anglo-Norman materials came to Norway via England as part of royal exchange of gifts.[49] This conjecture is supported by the fact that French courtly literature was patronised by the Angevin king and queen and would hence have been readily available and, more importantly, representative of the splendour of the English court at the time. Many of the translated romances contain inscriptions indicating that they were seemingly translated at the request of King Hákon. Similarly, Norwegian manuscript fragments of several of the texts exist, which otherwise survive only in Icelandic manuscripts, indicating their Norse origin. This is moreover supported by philological evidence in other extant manuscript copies. Several of these Norse translations were later converted into Swedish at the behest of Eufemia, the queen of King Hákon V of Norway (r. 1299–1319), which confirms their existence in Norway at the time.[50]

Textual Transmission

The Norse texts analysed here all belong (except perhaps the Norse version of *Partonopeu de Blois*, whose origin remains uncertain) to the reign of King Hákon and hence bear witness to the massive flow of literary material from northern France through England and ultimately to Iceland via Norway. They form a coherent group as literary works executed at a specific time and place and encompassing a specific intent, the deliberate import of foreign material by the Norwegian court.[51] They were also, as a group, translated significantly

---

[48] For information on King Hákon's reign and the relations between the English and the Norwegian court during the rule of Hákon and King Henry III see Knut Helle, 'Anglo-Norwegian Relations in the Reign of Håkon Håkonsson (1217–63)', *Medieval Scandinavia* 1 (1968), 101–14; Knut Helle, ed. *The Cambridge History of Scandinavia*, particularly 369–91; and Leach, *Angevin Britain and Scandinavia*. Despite its age, Leach's massive volume, describing the historical connections between Britain and Scandinavia during the reign of the Angevin kings, continues to be a comprehensive and by and large an accurate source for the period and the relations between the countries.

[49] It is known that Henry took pleasure in hunting birds, such as hawks and falcons, and that they frequently served as royal gifts to the English monarch from King Hákon (Helle, 'Anglo-Norwegian Relations', 105–6).

[50] Some of the French material translated in Norway in the thirteenth century has in fact only been preserved in Norse. The Norse *Tristrams saga ok Ísöndar*, for instance, is frequently used as guide in the editing of the Anglo-Norman *Tristan* by Thomas of Brittany. The immense Nordic collection of *chansons de geste*, *Karlamagnús saga*, similarly contains episodes now lost, indicating that there may have been entire branches of the epic genre that are no longer extant except in a Norse version.

[51] I agree here with the arguments presented in a remarkable article by Jody Enders, which proposes the reintroduction of 'intentionality' into literary discussion ('Medieval Death, Modern Morality, and the Fallacies of Intention', *New Medieval Literatures* 5 (2002), 87–114). The presumption in this study is that there is with any given literary work an underlying intent that influences the shape of the work. While such 'authorial intent' is obviously both elusive

earlier than their respective Middle English counterparts, bringing to the fore some interesting questions about authorial intent and the impact it might have had upon the reconfigurations of the material. The earliest English text discussed here, *Ywain and Gawain*, has been dated to the first half of the fourteenth century, at least half a century later than its Norse equivalent, *Ívens saga*. The latest, *Sir Launfal*, from the late fourteenth century, was composed over a century later than the corresponding Norse translation of Marie de France's *Lais*. Given the complex preservation history of these Norse texts, however, the time lapse is diminished by the fact that the texts discussed below – apart from *Strengleikar*, which is preserved in a thirteenth-century Norwegian manuscript – have all come down to us in fourteenth- and fifteenth-century Icelandic manuscripts, putting them much closer in terms of actual identifiable reading communities to their English counterparts.

The discussion thus encompasses not only the move from northern France through England to Norway, but the ensuing transmission of those texts to Iceland, where they were copied and preserved. Iceland lost its independence to the Norwegian throne during the rule of King Hákon. The first half of the thirteenth century had been beset with civil discord between the principal families battling over control over the country. In 1262–4 the Althing recognised the Norwegian king as ruler, ending the Icelandic commonwealth, but bringing peace to a country torn apart by the bloodshed of feud and discord. A cultural correlation that had always existed as a result of the common heritage of the Icelandic and Norwegian people was thus reinforced by their union under one monarch. It is therefore quite likely that the French material translated in Norway passed not long afterwards to Iceland and it is even conceivable that Icelanders took part in the translation activity itself in Norway, given their propensity for historical writing and their established reputation in Scandinavia as historians and royal biographers.[52]

The Norse texts thus contain within them the complex pattern of cultural transmission from Anglo-Norman, or French, into the Norse tongue in the thirteenth century, only to be rewritten and possibly reshaped as they continued their journey further north. The copying of the French translated material in the fourteenth and fifteenth centuries in Iceland forms a part of a greater interest in literary activity and textual preservation evident in the copying and gathering of texts, both native and foreign, in massive manuscript collections. The Icelandic scribes did not seem to make a distinction between translated and native texts, putting together both translated romances with native ones in collections of romances. The distinction seems to be based not on the origination of the material, but rather on the language in which it has been preserved, that is, Norse. There are relatively few texts preserved in Latin

and limited, its existence and the bearing it has had on the work is of value in deciphering the cultural conceptualisations that have impacted its creation.

[52] It is known that Snorri Sturluson (1178/9–1241) visited the Norwegian court at least twice and his nephew, Sturla Þórðarson (1214–84), wrote Hákon's biography, *Hákonar saga Hákonarsonar* (see Guðrún Nordal, Sverrir Tómasson and Vésteinn Ólason, eds., *Íslensk bókmenntasaga*, vol. 1, Reykjavik: Mál og menning, 1992, 309–401, for information on Snorri Sturluson, in particular 366–83).

in Iceland, in comparison to England, and almost none of these collections contain works in multiple languages, as is apparent in English manuscripts.[53] This discrepancy indicates a difference in approach to notions of linguistic and national coherence between thirteenth- and fourteenth-century England and Iceland. Neither seems to make much of a distinction between adapted and native material, yet the Icelandic manuscripts are noticeably monolingual, whereas many of the English manuscripts evince the facility with which English readers apparently moved between Middle English, French and Latin.

The discussion in the following chapters begins with the exploration of the interconnections between the Angevin dynasty in England and the Norwegian court, and of questions of literary and cultural incursion. The analysis of the Middle English and Old Norse versions of Marie de France's *Lais*, presumably written in England in the twelfth century and preserved in Anglo-Norman, probes questions of cultural dominance by drawing on the critical discourses of imperialism and post-colonial theory. The political implications of the interrelation between Anglo-Norman and Middle English in the fourteenth century, when both *Lay le Freine* and *Sir Launfal* were written, are explored in the analysis of the reconstruction of the French text in Middle English. The question of whether political authority comes into play in textual transmission and how that affects the possible reshaping of philosophical or political subtext through dissident representation is thus probed. The chapter plays on the conceptualisations of cultural autonomy and identity, linguistic and literary authority and the implication of textual refashioning for literary integration and assimilation, or conversely, for cultural and linguistic defiance.

The following chapter moves geographically further south as the attention shifts from the Angevin empire to northern France and the tradition of the *chanson de geste*. *La Chanson de Roland* was written some time around the turn of the eleventh and the twelfth centuries, and thus reflects a different and earlier historical and cultural context than the *Lais*. Both formed, however, part of the same import of French literary material into Norway in the thirteenth century. This is the only chapter depicting a two-way comparison as there is no comparable version of *La Chanson de Roland* in English.[54] The text of the *Chanson* is, nonetheless, important in the context of this discussion as it contains ethics of the heroic mentality that accords with the Germanic tradition of warrior ideals evident in Scandinavian literature. This epic mode of representation is absent from the romances, as they depict a fundamentally new stage of literary concerns and moral ideals. The comparative analysis of the reception of the epic text as opposed to the more lyric poetry of Marie de France, or the later courtly romances, thus

---

[53] The few instances where the amalgamation of Latin and Norse can be found occur in religious manuscripts, where a Norse translation might follow a Latin sermon, for instance.

[54] The extant fragment of 1,049 lines of the Middle English *Song of Roland*, preserved in the Lansdowne MS 388, is not based on the extant French text of *La Chanson de Roland*, or at least not exclusively, and is to a great extent indebted to Turpin's *Vita Caroli Magni*, often referred to as the Pseudo-Turpin (*The Sege off Melayne, The Romance of Duke Rowland and Sir Otuell of Spayne, The Song of Roland*, ed. Sidney J. Herrtage, Early English Text Society Extra Series 35, New York: Kraus Reprint, 1981, xviii–xxv).

provides a contrast that foregrounds the mode of reception, the nature of modifications, and the function the texts may have had within their reading communities. The emphasis in the analysis of the Norse version of the *Chanson* is on the transmission of behavioural patterns. These serve as evidence of the conceptualisation of culture as a semiotic system that is inherently destabilised in the process of translation owing to the different significations attached to the semiotic concepts within each linguistically defined community. It thus portrays translation essentially as the transfer of signs from one system to another, necessitating cultural adaptation of unfamiliar signs, or signs with a different (and sometimes opposite) meaning.

The third chapter returns to the time period of the formation of the courtly romance and the introduction of courtly literature in the examination of the Norse and English translations of Chrétien de Troyes's *Le Chevalier au Lion*, or *Yvain*. While the French text was written at approximately the same time as Marie de France's *Lais*, and the Norse text translated about a century later, the English text belongs to the same period as *Lay le Freine* and shows some signs of modifications similar to those in that text. Both show deceptive fidelity to their original, quite unlike the later *Sir Launfal*, for instance, that nonetheless conceal systematic modifications of the source texts, indicating a different authorial intent and purpose. The chapter focuses on narratological transformations evident in both the English and Norse texts as evidence of the narrative predilections of the English and the Norse audiences. The interconnections between the cultural traditions of those reading communities, versus that of the French courtly milieu that promoted the perfection of the romance form in the hands of Chrétien de Troyes, are similarly explored. Again, the disparity in modification agenda between the Norse and English translators highlights the cultural and social implications of the translation activity.

The final chapter addresses the longest and most complex text of all the works analysed here. *Partonopeu de Blois* pulls together many of the threads discussed in the previous chapters, while simultaneously throwing into relief the complexities and ambiguities of cultural and textual transmission. *Partonopeu* epitomises the multiplicity of medieval textuality, yet it has been curiously neglected by critics. The existence of two separate and defined versions of the story makes the comparative analysis particularly challenging. Yet at the same time it highlights some of the main arguments that have been put forth in the preceding chapters, which have dealt with the direct transmission of a single text from one language to another. The complexity is amplified by the existence of both versions in English, thereby interlinking the English translations to both the Norse and the French text. Here there is evidence of intricate and fascinating transmission patterns, of sophistication in literary adaptation that surpasses the other translations, of elaborate and perhaps surprising cultural and social interrelations. The discussion is complicated by the fact that it is unclear whether the text was translated in thirteenth-century Norway or not, which shifts the focus to the Icelandic manuscript copies. Evidence of romance translation activity in Iceland in the fourteenth century would have dramatic effects on the understanding of literary activity and audience interests in Iceland at that time. It has generally been assumed that the French material was translated in Norway and eventually transported to Iceland. If *Partalopa saga* was in fact translated in Iceland in the fourteenth century it would reveal direct and dynamic engagement with foreign literary material by writers in fourteenth-century Iceland. The fourteenth century in Iceland has frequently been regarded as the century of literary decline, marking the end of native saga composition, which was succeeded by the 'lesser' non-indigenous genres such as the romances. Recently, however, scholars have begun to direct their attention to the more marginal genres of *riddarasögur* (romances) and *fornaldarsögur* (legendary sagas) as evidence of a flourishing literary tradition that is moreover intimately interconnected with continental literary activity.[55] Christopher Sanders states, in his edition of *Bevers saga*, that there is in fact no conclusive evidence that points to a Norwegian origin of the translation, which suggests that not only may *Partalopa saga* have been translated in Iceland, but so may *Bevers saga*.[56] The relocation of the translation of *Bevers saga* and *Partalopa saga* would indicate the active engagement with foreign literary material in fourteenth-century Iceland. *Bevers saga* is a translation of the Anglo-Norman *Boeve de Haumtone* and Sanders argues for close correlations between the Icelandic version and the existing manuscript copies of the Anglo-Norman version, making it likely that the text came to Iceland (or Norway) via Britain.[57] The connections with England and English literary activity are of particular interest here as both the Norse and English translations of *Partonopeu de Blois* preserve the variant version of the Partonope legend.

The chapter contemplates this question of transmission patterns and the role the textual transmission has played in the reconstruction of the text. The focus is on the cultural impact in the analysis of modifications in gender structures and character representation. These modifications in turn indicate distinct differences in gendered social and cultural values. Perhaps more than anything, the chapter suggests a new mode of approaching such a study, one that favours the translation as an independent work representative of the social and literary context from which it originates and foregrounds the differences between source text and translation as evidence of cultural creativity. The chapter is therefore intended to both deepen and complicate the argument of cultural transmission.

[55] For a discussion of *riddarasögur* see for instance Kalinke, *King Arthur North-by-Northwest* and *Bridal-Quest Romance in Medieval Iceland*; Barnes, 'Romance in Iceland'; and Glauser, 'Romance (Translated *riddarasögur*)'. For approaches to *fornaldarsögur* see for instance Torfi Tulinius, *The Matter of the North. The Rise of Literary Fiction in Thirteenth-Century Iceland*, trans. Randi C. Eldevik (Odense: The Odense University Press, 2002); and Agnete Ney, Ármann Jakobsson and Annette Larsen, eds., *Fornaldarsagaerne: Myter og virkelighed* (Copenhagen: Museum Tusculanums Forlag, 2008).

[56] *Bevers saga* has been preserved in Icelandic manuscripts only, although the story is listed in an inventory written in Ryfylke in Norway in 1366. Sanders points out that while remarkable, the citation is not an indication of Norwegian origin as Icelandic manuscripts were frequently exported to Norway in the fourteenth century (*Bevers saga*, ed. Christopher Sanders, Reykjavík: Stofnun Árna Magnússonar á Íslandi, 2001, xc–xci).

[57] Ibid. clii–clvi.

Introduction

The structure of the book is thus neither linear nor geographically organised, but is based instead on a thematic development. It moves from the notion of literary imperialism in the first chapter to examination of behavioural patterns in the second, through analysis of narrative transformations in the third and ultimately to investigation of representational modifications as evidence of intrinsic disparities in societal perceptions of gender and social structures. The broad scope, both in terms of texts and methodology, is intended to denote the complexity of cultural transfer. The exploration of literary and cultural influence in the first chapter serves to foreground the concept of *mouvance* on a national scale, or perhaps more accurately on an international scale. The movement of texts and their implicit cultural content across linguistic and territorial boundaries underlies the entire topic of the volume and hence is addressed in the first chapter on the expansive level of cultural and social contact. The second chapter in turn narrows the focus from the encounter between the sometimes conflicting ideologies of separate cultural domains to the study of behavioural and emotional modifications. The view thus shifts from the trans-national movement of texts to the examination of behavioural codes intrinsic to every community and the way in which those existing codes shape the substance of the translation.

The third chapter maintains the more restricted perspective by analysing narrative and formal conventions as means of establishing the mobility and regenerative quality of literary traditions. In the fourth chapter the scope is broadened again to explore the ideologically prescribed perceptions of such concepts as masculinity, femininity and authority. This in a way completes the circle and returns to the first chapter in the questioning of the inherent qualities of the societal perception of gender. It seeks to illuminate through the comparative reading of the various versions of the Partonope story how such structures are culturally determined and hence unstable and variable. In a sense, the last chapter thus confirms the notion of cultural resistance proposed in the first chapter through the depiction of the literary transformations of the socially prescribed codes of gendered behaviour. The discussion therefore seeks to capture the multiplicity of cultural movement in the late Middle Ages through the exploration of the various aspects of textual transmission, such as the impact of culturally prescribed codes of conduct and narrative conventions as well as the significance of pre-existing literary traditions in translation. Similarly it aspires to reveal how the reception of ideologically determined narrative functions and character portraits affects the refashioning of those texts and what that tells us about their ultimate reading communities.

CHAPTER ONE

The Imperial Implications of Medieval Translations: Textual Transmission of Marie de France's *Lais*

BY EXAMINING THE ADAPTATIONS of Marie de France's *Lais* into Old Norse and Middle English, this chapter seeks to explore issues of cultural dominance and imperial influence in textual transmission during the late Middle Ages in Northern Europe. The interrelations of the various cultures and the respective medieval vernaculars, Old French, Middle English and Old Norse, will be explored through linguistic and contextual analysis of the translations.[1] The intention is to provide a comparative model of translation as intercultural by drawing on and conversing with post-colonial studies.

Critical discourse about imperialism tends to focus on the aggression of a dominant nation, the empire, upon an ethnically defined 'other'. Despite the complex interplay of cultural authority and subordination in late-medieval Europe, the definition of 'empire' tends to shift such discussions away from the Middle Ages towards latter periods of *post*-colonial activity. Recent studies, however, have borrowed the theoretical approaches of post-colonial studies to examine the complexities and ambivalences of intercultural relations in the medieval period.[2] While many adherents of post-colonial theories warn against their geographical and temporal displacement in this way, I agree with Patricia Clare Ingham's counter-argument that 'the modernity of post-colonial studies blocks certain routes to the past, and thus maintains

---

[1] By 'cultures' I mean the respective cultural realms of the texts, i.e. the Norwegian royal court in the thirteenth century, at which the *lais* were presumably translated, the geographically demarcated and linguistically defined realm in which Middle English would have been spoken and written, and the French-speaking courtly environment out of which and into which the *lais* were composed. The fact that the geographical locations of these 'cultures' might in fact overlap does not negate the fact that the transfer from one language to another involves a cultural transfer in so far as linguistic conceptions are of necessity culturally determined.
[2] See Ananya Jahanara Kabir and Deanne Williams, eds., *Postcolonial Approaches to the European Middle Ages* (Cambridge: Cambridge University Press, 2005); Patricia Clare Ingham and Michelle R. Warren, eds., *Postcolonial Moves: Medieval through Modern* (New York: Palgrave Macmillan, 2003); Patricia Clare Ingham, '"In Contrayez Straunge": Colonial Relations, British Identity, and *Sir Gawain and the Green Knight*', *New Medieval Literatures* 4 (2001), 61–94; Jeffrey Jerome Cohen, ed., *The Postcolonial Middle Ages* (New York: St Martin's Press, 2000); Sharon Kinoshita, *Medieval Boundaries. Rethinking Difference in Old French Literature* (Philadelphia: University of Pennsylvania Press, 2006).

certain nationalist and historicist exclusions'.[3] The deliberate distancing of post-colonial studies from the dynamics of both cultural and geographical conflicts in pre-modern civilisations re-enacts the binary oppositions of modern and archaic, civilised and barbaric. The shifting of those temporal boundaries challenges this conception of modernity as oppositional to the medieval as 'other' by allowing for the inclusion of the medieval as a site of potential imperial dynamics.

By drawing on imperial theorising to explore pre-colonial issues of power and cultural marginality, I do not mean to question its later historical relevance, but rather to expand the concept to include 'cultural' imperialism.[4] By using the metaphor of national expansions to incorporate cultural expansionism one can examine power dynamics without prejudging the stability of such categories as race, ethnicity and nationality in medieval times. I conceptualise empire as the perceived cultural and political superiority of a cohesive sovereign, in this case the 'Francophone court'.[5] This does not entail the imposition of national borders and ethnic distinctions – constructions that form a part of modern sensibilities rather than medieval – so much as the perception of regal rule based on political authority and linguistic coherence.

Admittedly, the medieval imperium is to be found in Christendom and its propagation, rather than in secular rulers. The impact of the teachings of the Roman Church upon its adjacent domains is, however, replicated on a cultural and linguistic level in the relationship between a culturally and politically dominant society and the surrounding territories. The authority of that cultural centre is amplified by the dispersal of the imperial power of Christian ideology through missionary activity and religious dissemination.[6] In England this becomes apparent when Anglo-Normans are installed in positions of power within the English Church after the Conquest and thus placed in control of the interpretation and representation of Christian ideas

---

[3] Ingham and Warren, *Postcolonial Moves*, 2. For argument against such usage see for example Bill Ashcroft, Introduction, in Bill Ashcroft, Gareth Griffiths and Helen Tiffin, eds., *The Post-Colonial Studies Reader* (London: Routledge, 1995), 1–4, and Gabrielle Spiegel, 'Épater les médiévistes', *History and Theory* 39 (2000), 243–50.

[4] The term 'cultural imperialism' is used by John Tomlinson in his book, *Cultural Imperialism* (Baltimore: Johns Hopkins University Press, 1991), which, however, addresses the supposed negative impact of the modern ethos of capitalism and consumerism on the Third World, not perceived cultural superiority in the Middle Ages. For a discussion of the history of the term see ibid., 2–8.

[5] 'Francophone court' serves here as a term for the literary and cultural traditions of the French-speaking aristocratic courts (including such dialects as Francien of the royal court of France, Anglo-Norman in England, and Picard in the north-east).

[6] The complex pattern of cultural transmission, such as the diffusion of Christian doctrine from Rome through France, arriving ultimately in Norway via England, obviates any clear distinction between centre and margins. Similarly the ethnic migrations (for example the Norsemen to Normandy) and the often convoluted flow of literary themes and ideas (the Breton *lais* for instance) preclude any rigid definition of cultural hierarchy. There is, however, a clear sense of cultural dispersion and receptivity evident in the dissemination of French literary material into Middle English and Old Norse in the thirteenth and fourteenth centuries, which draws on the perceived cultural and literary pre-eminence of northern France.

and principles.[7] The interrelations between the ecclesiastical domain, education and writing make literature the prime location for manifestations of imperial influence. The study of translations, particularly translations from a dominant language into a language with a less authoritative status, provides the ideal locus for examining problems of power and cultural transposition.[8]

Cultural Authority and Linguistic Resistance

The corpus of *Lais* customarily ascribed to Marie de France is believed to have been written in England between 1155 and 1170. The twelve *lais* have been preserved in only one complete Anglo-Norman manuscript, British Library Harley 978, written in the mid-thirteenth century in England. There are additionally four extant manuscripts containing one or more of her *lais*.[9] During the reign of Hákon Hákonarson, king of Norway from 1217 to 1263, several translations of French literature into Old Norse were commissioned, ostensibly by the king himself, one of which was a collection of *lais*, called *Strengleikar*: '<E>N bok þessor er hinn virðulege hacon konongr let norræna or volsko male ma hæita lioða bok. þui at af þæim sogum er þæssir bok birtir gærðo skolld i syðra brætlande er liggr i frannz lioðsonga' (4) (This book, which the esteemed King Hákon had translated into Norse from the French language, may be called 'Book of Lais', because from the stories which this book makes known, poets in Brittany – which is in France – composed *lais*) (5).[10] It contains eleven of Marie's *Lais* (*Eliduc* is omitted) along with ten other

---

[7] The division between the French-speaking ecclesiastical leaders and the English-speaking congregation foregrounds the inevitability of either a complete alienation and subjugation of the subjects, often observed in modern post-colonial states, or, conversely, the integration and assimilation of the dominating force into the existing social realm, as evinced in late-medieval England.

[8] The editors of *The Idea of the Vernacular* point out that recent scholarship on medieval translations has been 'less concerned with translation as a pragmatic or creative practice than as a site where cultural relations of dominance and subservience might be played out' ('The Notion of Vernacular Theory', in *The Idea of the Vernacular*, ed. Jocelyn Wogan-Browne, Nicholas Watson, Andrew Taylor, and Ruth Evans, University Park: The Pennsylvania University Press, 1999, 314–30, at 317). For works adopting this approach see for instance A. J. Minnis, *Medieval Theory of Authorship* (Philadelphia: University of Pennsylvania Press, 1988) and Rita Copeland, *Rhetoric, Hermeneutics, and Translation in the Middle Ages. Academic Traditions and Vernacular Texts* (Cambridge: Cambridge University Press, 1991).

[9] *Les Lais de Marie de France*, ed. Jean Rychner (Paris: Éditions Champion, 1966), and *The Lais of Marie de France*, trans. Robert Hanning and Joan Ferrante (New York: E. P. Dutton, 1978). The intricacies of the Anglo-Norman and Old French linguistic and cultural interrelations will not be addressed directly in this chapter and a common 'French' cultural background of those texts will be assumed. This approach does not reject existing internal differences, but rather seeks to foreground the commonality of the cultural heritage of French and Anglo-Norman linguistic and literary traditions as it pertains to literary transmission of French material in England and Scandinavia.

[10] *Strengleikar. An Old Norse Translation of Twenty-one Old French Lais*, ed. Robert Cook and Mattias Tveitane (Oslo: Norsk historisk kjeldskrift-institutt, 1979). Quotations will hereafter be given with page number in parentheses in the text with the relevant poem identified if necessary. Cook's English translation of the Norse prose is used throughout the paper with only minor amendments when needed for comparison purposes.

lais, some of which have no known Old French originals. The Old Norse text has been preserved in a single manuscript, Codex De la Gardie 4–7 in the Uppsala University Library, dated approximately 1270, which is no longer in a complete state. Fragments varying in size are now conserved as manuscript AM 666b 4to in the Arnamagnæan collection in Copenhagen.[11] The codex is missing several leaves from the end, indicating that it may have contained more *lais*. It is, however, unlikely that *Eliduc* formed part of the compilation as it could scarcely have fitted on the lost leaves.[12]

Prior to King Hákon's ascent to the throne in 1217, Norway had been wracked by civil wars and strife for almost a century. It was during his reign that peace was brought to the country under one rule.[13] His grandfather, King Sverrir Sigurðsson (r. 1184–1202), had instituted a central government and established the close connection to the English court that would only be reinforced during the sovereignty of his grandson. The Church was similarly dependent on English religious houses, both in terms of ecclesiastical organisation and education, since the institution and dispersal of Christian doctrine in the thirteenth century was almost exclusively accomplished through England.[14] The ensuing peace and relative prosperity allowed the king to pursue his more refined interests. The burst of literary and translation activity in Norway during his rule testifies to his interest in such cultural activities. Several romance translations name him as patron and instigator of the translation activity and the majority of the translated romances have been attributed to his reign. *Tristrams saga* contains, for instance, a prologue, similar to that of *Strengleikar*, indicating that the text was supposedly commissioned by King Hákon:

> Hér skrifaz sagan af Tristram ok Ísönd dróttningu, í hverri talat verðr um óbæriliga ást, er þau höfðu sín á milli. Var þá liðit frá hingatburði Christi 1226 ár, er þessi saga var á norrænu skrifuð eptir befalningu ok skipan virðuligs herra Hákonar kóngs. En Bróðir Robert efnaði ok upp skrifaði eptir sinni kunnáttu með þessum orðtökum, sem eptir fylgir í sögunni ok nú skal frá segja.[15]

---

[11] The De la Gardie manuscript is the oldest and most important Norwegian source of Old Norse translations of courtly literature, as most of the romance translations have been preserved only in later Icelandic manuscripts.

[12] The major part of the codex 'was originally made up of six regular gatherings, consisting of 8 leaves, or 4 double leaves each. It would, therefore, be natural to suppose ... that the seventh and last gathering also consisted of 8 leaves, of which only the outer pair, leaves 1/8, is now preserved' (ibid. xiii–xvii). For a description of the manuscript see *Elis saga, Strengleikar and Other Texts. Uppsala University Library Delagardieska Samlingen Nos. 4–7 Folio and AM 666 b Quarto*, ed. Mattias Tveitane. Corpus codicum norvegicorum medii aevi, quarto serie, vol. 4 (Oslo: The Society for Publications of Old Norwegian Manuscripts, 1972).

[13] For information on the historical context of King Hákon's rule see Knut Helle, ed. *The Cambridge History of Scandinavia*, vol. 1, *Prehistory to 1520* (Cambridge: Cambridge University Press, 2003), particularly 369–91.

[14] Religious houses were not only founded on Anglo-Norman traditions and through English sister houses, but were often ruled by Anglo-Norman abbots. The Norwegian Cistercian houses Hovedøya and Lyse near Bergen, which are linked to the production of texts during King Hákon's rule, were founded as the daughter houses of the English Fountains Abbey in 1146 (*Elis saga, Strengleikar and Other Texts*, 32).

[15] *Tristrams saga ok Ísöndar*, ed. and trans. Peter Jorgensen, in *Norse Romance*, ed. Marianne

[Written down here is the story of Tristram and Queen Ísönd and of the heart-rending love they shared. This saga was translated into the Norse tongue at the behest and decree of King Hákon when 1226 years had passed since the birth of Christ. Brother Robert ably prepared the text and wrote it down in the words appearing in this saga. And now it shall be told.][16]

The prologue moreover states the presumed date of the translation, 1226, and provides the name of the translator, or scribe, as Brother Robert. The name may link the text to *Elis saga*, contained in the De la Gardie manuscript, which refers to a translator by the name of 'Roðbert ábóti' (Abbot Roðbert), who purportedly translated the text at the request of King Hákon.[17] If the preamble is accurate it confirms King Hákon as the patron of *Tristrams saga* and quite possibly the other stories dedicated to him, i.e. *Ívens saga, Elis saga, Strengleikar* and *Möttuls saga*. While such dedications are quite common and often form part of the rhetoric of the text, the fact that several texts name King Hákon as a patron of the translation supports the claim. It can furthermore be shown by means of manuscript preservation, linguistic and stylistic analysis that the texts are likely to have been translated in Norway in the thirteenth century. Similarly, the opulence of Hákon's court at Bergen, in comparison with prior and other Scandinavian royal sites, as well as the education of his sons bear witness to a predilection for the sophistication evidenced by his English and French neighbours.[18]

It is not unreasonable to assume that the king would seek to emulate the courtly refinement of his royal allies in the British Isles, particularly considering the close and cordial relationship he enjoyed with King Henry III and the English throne. Henry Goddard Leach argues that the Norse translations were literally intended as manuals in the customs of chivalry.[19] Marianne E. Kalinke rejects this notion, arguing that their main purpose was entertainment, not instruction, since the very elements of courtly etiquette, such as descriptions of dresses and passages of love, were greatly condensed or omitted.[20] The fact that the texts were adjusted to Nordic audiences by excluding or reducing elements that had no meaning within the receptive culture does not preclude their function as guidance in courtly mannerisms. Similarly the very notion that

---

E. Kalinke, vol. 1, *The Tristan Legend* (Cambridge: D. S. Brewer, 1999), 23–226, at 28.

[16] Ibid. 29. The English translation is based on the facing-page translation of the saga.

[17] *Elis saga ok Rósamundu*, ed. Eugen Kölbing (Heilbronn: Verlag von Gebr. Henninger, 1881), 116. It is conceivable that the same individual, a monk by the name of Robert or Roðbert, translated both *Tristrams saga* and *Elis saga* and that at the time of the translation of *Elis saga* he had become an abbot. The name is not Scandinavian and it has generally been assumed that he was an English (Anglo-Norman) monk and that he resided perhaps at Lyse (*Elis saga, Strengleikar and Other Texts*, 32). For information on Brother Robert, see for instance Sverrir Tómasson, 'Hvenær var *Tristrams sögu* snúið?', *Grípla* 2 (1977), 47–78, and works cited there.

[18] The young Hákon (1232–57) was instructed in the arts of the Norman knights and his brother, Magnús (1238–80), later king of Norway, became patron of Icelandic writers who visited the court at the king's request (Henry Goddard Leach, *Angevin Britain and Scandinavia*, Cambridge: Harvard University Press, 1921, 154–5).

[19] *Angevin Britain and Scandinavia*, 153.

[20] *King Arthur North-by-Northwest. The 'matière de Bretagne' in Old Norse-Icelandic Romances*. Bibliotheca Arnamagnæana 37 (Copenhagen: C. A. Reitzels boghandel, 1981), 28.

they were intended as 'entertainment' rather than for educational, doctrinal or documentary purposes, indicates the extent to which the ideology represented within the text, that is the nobility's leisure to pursue such frivolous matters, has been assumed. It is therefore quite plausible that the succession of translations, apparently commissioned by King Hákon and carried out during his reign, formed part of an introduction and institution of the courtly tradition of the French and Anglo-Norman rulers among his entourage.

This influx of French literature into Norway in the thirteenth century brings to mind the question of cultural dominance in textual transmission. Those texts contained embedded within them the ideology of a dominant linguistic and cultural centre that would have an impact on the reading communities receiving them. The fact that the foreign material may have been imported on purpose to influence social behaviour draws attention to the volatility of cultural stability. Michael Doyle's definition of empire as a relationship between two political societies, defined by control and achieved by either direct violence or by indirect social and cultural dependency, points to the significance of the underlying civilising force in the imperial endeavour.[21] The cultural and political authority of the Francophone court versus that of Norway establishes a connection between a dominant territory and a marginal one. The resulting unilateral communication of ideas thus reaffirms conventional imperialist tenets. The Norwegian manual for princes, *Konungs skuggsjá* (Latin: *Speculum Regale*), presumably written during King Hákon's reign, contains a paragraph specifying the status of the French tongue as a language of political value: 'oc æf þu willt wærða fullkomenn í froð- | leic. Þa næmðu allar mallyzkur *en* | *alra hælz latinu oc walsku. Þwiat* | *þær tungur ganga wiðazt.* En þo | dynþu æigi at hældr þinni tungo'[22] (And if you wish to become perfect in knowledge, you must learn all the languages, *first and foremost Latin and French, for these idioms are most widely used.* And yet, do not forget your native tongue or speech).[23] The fact that the Francophone court was only inadvertently implicit in its imperial mission does not negate the relationship established between the two sovereigns. It is the *perception* of superiority, rather than a forceful imposition of values by an empire, which results here in the dynamics of cultural supremacy and dependence.[24] The

---

[21] *Empires* (Ithaca: Cornell University Press, 1986), 45.
[22] *Speculum Regale. Ein altnorwegischer Dialog nach Cod. Arnamagn. 243 Fol. B und den ältesten Fragmenten*, ed. Oscar Brenner (Munich: Christian Kaiser, 1881), 8, my italics.
[23] *The King's Mirror (Speculum Regale – Konungs skuggsjá)*, trans. Laurence Marcellus Larson (New York: The American-Scandinavian Foundation, 1917), 81, my italics. Minor adjustments have been made to Larson's translation to more accurately reflect the Norse text. It is of note here that the manual underlines the significance of not neglecting the native tongue or allowing it to be corrupted by foreign influence, revealing an awareness of the correlation between language and identity, past and history.
[24] The modern world is witnessing similar imperial tendencies in the incursion of American language and popular culture into the global community. The absence of direct political aggression therefore in no way diminishes the impact of the dominating culture upon those receiving the foreign material. These relationships undergo constant realignment as the native cultures try to resist the foreign influence on the basis of on linguistic policy, cultural integrity and national identity. The very same impulses of resistance, albeit perhaps less overt

infiltration of a dominant ideology into a marginal society highlights the imbalance of power and the imperial implication of the literary incursion.

A closer look at the text will reveal the complex interrelations of cultural authority and reception in textual transmission. The Norse translator transforms the verse form of Marie de France's *Lais* into prose, resulting in adjustments both in the aural effect of the text and in the condensation of the matter. The existing native metres of eddic and skaldic verse (*dróttkvætt*) were singularly unsuited for the octosyllabic couplets of Marie de France's *Lais*.[25] Moreover, there was already an established custom of prose narration in Scandinavia at the time in the writings of *konungasögur* (sagas of kings) and *Íslendingasögur* (sagas of Icelanders).[26] Given the lack of suitable verse form and the strong tradition of vernacular prose writing, the choice of prose over verse as medium seems logical as it would ensure the reception of the foreign material by an audience already accustomed to such narrative presentation. Yet the transfer from the evocative lyricism of Marie de France's poems to the traditionally austere and objective narrative mode of the native prose is particularly challenging.

The opening lines of the first poem in the collection, the Anglo-Norman *Guigemar* and the Old Norse *Guiamars lioð*, will serve to elucidate similarities and divergences in the translation process:

> Les contes ke jo sai verrais,
> Dunt li Bretun unt fait les lais,
> Vos conterai assez briefment.
> El chief de cest comencement,
> Sulunc la lettre e l'escriture,
> Vos mosterai une aventure
> Ki en Bretaigne la Menur
> Avint al tens ancïenur.   (19–26)[27]

and conscious, can be observed in the Nordic reception of the French literary matter.

[25] The eddic verse form is based on short lines, with a limited number of syllables, that are linked together by alliteration. The skaldic metre is ornate with complex syntactical constructions interspersed with compound metaphors called *kennings*. For an astute and original recent study of skaldic verse see Guðrún Nordal, *Tools of Literacy: The Role of Skaldic Verse in Icelandic Textual Culture of the Twelfth and Thirteenth Centuries* (Toronto: University of Toronto Press, 2001). For a general overview of eddic and skaldic verse see Margaret Clunies Ross, *A History of Old Norse Poetry and Poetics* (Cambridge: D. S. Brewer, 2005).

[26] It is likely that some form of native literature (whether oral or written) was being produced in Norway with similarities to that extant from Iceland, or that Norwegians were at least familiar with what was being produced in Iceland, in view of the close cultural connections between the two countries. *Konungs skuggsjá* was written around 1250, indicating that vernacular prose was an accepted medium in the mid-thirteenth century. The historian Snorri Sturluson (1178/9–1241) resided at the royal court in Norway before writing *Heimskringla*, the story of the Norwegian royal family. At least two Icelanders, Karl Jónsson (c.1135–1213), who wrote *Sverris saga*, and Sturla Þórðarson (1214–84), who wrote the sagas of King Hákon Hákonarson and Magnús the Law-mender, were employed at the court (see Guðrún Nordal, Sverrir Tómasson and Vésteinn Ólason, eds., *Íslensk bókmenntasaga*, vol. 1, Reykjavík: Mál og menning, 1992, 358–401).

[27] Quotations are taken from *Les Lais de Marie de France*, ed. Jean Rychner, and will hereafter

[The tales which I know are true –
and from which the Bretons made their lais –
I'll now recount for you briefly;
and at the very beginning of this enterprise,
just the way it was written down,
I'll relate an adventure
that took place in Brittany,
in the old days.]²⁸

The Norse version follows the text closely and can be read almost line by line: 'SOgur þær er ec væit sannar oc brættar hava lioðsonga af gort. vil ec segia yðr sem ec ma með fæstom orðum. En sua sem ritningar hava synt mer vil ec sægia yðr atburði þa sem gerðuzt a hinu syðra bretlande i fyrnskunni' (12) (The stories which I know are true and from which the Bretons have made *lais* I want to tell you as best I can in a very few words. And just as writings have revealed to me, so will I tell you the adventures which took place in Brittany a long time ago) (13). The soft, playful tone of the original is to a great extent lost in the adaptation of the material to the linguistic structure of Norse prose, where sentences become generally shorter and more abrupt. The result is often a more powerful and swift narration which shifts the focus from the inner perspective of the characters to the action.

The impartial narrative tone, adopted from the native literary tradition, and the apparent lack of interest in the psychology of the characters, differ fundamentally from the ostensibly light-hearted yet subtly judicious narrative presence in the Anglo-Norman poems. The general prologue to the *Lais* is, in fact, a declaration of personal voice and authorship. The statement that 'ki Deus ad duné escïence / E de parler bone eloquence / Ne s'en deit taiser ne celer, / Ainz se deit voluntiers mustrer' (1–4) (whoever has received knowledge / and eloquence in speech from God / should not be silent or secretive / but demonstrate it willingly) (Prologue 1–4) is a direct reference to the authorial self.²⁹ The compelling personal voice in the *Lais* is, however, undermined

---

be given with line numbers for the relevant poem in parenthesis in the text. Unless specified in the text the *lai* in question is also identified.

²⁸ Robert Hanning and Joan Ferrante's English translation is used in this paper with some minor adjustments (*The Lais of Marie de France*). Line numbers are given in parenthesis following the citation in the text. If necessary the relevant *lai* will be identified as well.

²⁹ Even if one assumes the prologue containing the reference to Marie in the Harley manuscript to be an addition, the *lais* themselves nevertheless form a corpus inasmuch as they interact with each other through recurring themes, symbols, repetition and intertextual dialogue. Moreover, the narrative voice throughout the *lais* as well as the perspective is quite distinctly (and uniquely) feminine. For further information about Marie as an author see Howard R. Bloch, *The Anonymous Marie de France* (Chicago: The University of Chicago Press, 2003). For information on the narrative voice see for instance Roberta L. Krueger, 'Marie de France', in *The Cambridge Companion to Medieval Women's Writing*, ed. Carolyn Dinshaw and David Wallace (Cambridge: Cambridge University Press, 2003), 172–83, and H. Marshall Leicester, Jr, 'The Voice of the Hind. The Emergence of Feminine Discontent in the *Lais* of Marie de France', in *Reading Medieval Culture. Essays in Honor of Robert W. Hanning*, ed. Robert M. Stein and Sandra Pierson Prior (Notre Dame, Indiana: University of Notre Dame Press, 2005), 132–69.

in the Norse text as the translator adds a preamble to the actual prologue displacing Marie's voice with his own:[30]

> <A>T hæve þeirra er i fyrnskun*n*i varo likaðe oss at forvitna ok ran*n*zaka ... ok fyr*i*r þui at i fyrnskun*n*i gerðuzc marger undarleger lut*i*r ok ohæyrðir atburðir a varu*m* dogum. þa syndizc oss at fræða verande ok viðrkomande þæim sogum er margfroðer men*n* gærðu um athæve þæirra sem i fyrnskun*n*i varo ok a bokom leto rita. (4)
>
> [It pleased us to inquire about and examine the deeds of those who lived in olden days ... And because many marvelous things and events unheard of in our time took place in olden days, it occurred to us to teach men living and those to come these stories, which men of great learning made about the deeds of those who lived in olden days and which they had written down in books. (5)]

The narrative 'us' here shifts the authority within the passage away from the personal voice in the French text, which is subtly seeking to establish its own feminine voice as authoritative through reference to God as the ultimate source of her literary talent.[31] The narrator moreover grounds this authority in 'men of great learning', which is precisely the canon of secular authority that the narrative voice in Marie's *lais* is contending and into which she is inserting her text (if we presume the author indeed to be a women, whether or not with the name of Marie). Once the translator therefore commences with the French prologue, the context is radically different and the words 'vizsku ok kun*n*asto ok snilld' (6) (wisdom and knowledge and eloquence) (7), echoing the French 'escïence' and 'eloquence' (1–2), assume a different meaning altogether in light of the translator's addition. The depersonalisation of the narrative voice is reinforced in a slight omission in the following lines in the otherwise rather faithful translation. The narrative voice, ostensibly Marie's as the presumed author, claims in the French text to have stayed awake frequently to work on her poems: 'Rimé en ai e fait ditié, / Soventes fiez en ai veillié!' (Prologue 41–2) (To put them into word and rhyme / I've often stayed awake) (Prologue 41–2). The statement foregrounds the actual labour that has gone into creating the texts as she has stayed awake for nights to reconstruct the material. This short

---

[30] I assume the translator was male as it is unlikely, although not inconceivable, that it was in fact a woman. While there is clearly a distinction between the historical (and obscure) author and the implied author in the text, the authorial voice (the 'I' in the text) affects the reading of the poems inasmuch as it declares itself to be feminine (Marie's), established (as it is subject to the envy of others) and imbued by God (and hence authoritative).

[31] It is to be noted here that according to Robert Cook and Mattias Tveitane there are numerous linguistic differences present in the poems that must have been present in the first versions of each of the poems. The translations must therefore originally have been made by 'different persons (at least two, but quite as likely three or four) with clearly different Norwegian dialects' (*Strengleikar* xxvii). The plural of the narrative instance, i.e. 'us' as opposed to the personal 'I' of the French text, lends some likelihood to the theory of multiple translators working together on the collection, possibly in connection with the royal court. The idea is further supported by the fact that many of the translated *lais* in fact retain, or add a secondary narrative 'I' instead of the plurality of the initial narrative voice.

sentence is, however, omitted in the Norse text, which nevertheless relates the surrounding material fairly accurately. By removing the emphasis on the labour of creativity the translation undermines the narrative voice and subverts the feminine subtext. The prologue to *Guigemar*, which affirms the narrative voice as Marie's in her request to the lords to listen to her words, 'Oës, seignurs, ke dit Marie' (3) (Listen, my lords, to the words of Marie) (3), is omitted entirely in the Norse translation, which resumes at the beginning of the tale quoted earlier.[32] The shift in perspective from the feminine to the masculine viewpoint in the translation may be due to a conscious commiseration by the translator, being almost certainly male himself, with the male protagonist of *Guigemar*. The meticulous removal of all traces of a feminine narrative voice would again suggest the deliberate re-assertion of a masculine narrative voice (or voices), perhaps as deference to the text's new linguistic re-presentation in Old Norse, a conceivably 'masculine' language in its aural resonance when compared with the melodious tone of the French poems.

The majority of alterations evident in the transmission from Anglo-Norman to Old Norse can be categorised as omission of inconsequent detail, reduction in sentimentality, increased focus on action and the interpolation of explicative passages clarifying French words or concepts that would have been unfamiliar to the audience. In *Laustiks lioð* the translator adds a paragraph explaining the naming of the French poem, *Laüstic*, and the symbolic connotation of the nightingale, thereby indicating that those symbolic connotations might not have been associated with the bird among the Nordic audience: 'sua er kallat i bræzko male. en i volsku russinol. en i ænsku nictigal. En þat er æinn litill fugl. er þægar sumra tækr þa syngr hon ok gellr um nætr sua fagrt. ok miori roddu at yndeltgt oc ynnelegt er til at lyða' (102) (So it is called in the Breton language, but in French 'russinol', and in English 'nictigal'. That is a little bird which, when summer begins, sings and chants at night so beautifully and in such a thin voice that it is delightful and delicious to listen to) (103). The immediate and unconscious associations that the French speaking readers would have drawn have to be explained verbally. The translator does so by depicting the song of the nightingale as emblematic of the unspoken love and feelings created by the thought of a loved one.

This is reinforced later in the poem in a second addition conveying again the symbolic surplus of the bird image in the poem through textual augmentation. In the French *Laüstic* the culmination of the couple's doomed love is staged amidst images of summer's fecundity:

> Tant que ceo vint a un esté,
> Que bruil e pré sunt reverdi

---

[32] It is, of course, quite conceivable that the manuscript version the Norse translator was working from did not have the relevant passage. The manuscript used must, nevertheless, have been quite close to the Harley manuscript, which stems from the mid-thirteenth century, or approximately the same period as the De la Gardie manuscript containing the *Strengleikar* collection. The translations are generally very close, and in those instances where individual *lais* have been preserved in other manuscripts the readings accord most frequently with those of the Harley manuscript (*Strengleikar*, xvii).

> E li vergier ierent fluri;
> Cil oiselet par grant duçur
> Mainent lur joie en sum la flur. (58–62)
>
> [Until one summer
> when the woods and meadows were green
> and the orchards blooming.
> The little birds, with great sweetness,
> were voicing their joy above the flowers.]

The opulence of nature's fertility and the 'joie' of the birds accentuates the sterility of the couple's love, which is limited to words and looks without any possibility of physical love.[33] The Norse translator conversely explicates the impressions of fertility in the image of the nightingale: 'Nu æinu sinni sem sumra tok. þa tok laustik at syngia með hinum fægrsta song. ok kallaðe maka sinn til astar auka undir viðar / laufom ok blomum' (102) (Now once at the beginning of summer the nightingale started to sing a very beautiful melody and summoned its mate to augment love under forest leaves and blossoms) (103). The passage no longer serves as background for human love, but literally replicates it in the act of the nightingale who summons the object of his affection to love-making.[34] Moreover, the translator adds that the bird's song incites the couple to love: 'gaðe hann með ollum hug songanna fuglanna. er huatto hann til astanna' (102) (he heeded with all his heart the songs of the birds, which were inciting him to love') (103). The song of Laustik therefore encourages them to act on their love in the Norse version, whereas in the French text the singing of the birds in fact foregrounds the barrenness of their love. The minor adjustments of the text – in the effort to convey the symbolic substance of an object – therefore leads to the interpretative re-engagement with the text. The symbolic connotations are actualised within the text itself, causing a shift in the defining pattern that affects the remaining figurative framework of the text. The entreaty to love-making leads directly to the death of Laustik, the symbol of love, and the end of the affair. In the French text, however, the encasement of the bird in the ornamented casket (wrapped in the cloth covered in symbols) signals the transference of the desire from barren love-making to productive creation and the continuation of their love through symbolic representation, that is, in Marie de France's text. The Norse translation faithfully conveys the ending with the bird in the casket, but the underlying suggestive symbolism of desire, *joie*, words and creativity that is highlighted in Marie's text is undermined in the translation. By shifting the emphasis from the transferrance of desire in the French text to the concentration of that desire in the image of the bird, which is then killed, the entire defining framework of the text is destabilised.[35]

---

[33] The French text in fact emphasises that they are limited quite literally to 'de parler e de regart' (68) (to words and looks).

[34] The sentence 'kallaðe maka sinn til astar auka' literally means to summon the mate for procreation.

[35] Significantly, the reference to to 'de parler e de regart' (68) is missing in the Norse text,

In *Bisclarets lioð* (French *Bisclavret*) the translator interposes an account of a personal experience related to the topic of the story at the end of the translation: 'En sa er þessa bok norrænaðe ha*nn* sa i bærnsko sin*n*i æin*n* ʀikan bonda er hamskiftisk stundum var ha*nn* maðr stundum i vargs ham. ok talde allt þat er vargar at hofðuzt mæðan er fra ho*n*om ækki længra sægiande' (98) (He who translated this book into Norse saw in his childhood a wealthy farmer who shifted his shape. At times he was a man, at other times in wolf's shape, and he told everything that wolves did in the meantime. But there is no more to be said about him) (99). The addition bears witness to a conscious effort by the translator to adapt the foreign text to the collective psyche of his readers by making the text more familiar through the medium of his own experiences. The precise translation reveals the underlying intent to convey the emotional and social mannerisms implicit in the linguistic presentation of the original poems. Yet there is a distinct attempt at integrating the foreign text into the existing Norse literary tradition, indicating an acute awareness of cultural disparity and the need to merge the translated text and its environment to ensure successful adaptation.

It is in the transmission and imposition of a univocal discourse of a dominating culture upon a marginal society that the imperial agenda, implicit in the Norse translations of the Anglo-Norman poems, can be found. The formal and linguistic alterations evident in the Old Norse translations, however, undermine the process of cultural conversion, intrinsic to the original translation objective. The textual modifications signal the effort of integrating the material into an existing tradition rather than supplanting that tradition. The French material is replanted in the foreign Nordic soil and the result is a distinctly different text, intimately interconnected with its source, yet unexpectedly unique. The shift in tone and aural quality from the Anglo-Norman verse to Old Norse prose accentuates the capacity of language as a site of resistance to imperial control. While the Nordic tongue is made to expand to incorporate the unfamiliar elocution of the courtly lyrics, the linguistic subtleties integral to the French mentality are abandoned as the text assumes the character and texture of Nordic expression.

Translation as Dialogue and Dissent

The editors of *The Post-Colonial Studies Reader* draw attention to the fact that 'the control over language by the imperial centre – whether achieved by displacing native languages, by installing itself as a "standard" against other variants . . . or by planting the language of empire in a new place – remains the most potent instrument of cultural control'.[36] The notion of political control through linguistic displacement is, of course, of particular relevance to

---

indicating the shift in interpretative direction of the translator. It is, of course, conceivable that this minor omission represents a scribal oversight, yet the absence of the comment supports the overall shift in focus that indicates an active re-engagement with the text rather than an accidental scribal omission.

[36] 'Language', in Ashcroft *et al.*, *The Post-Colonial Studies Reader*, 283.

Middle English literature. The invasion of a 'foreign' ruler and his followers into England in 1066 emulates in many aspects later colonial excursions into marginal territories, notwithstanding the fact that with the Norman invaders the connection to an 'empire' was neither direct nor political, but rather linguistic and cultural.[37] Ethnic or regional aggression is, of course, played out on English borders more or less throughout the medieval period, but also significantly in the early Middle Ages through Viking invasions of Anglo-Saxon territory and the Scottish isles, which again replicates earlier movements of peoples and regional discords.[38] The substitution of the French language as the language of political and social distinction signals, however, the colonising implications of the Norman Conquest of England.[39] There are indications that the imposition of the language upon the 'occupied' country may not have penetrated through the various class layers.[40] English remained the language of the peasantry and lower classes – hence its demotion in status – and the majority of the upper and middle class simply adopted the new language in their official engagements while retaining the old. Most became bilingual (or multilingual) and French thus never displaced English as a common language used in everyday speech except perhaps among the exclusive and restricted circle of nobility.[41]

While the three languages, Latin, French (Anglo-Norman) and English, co-existed in relative harmony, albeit in a distinct hierarchical order and role, from the Conquest to the end of the thirteenth century, the fourteenth century saw a swift decline in Anglo-Norman use, both official and literary.[42] The

---

[37] This discussion does not explore the existing ethnic diversity of Anglo-Saxon England, or the inherent cultural multiplicity of the Normans. Such existing multiculturalism does not, however, detract from the argument of imperial dynamics of the cultural interrelations as they are not based on conceptions of ethnic homogeny, or national identity. In fact, it supports the argument of pre-modern patterns of conquest, dominion, settlement and native integration.

[38] For further information on colonial histories and border cultures in medieval Britain see Michelle R. Warren, *History on the Edge. Excalibur and the Borders of Britain 1100–1300* (Minneapolis: University of Minnesota Press, 2000), and Randy P. Schiff, 'Borderland Subversions: Anti-imperial Energies in *The Awntyrs off Arthure* and *Golagros and Gawane*', *Speculum* 84 (2009), 613–32.

[39] The discussion here does not go into the details of the dialectal variations spoken by the invading army and the subsequent followers. The major colonising implication is to be found in the substitution of a language other than the one spoken – regardless of the existing multiplicity of languages and dialects spoken within insular borders – by an invading and dominating force. The resulting hierarchical power structures that are contingent on linguistic capacities underlie the analysis here.

[40] Susan Crane points out that the majority of the population in England remained monolingual and that soon after the Conquest the two vernaculars, English and French, became associated with 'differing spheres of activity and registers of formality', indicating that social ranking was based on linguistic attributes. The language spoken served therefore as an indicator of both social status and function ('Anglo-Norman Cultures in England, 1066–1460', in *The Cambridge History of Medieval English Literature*, ed. David Wallace, Cambridge: Cambridge University Press, 1999, 35–60, at 44).

[41] Derek Pearsall, *Old English and Middle English Poetry* (London: Routledge & Kegan Paul, 1977), 86–90.

[42] For a discussion of the usage of English, Anglo-Norman and Latin in thirteenth- and

lack of dominating outside force allowed for the rapid assimilation and integration of Anglo-Norman descendants and their traditions into the existing way of life, creating a hybrid culture that would reflect the multitude of ethnic and cultural influences that came to be known as 'English' culture. The English tongue, itself a hybrid and continually regenerating language, becomes in the course of the fourteenth century the dominating literary language. This has frequently been seen as the result of the decay of the Anglo-Norman language owing to its isolation and lack of regenerative capacity of a mother tongue. Richard Ingham rejects the notion of Anglo-Norman as a degenerate and artificial language and points out that the grammar of Anglo-Norman in fact 'maintained the characteristics that would be expected of an evolving variety of medieval French at that time'.[43] Nevertheless, the previous apparently peaceful co-existence of the two languages, encouraged perhaps by the shifting boundaries of both the French kingdom and English ownership of continental land, seems to fade in the fourteenth century, and by the end of the century Anglo-Norman seems no longer to be following that of continental French, while English has mostly taken over.[44] The co-existence of diverse languages probably promoted the mobility and resilience which ultimately made the re-establishment of English as a literary language possible, albeit much changed by those very influences upon it.

The act of writing in the English vernacular thus assumes a completely different dimension, in relation to the source language and text, than that of writing in Old Norse, where those internal linguistic ambivalences were non-

fourteenth-century England see W. M. Ormrod, 'The Use of English: Language, Law, and Political Culture in Fourteenth-Century England', *Speculum* 78.3 (2003), 750–87; W. Rothwell, 'The Role of French in Thirteenth-Century England', *Bulletin of the John Rylands University Library of Manchester* 58 (1976), 445–66; W. Rothwell, 'The Trilingual England of Geoffrey Chaucer', *Studies in the Age of Chaucer* 16 (1994), 45–68; Rolf Berndt, 'The Period of the Final Decline of French in Medieval England (Fourteenth and Early Fifteenth Centuries)', *Zeitschrift für Anglistik und Amerikanistik* 20 (1972), 341–69; Jocelyn Wogan-Browne *et al.*, eds., *Language and Culture. The French of England c.1100–c.1500* (York: York Medieval Press, 2009); and Thorlac Turville-Petre, *England the Nation. Language, Literature, and National Identity, 1290–1340* (Oxford: Clarendon Press, 1996).

[43] 'The Persistence of Anglo-Norman 1230–1362: A Linguistic Perspective', in *Language and Culture. The French of England c.1100–c.1500*, ed. Wogan-Browne *et al.*, 44–54, at 54. W. Rothwell similarly rejects the concept of Anglo-Norman's extinction as due to its status as a dialect and argues against the notion of the standardisation of Francien as a source of modern French in his article 'The Trilingual England of Geoffrey Chaucer'. He points out that English and French were both living vernaculars, whereas Latin was a dead construct, but does concede that during the fourteenth century Anglo-French became increasingly a 'written language of record' as opposed to a dynamic spoken vernacular (54). For an opposing perspective see for instance D. Kibbee, 'Emigrant Languages and Acculturation: The Case of Anglo-French', in *Origins and Development of Emigrant Languages. Proceedings from the Second Rasmus Rask Colloquium, Odense University, November 1994*, ed. Hans F. Nielsen and Lene Schøsler (Odense: Odense University Press, 1996), 1–20.

[44] This is evident in the 'collapse of its formal systems', which can be detected from the French used in lawbooks in England in the fifteenth century (Richard Ingham, 'The Persistence of Anglo-Norman 1230–1362: A Linguistic Perspective', in *Language and Culture in Medieval Britain. The French of England c.1100–c.1500*, ed. Jocelyn Wogan-Browne *et al.* York: York Medieval Press, 2009, 44–54, at 54).

existent. The social and political implications of linguistic choice in textual production in fourteenth-century England make the correlation between source text and translation inherently more complex than in Norway. Similarly the interconnectedness of the two cultures co-existing within the same locality almost certainly had an impact on authorial attitude in a manner inherently absent from the Nordic translations. Whereas England was inherently a polyglot culture where the existing languages continually influenced each other, Norway had more distinct linguistic boundaries. As with England there were of course existing dialectal differences, influenced to a greater and lesser extent by exposure to other languages and hence to a certain extent geographically determined. Also, Latin held an ecclesiastic authority over the vernacular. Nevertheless, Norway did not contain multiple different languages within its borders competing for literary, political or bureaucratic dominance. Norse was the common language spoken by the inhabitants, subject to dialectal variations, but less heavily influenced by encounters with other languages. And unlike English, Norse remained a dominant language across the various classes. The ethnic distinctions and those of definable borders may have demarcated the linguistic distinctions more clearly than within the multilingual environment of England where English, Norse, French, Welsh, Gaelic and other languages struggled to assert themselves. Nicholas Watson draws attention to the preoccupation with legitimacy and status of the vernacular as well as the political implications of the use of written English in the fourteenth century. He points out that 'fourteenth-century English texts often refer to the language in which they are written, giving various reasons for using English.'[45] This suggests a certain conflict with respect to the choice of language that is absent in Norway. It also intimates a particular authorial stance with respect to choice of language as medium, one that reflects potential political volatility, identity crisis, or an agenda. The ambiguity of the relations between the French originals and the English redactions is compounded for the modern reader by the fact that only two of Marie's *lais* have been preserved in Middle English; *Lay le Freine* and *Sir Launfal*, along with *Sir Landevale*.

The anonymous *Lay le Freine* is a relatively close translation of *Lai le Fresne* dating from the early fourteenth century and exists in only one manuscript copy, the Auchinleck compilation, which is partially damaged.[46] Thomas Chestre's *Sir Launfal* is a loose adaptation of the story of *Lanval* written in the late fourteenth century and preserved in only one mid-fifteenth-century manuscript, British Library Cotton Caligula A.ii.[47] The temporal disparity

---

[45] 'The Politics of Middle English Writing', in *The Idea of the Vernacular*, ed. Wogan-Browne et al., 331–52, at 334.

[46] Anne Laskaya and Eve Salisbury point out in their edition that the dialect of *Lay le Freine* is similar to Chaucer's and place its point of origin therefore near London or Middlesex (*The Middle English Breton Lays*, TEAMS Middle English Text Series. Kalamazoo: The Medieval Institute Publications, 2001, 9–10).

[47] The primary source for Thomas Chestre's tale is the anonymous Middle English *Sir Landevale*, which is similarly an adaptation of Marie de France's *Lanval* preserved in three manuscripts (Bodleian MS Rawl. C.86, Cambridge University Library MS Kk v.30, and British Library MS Add. 27897) and in two fragments of early printed books (Malone 541 and Douce

between the source text and the two Middle English versions makes the discussion of translation aim and textual representation of the source material especially difficult. Whereas the Norse text was translated within a generation or so of the originals and was therefore still embedded within the intellectual realm that produced the *lais*, the Middle English texts are not only written at a much later date, but they are also separated from each other by up to a century.

The later text, Thomas Chestre's *Sir Launfal*, is written in a period that witnessed significant changes in the political structures of English society that are to a certain extent reflected in the shift in the hierarchy of the two vernaculars. The poem is written in a tail-rhyme stanza, a 'native' stanzaic form used in a number of other Middle English romances. The change in verse form in and of itself necessitates some dramatic changes owing to the conversion from the four-stress couplets to the twelve-line tail-rhyme stanza, which results in a different rhythmical pattern and expands the text significantly. Similarly it indicates the shift that has occurred from the mainly aristocratic audience of Marie de France's *Lais* to the more mixed social classes among whom the tail-rhyme romances were popular.[48] The discussion of *Sir Launfal* is complicated by its relation to its sources as it derives partly from an earlier translation, *Sir Landevale*, likely translated in the early fourteenth century as *Lay le Freine* was.[49] *Sir Launfal* engages the contemporary social conditions through the recreation of Marie de France's original as well as its earlier (and more faithful) rendition, revealing ultimately the contestatory relationship between source and target text.

While the Anglo-Norman version of *Lanval* is courtly, with a simple yet eloquent verse structure and a compassionate narratorial attitude towards its protagonist, *Sir Launfal* exhibits quite the opposite tendencies. The language is brusque with a large amount of added phraseology. The initial lines of the texts serve to demonstrate the divergence in tone and attitude as well as formal representation:

> L'aventure d'un autre lai,
> Cum ele avint, vus cunterai.

Fragments e. 40, both in the Bodleian Library). The other known source is the anonymous Old French *lai* of *Graelent*. Most scholars assume there to be a third lost source containing episodes missing in both *Graelent* and *Sir Landevale* (see Thomas Chestre, *Sir Launfal*, ed. A. J. Bliss, London: Thomas Nelson and Sons, 1960, 1–31, and *The Middle English Breton Lays*, ed. Laskaya and Salisbury, 201–2).

[48] Bliss states in his edition of *Sir Launfal* that the tail-rhyme romances were the work of 'travelling minstrels, intended for a mixed audience' (31). The tail-rhyme metre was a native form particularly suited to the communal recital of popular narratives favoured by the middle class and the diverse audiences of public places. For a discussion of the tail-rhyme tradition see A. McI. Trounce, 'The English Tail-Rhyme Romances', *Medium Ævum* 1 (1932), 87–108, continued in *Medium Ævum* 2 (1933), 189–98, and in *Medium Ævum* 3 (1934), 30–50.

[49] Laskaya and Salisbury assume that *Sir Launfal* derives from the south Midlands (*The Middle English Breton Lays*, 9–10). Bliss assumes *Sir Launfal* originated in Kent or the neighbouring area, possibly Essex, while he places *Sir Landevale* in the south Midlands (Thomas Chestre, *Sir Launfal*, 5–12)

> Faiz fu d'un mut gentil vassal:
> En bretans l'apelent *Lanval*
>
> A Kardoel surjurnot li reis
> Artur, li pruz e li curteis,
> Pur les Escoz e pur les Pis,
> Ki destrueient le païs   (*Lanval*, 1–8)
>
> [I shall tell you the adventure of another *lai*,
> just as it happened:
> it was composed about a very noble vassal;
> in Breton, they call him Lanval.
>
> Arthur, the brave and courtly king,
> was staying at Cardoel,
> because the Scots and the Picts
> were destroying the land.]

The narrative voice establishes itself at the outset of the octosyllabic couplets announcing that it will recount 'another *lai*', indicating that it belongs to a corpus of *lais*, some of which have presumably been delivered beforehand by that very same voice. The tone is subdued, courteous, personal (through the address), yet simultaneously absent in its narrative distance from the material she (or he) is about to recount. The setting is established through the reference to 'Artur, li pruz e li curteis' (Arthur, the brave and courtly) and the chivalric context is reinforced through the depiction of the protagonist as 'mut gentil vassal' (very noble vassal). The narratorial voice is therefore positively predisposed towards its protagonist at the outset of the story, thereby positioning the audience in terms of context and perspective.

Chestre's version reveals some dramatic divergences from the narratorial contextualisation of the French original:

> Be douȝty Artours dawes,
> Þat held Engelond yn good lawes,
> Þer fell a wondyr cas
> Of a ley þat was ysette,
> Þat hyȝt 'Launual', & hatte ȝette:
> Now herkeneþ how hyt was.
> Douȝty Artour somwhyle
> Soiournede yn Kardeuyle,
> Wyth joye & greet solas,
> And knyȝtes þat wer profitable
> Wyth Artour, of þe Rounde Table –
> Neuer noon better þer nas   (1–12)[50]

It is readily apparent that the text is not a direct transposition of the French original. More importantly, however, is the shift that has occurred not only

---

[50] Thomas Chestre, *Sir Launfal*, ed. Bliss. Hereafter referred to by line numbers following quotation as above.

in terms of the material presented, but in the manner of its presentation. The tail-rhyme metre radically changes the rhythm and delivery of the material. The internal emphasis is shifted within each line, creating a discursive directness in Chestre's version that is underscored by a certain amount of standardisation of rhyme words and vocabulary. While the text is apparently intended for delivery, the persistent narrative presence of the French text has been replaced by a traditional invocation to 'herken' to a tale about to be told. There is no mention of a conflict with the Scots and Picts and instead Chestre proceeds to recount the various members of the Round Table. Significantly, there is no further reference to Launfal's character, leaving the audience to draw conclusions as to his position among Arthur's knights from the story itself.[51]

The characterisation of Sir Launfal is additionally rather unconventional. He is less idealised and his representation frequently deviates from that appropriate to the traditional romantic hero. Shortly before encountering Dame Tryamour, Sir Launfal leaves the court dejected after being excluded from the festivities of Trinity owing to this poverty. The text shows him harnessing his horse and then proceeds to deride its protagonist: 'He roode wyth lytyll pryde. / Hys horse slod, & fel yn þe fen / Wherfore hym scornede many men' (213–15). The insult of the exclusion from the festivities is redoubled by the scorn of the men. Moreover, the slipping of the horse in the mud is an exercise in realism rarely present in chivalric romance. The conventional romantic exploit is thus undercut by an impression of realism through references to poverty, ostracism and the reality of knightly tribulations, such as muddy roads and unsteady horses. The story draws attention to the mundane problems of Launfal's existence, whereas the focal point in Marie's version is on the failure of courtly society as an ideological construct, not its physical and financial ramifications. In the French text Lanval finds himself the object of envy at a foreign court that fails to recognise his worth, a statement that echoes Marie's self-proclaimed narrative voice in the prologue to *Guigemar*:

> Mais quant il ad en un païs
> Hummë u femme de grant pris,
> Cil ki de sun bien unt envie
> Sovent en dïent vileinie:
> Sun pris li volent abeissier   (7–11)

---

[51] The earlier translation, *Sir Landevale*, recounts the French text more closely, yet some of the shifts in representation are already present there: 'Sothly, by Arthurys day / Was Bretayn yn grete nob*ley*, / For, yn hys tyme, a grete whyle / He soiourned at Carlile; / He had with hym a meyné there, / As he had ellyswhere, / Of the Rounde Table the k*n*yghtys all, / With myrth and joye yn hys hall' (*Sir Landevale* in Thomas Chestre, *Sir Launfal*, ed. Bliss, 105–28, lines 1–8). All references to the conflict of the northern borders have been eliminated and the insistent narrative voice of the French poems has vanished as well. The text of *Sir Launfal* reveals, however, the active engagement with both source texts, i.e. the Anglo-Norman and the Middle English version, in a particular manner that is no less subversive to *Sir Landevale* than it is to the French original. It should be noted that while this particular passage does not agree with *Sir Landevale* there are several instances where Chestre shows his direct indebtness to the text.

> [But anywhere there is
> a man or a woman of great worth,
> people who envy their good fortune
> often say evil things about them;
> they want to ruin their reputations.]

The prologue establishes a parallel between the unfortunate Lanval and the authorial self as they are both subject to the envy and resentment of others. The predisposition of the narrative voice towards Lanval thus foregrounds the failure of the court of Arthur, and hence of Arthur himself, to adequately provide for the noble Lanval.[52] The material preoccupations in Marie's tale reflect that of the chivalric code and the courtly expectations of knighthood. In *Sir Launfal*, however, the focus is directed away from the ideological structures of courtly ethics to the socio-economic conditions of the individual in society and the necessity of something as mundane as money for survival. Dinah Hazell points out that Chestre is writing at a time of pervasive impoverishment within the lower strata of society and increasingly within the upper classes.[53] The mounting demands on all classes, brought on by post-Plague conditions of mobile work forces, taxation and rising prices, suggest a fundamental shift in authorial objective and a growing relevance of the threat of impoverishment apparent in Chestre's text.[54] In fact, the entire passage relating the degradation of Sir Launfal owing to poverty and the resulting exclusion from the community is absent in both Marie's version and *Sir Landevale*, where the text moves directly from the disillusionment with the court to the encounter with the enigmatic lady who becomes his lover.

While Marie's text emphasises the sense of displacement and the failure of the court to maintain or uphold the courtly ideal, Sir Launfal's problems arise implicitly from his antagonism towards the queen. The text states that Sir Launfal did not like her 'for þe lady bar los of swych word / Þat sche hadde lemmannys vnþer her lord' (45–6), which leads to her (not Arthur) withholding gifts. While the queen does not appear until after the encounter with the mysterious maiden in *Lanval*, the encounter is in fact an indirect result of the reputation of the queen and Sir Launfal's judgement of her moral character in

---

[52] Whether the *lais* were originally conceived of as a corpus, or are in fact individual and separate *lais* randomly collected, they are nevertheless presented in a particular order and in a particular context within the Harley manuscript. They were therefore received as a corpus by the audience and/or readers of that particular manuscript, and this must necessarily have influenced their perception of the tales. Even if one assumes the tales were independent, or that the prologue to *Guigemar* was a later addition having little or nothing to do with the presumed author (or authors) of the *lais*, the perspective remains with Lanval throughout the story. He is associated with positive qualities such as nobility, valour, generosity, beauty and bravery (see lines 21–2), whereas Arthur's court is associated with envy, disregard (as Arthur simply forgets him) and artificiality (the courtiers feigning love while simultaneously delighting in his misfortunes) (see lines 5–38).
[53] 'The Blinding of Gwennere: Thomas Chestre as Social Critic', *Arthurian Literature* 20 (2003), 123–43, at 132.
[54] Ibid. 132–5.

Chestre's version.[55] The moral condemnation of female behaviour therefore underlies the entire narrative framework of Chestre's text and destabilises the original conflict between the courtly ideal, love and the otherworld, represented by the vanishing of Lanval along with his maiden to Avalon.[56]

The distancing of the narrative voice from the protagonist similarly generates a detachment between Sir Launfal and the reader which detracts from a generic reading and thus actively involves the reader in the re-interpretation of the text. The satirical tone in the following example, where Launfal is unable to dine with the aristocracy, or go to church, due to his lack of appropriate accessories and clean clothes, underlines this disassociation:

> 'Damesele,' he sayde, 'Nay!
> To dyne haue J no herte:
> Þre dayes þer ben agon,
> Mete ne drynke eet y noon,
> And all was for pouert.
> Today to cherche y wolde haue gon,
> But me fawtede hosyn & schon,
> Clenly brech & scherte   (194–201)

It is hard to imagine Marie de France discussing her protagonists' 'dirty breeches' or otherwise 'demoting' her characters to confront such ordinary and pragmatic problems. In fact A. C. Spearing criticises the poem for its apparent lack of sophistication, stating that 'Thomas Chestre either failed to grasp or failed to value the true nature of the Lanval story', and proceeds to call it a 'fascinating disaster'.[57] Yet he, along with Anne Laskaya and Eve Salisbury, suggests that the poem 'rather masterfully satirizes a bourgeois mentality' in its sometimes mocking depiction of the courtly realm and urban society.[58] Rather than dismissing the text as a 'disastrous' adaptation of Marie de France's *Lanval*, we may see it as an independent reworking of the French *lai* to produce a 'commentary' on contemporary culture. Whatever its success

---

[55] In *Sir Landevale* the queen does not appear until after the meeting and Sir Landevale's impoverishment is due to his own excessive spending (see *Sir Landevale* in Thomas Chestre, *Sir Launfal*, ed. Bliss, 105–6). Chestre may be adopting a theme from *Graelent* here, where Arthur neglects the hero at the suggestion of the queen (see *'Graelent' and 'Guingamor': Two Breton Lays*, ed. and trans. Russel Weingartner, New York: Garland Publishing, 1985).

[56] Dinah Hazell focuses on the blinding of Gwennere in the end of *Sir Launfal* as the fundamental valuation of justice, morality and Arthurian society in her article 'The Blinding of Gwennere: Thomas Chestre as Social Critic', *Arthurian Literature* 20 (2003), 123–43. For a discussion of the queen's function in *Lanval* see for instance Leicester, 'The Voice of the Hind'. The shift in representation of feminine behaviour and its moral implications is reiterated in the Middle English translation of *Partonopeu de Blois*, discussed in Chapter 4, where the English translation reveals similar behavioural modifications and conflicting stance towards female sexuality.

[57] 'Marie de France and her Middle English Adapters', *Studies in the Age of Chaucer* 12 (1990), 117–57, at 148.

[58] *The Middle English Breton Lays*, ed. Laskaya and Salisbury, 203, and A. C. Spearing, 'The Lanval Story', in his *The Medieval Poet as Voyeur* (Cambridge: Cambridge University Press, 1993), 97–120.

on the level of literary achievement, it can then be seen as fully embedded within the historical and cultural framework of the author.

As was the case with the Norse translations, the Middle English version has been adjusted to its new reading community, probably the aspiring middle class where the intricacies of courtly etiquette had less immediate relevance than with the presumably mostly aristocratic audience of Marie de France's *lais*. Dieter Mehl notes that the 'same period that saw the emergence of the English romances, also saw the steady decline of the knight, who had been such an essential part of courtly society', signalling the disintegration of the fundamental societal structures and elements that had supported the courtly value system.[59] While the material was translated precisely for the novelty of its content in Norway, the Anglo-Norman text had, in all probability, existed for over two centuries in England and the courtly system of values embedded within it was therefore not only already in place, but had no longer such practical relevance to its audience.[60]

The refined elocution of courtly love and knightly adventures of Marie's *Lanval* assumes a burlesque tone of practical and ordinary problems in the English text. Sir Launfal is denied hospitality by the mayor, who refuses to lodge him and his fellow knights in his house and sends him to 'a chamber by my orchardsyd(e)' as a means of ridding himself of this presence (124). The refusal of the mayor to provide lodging calls into question the entire foundation of the romantic ideology of noble behaviour. The concept of 'largesse', which is the foundation of the economy of gift exchange in the eleventh and twelfth centuries, passed from the social realities of the early Middle Ages into romance, where it reigned supreme. John W. Baldwin notes that largesse not only serves as the underpinning of the Arthurian court, but, moreover, 'generates and perpetuates chivalric society'.[61] As noted before, the failure to uphold the duties of the chivalric code of generosity leads ultimately to the crossing over into an otherworld in *Lanval*, a frequent means of escape from disenchantment and failure of love in the *lais*. The lack of munificence in *Lanval* is a sign of the degeneration of the court, whereas the mayor's reaction assumes a personal affront in *Sir Launfal*. Hospitality figured as an obligation

---

[59] *The Middle English Romances of the Thirteenth and Fourteenth Century* (New York: Barnes & Noble, 1969), 4.

[60] It is of relevance here that the Norse translators translated an entire corpus of *lais*, although these may not necessarily have formed the volume we know today as the *Strengleikar* collection. The import of the *lais* as a collection supports the idea that the translations of the *lais* served a specific agenda as the intentional influx of cultural capital. This is quite different with respect to the Middle English translations. It is, of course, quite possible that several or all of Marie de France's *lais* were translated at some point or another and the existence of *Sir Landevale* supports the notion that the *lais* may have existed in various forms in the centuries following Marie's presumed composition. There is, however, no evidence of a conscious effort to import the *lais* into Middle English as an object of a specific value (as a collection). The fact that *Lay le Freine* was translated almost a century earlier than *Sir Launfal* and, moreover, that they probably belong to different regions shows that they form part of separate and probably individual engagements with the existing literary matter in French (or Anglo-Norman).

[61] *Aristocratic Life in Medieval France. The Romances of Jean Renart and Gerbert de Montreuil 1190–1230* (Baltimore: The Johns Hopkins University Press, 2000), 98–121, at 100.

of largesse and the mayor's refusal to host Sir Launfal reveals the subversion of the entire protocol of chivalric behaviour that is furthermore directed at the individual rather than the courtly ideal.

The departure of Sir Huwe and Syr Jon owing to Launfal's lack of the necessary financial means to support their knightly lifestyle similarly undermines the very courtly ideology the text is drawing on: 'Þey seyd, "Syr, our robes beþ torent, / And your tresour ys all yspent, / And we goþ ewyll ydy3t"' (139–41). The focus on money as an economic necessity for maintaining appropriate clothing and equipment rather than a symbolic feature of social status indicates the fundamental shift that has occurred from the courtly tone of Marie de France's text to the Middle English version. It is possible that this may reflect an earlier generic shift: the author may have come into contact with the works of the early-thirteenth-century French writer Jean Renart, whose unusual narrative approach to the genre could have provided the creative motivation for the rewriting of *Sir Launfal*.[62] The focus on the economic aspect of the knight's search for glory and the subtle undermining of the conventional narratives structures of the romance that occur throughout Renart's *Romance of the Rose or Guillaume de Dole*, are reminiscent of *Sir Launfal*'s generic instability.[63]

Whether or not the author was familiar with the text and influenced by it in the composition of his texts, the Middle English version of *Lanval* deviates from the original in a particular and specific manner that places it in a discordant relationship with its source text. This refashioning of the French tale indicates the disparity between the function of the original and the purpose of its translation. Rather than imitating the tone and presentation of the French poem, as the Norse text does, the material is appropriated in favour of a contemporary political agenda. Where the Norse text seeks to internalise the courtly discourse of the French text (whether it succeeds or not) *Sir Launfal* engages in a contestatory dialogue with the original. The text thus plays on the resulting discord between the French courtly ideology, inherent in the original, and the contemporary English social conditions which the English version implicitly addresses.

By contrast, the anonymous *Lay le Freine*, dating from the early fourteenth century, shows a much closer correlation to the original. It is written in short

---

[62] It is not implausible that the writings of Jean Renart were known in England. For the suggestion that the Bohun family may have owned a manuscript containing the romances *Guillaume de Palerne* and Jean Renart's *L'escoufle*, see the forthcoming edition of *William of Palerne*, ed. David Lawton, TEAMS Middle English Text Series (Kalamazoo: The Medieval Institute). This would support the strong possibility that at least one of Renart's works existed in England during the time *Sir Launfal* was written and that the English author, and possibly even his intended reading community, may have been familiar with this alternative, more ironic approach to romance writing.

[63] Critics differ in their interpretations of the 'problem spots' of Renart's *Guillaume de Dole*, but later critics seem to agree that the inconsistencies in the text are due to the intentional and deliberate undermining of the romance genre, into which Renart is placing his own work, rather than demonstrating his lack of skills as a writer. The critical debate over his works in many ways reflects the debate over *Sir Launfal*'s literary quality (see Introduction, *Romance of the Rose or Guillaume de Dole*, trans. Patricia Terry and Nancy Vine Durling, Philadelphia: University of Pennsylvania Press, 1993, 1–15).

couplets, which would have been the most comparable Middle English metrical form to the French *Le Fresne*'s octosyllabic couplet. Despite remaining close to the original, the text shows signs of a deliberate adaptation to its new linguistic and geographical sphere in two minor modifications in the text. The translator moves the scene of the poem from 'Bretaine' in Marie's version to the 'west cuntré', thereby thematically localising it and hence reclaiming it as a part of Britain's literary heritage.[64] The shift in localisation of *Lay le Freine* further complicates the existing multiple cultural layers that make up Marie's *Le Fresne* and draws attention to textual instability and the convoluted relationship between source and target language.[65] The inherent marginalisation of the text itself (as the presumed creation of a female author) and the fluctuating borders of text, geography and language create a dynamic subtext of transformative potential within the *lais* themselves. In his brilliant study, Peter Haidu locates Marie 'geographically at the Anglo-Norman colonial margin of French culture and semiotically at the borderlines of a male-dominated textual culture', pointing to her self-representation within the texts as located at 'crossings, linguistic and geographic, repeatedly invoking the fiction of a prior subjectivity'.[66] If one perceives Marie's text as marginal in its conception it becomes, by means of the Norse translation, paradoxically a representative of the imperialised authority of a dominating culture. The unstable hierarchical structures of textual authority are appropriated and simultaneously reconstructed as signifiers of cultural authority by rejecting it origins, i.e. the presumed feminine voice. It is noteworthy that even in the Middle English *Lay le Freine* those boundaries (gender, geographic, linguistic) are disrupted, signalling the reconfiguration of the borders of the text through the act of translation. Not only has the perceived origin of the tale and the location of the story been shifted in the Middle English translation, but the narratorial voice has been appropriated and reconfigured as a presumably male voice asking the 'lordinges' to 'herkneth' to the tale to be told (68).

The Middle English translator furthermore inserts an explication of the French name of the poem suggesting that he assumes his audience might no longer be capable of comprehending the French word:

---

[64] The geographical change from Brittany to the 'west cuntré' of England is noted by most critics. Anne Laskaya and Eve Salisbury comment in their edition of *The Middle English Breton Lays* that the 'west country' was often associated with Wales and with the Celtic fairy world, and on that basis one could intimate that the move was possibly a conscious attempt at relocation back to the assumed place of origin of the tales by the Middle English redactor (8, 80 notes). This chapter will not go into the complexity of the English/Welsh relationship, both linguistic and ethnic, and the anglicisation of the British Isles.

[65] Warren notes that 'Arthurian histories . . . all emerged from border cultures and engage the dynamics of boundary formation into the thirteenth century and across the Channel', which raises intriguing questions of identity formation, boundary demarcation and the role of literature therein, particularly in the fourteenth century (*History on the Edge*, xi). For a discussion of border zones in Marie de France's *Lais*, see chapter 4 in Kinoshita's *Medieval Boundaries*.

[66] Peter Haidu, *The Subject Medieval/Modern. Text and Governance in the Middle Ages* (Standford, California: Stanford University Press, 2004), 138.

> Bifel a cas in Breteyne
> Whereof was made Lay le Frain.
> In Ingliche for to tellen ywis
> Of an asche for sothe it is   (23–6)[67]

This is reinforced later in the poem where the translator adds a passage explaining the signification of the heroine's name:

> Sche cleped it *Frain* in that stounde.
> (The Freyns of the 'asche' is a *freyn*
> After the language of Breteyn;
> Forthe *Le Frein* men clepeth this lay
> More than *Asche* in ich cuntray).   (230–4)

The explication reveals, as before with the Norse text, the recognition of linguistic boundaries and the attempt to bridge them through semantic exposition. The translator retains the French word, which no longer has the relevant semantic connotations within its new linguistic context, requiring the clarification of its meaning. In the case of the Norse version of *Le Fresne*, the translator has, on the other hand, opted to translate the name itself, calling the *lai Eskia* (Ash).

The Middle English translator in a similar manner omits the passage containing the play on the connotations of the twin sisters' names, Ash and Hazel:

> La Codre ad nun la damesele;
> En cest païs nen ad si bele.
> Pur le freisne que vus larrez
> En eschange le codre avrez;
> En la codre ad noiz e deduiz,
> Li freisnes ne porte unke fruiz!   (*Le Fresne* 335–40)
>
> [The girl's name is Codre [Hazel];
> there isn't one so pretty in this region.
> In exchange for the ash, when you get rid of her,
> you'll have the hazel.
> The hazel tree bears nuts and thus gives pleasure;
> the ash bears no fruit.]

The semiotic play on the semantic content of the names of the sisters in the French text foregrounds the way in which the symbolism works on all levels of the narration. The sign thus proliferates beyond its rhetorical function within the text. The translator, on the other hand, replaces the passage with a comment clarifying the French names: 'Better than Ash is Hazle y ween! / (For in Romaunce *Le Frain* 'ash' is, / And *Le Codre* 'hazle', y-wis)' (*Lay le Freine* 346–8). The repeated gestures to the French source throughout the text reveals the rhetorical self-consciousness of the writer regarding the material

---

[67] *Lay le Freine* in *The Middle English Breton Lays*, 61–87. Hereafter referred to by line numbers in parantheses following citation.

he is transmitting and the cultural and linguistic diversity of the reading community into which he is inserting his text. The Anglo-Norman ruling class was steadily being integrated with their English counterparts resulting in the disintegration of the existing cultural barriers. The established framework of linguistic order and function was beginning to come apart as there emerged a new class of people unable (or unwilling) to read French any more, but still existing within the cultural realm shaped by Anglo-Norman literature and tradition.[68] The recurring textual reference to a French original in *Lay le Freine* calls attention to the ambivalent relationship between class, identity and language in fourteenth century England.[69]

Cultural Rhetoric

Given that translation was in effect the mode through which reading and writing was taught within the multilingual context of England, it can be conceived of as simply another form of writing. Children learning to read and write in England were in fact to learning to read and write a foreign language. While boys were instructed in Latin and often French, girls were generally taught French. The translations of words and concepts back into the mother-tongue served to conceptualise the foreign vocabulary, intimately connecting the act of translation and move between languages with the act of writing itself.[70] While the Norse texts were translations of foreign work and culture, the Middle English version of *Le Fresne* can be better described as a refashioning of an existing authoritative text within a more local and diverse context of its English-speaking audience. Rita Copeland claims that 'as a rhetorical act, literary translation seeks to erase the cultural gap from which it emerges by contesting and displacing the source and substituting itself'.[71] The Middle English translation can be seen as an effort to bridge the cultural gap by forging a

---

[68] The approval of the Statute of Pleading by Parliament in 1362, which banned pleading in French in the English court on the premise that French was not adequately known, signals a shift in the fourteenth century in terms of linguistic competence in French within insular borders. W. Rothwell notes that the ban applied to the spoken, not the written language, but the proceedings of the court continued in fact to be recorded in French after the statute was issued ('English and French in England after 1362', *English Studies* 82 (2001), 539–59, particularly 539–42). The statute does, nevertheless, indicate that the general knowledge of French may have been decreasing. The statute may have been intended to prevent potential complications arising from legal proceedings taking place in a language the defendant and/or plaintiffs may have been unable to understand, or understood only poorly.

[69] It was, paradoxically, during the latter part of the period that saw the most substantial writing in Anglo-Norman that the resurgence of English occurred most extensively in literary writing (Crane, 'Anglo-Norman Cultures in England', 49–51).

[70] For information on French instruction in England in the Middle Ages see for instance Douglas A. Kibbee, *For to speke French trewely. The French Language in England, 1000–1600: Its Status, Description and Instruction* (Amsterdam: Benjamins, 1991), and W. Rothwell, 'The Teaching of French in Medieval England', *Modern Language Review* 63 (1968), 37–46. For a discussion of pedagogy and Latin in medieval England see Rita Copeland, 'Childhood, Pedagogy, and the Literal Sense', *New Medieval Literatures* 1 (1997), 125–56.

[71] *Rhetoric, Hermeneutics, and Translation in the Middle Ages*, 30.

connection to the original, through the repeated gestures to the French source, while simultaneously replacing the French text with the new English version. The fact that the cultural gap is linguistic in character does not invalidate the act of functional displacement. The translation in this case reaffirms the original by virtue of its translation, but simultaneously renounces the French text by replacing it with an English version.

Lay le Freine also shows signs of what A. C. Spearing terms 'a move down the social scale' similar to those of *Sir Launfal*.[72] The polite tone and attention to manners is reduced and many of the linguistic transformations are of the same variety, where the shift is from an inward perspective to an outward spatial and sequence-based focus. It is nevertheless quite possible that what appears as primitive structure may simply indicate a cultural preference for stories based on action rather than sensitivity to imagery and emotion, and may not always be indicative of the inadequacy of writers. Both Nordic and English reading communities show a predilection for compact and rapid narrative sequencing and lack of interest in extended rhetorical flourish of emotive or psychological characterisations.

The difference between the Old Norse and Middle English texts, however, is intimately related to the question of geographic and cultural demarcation. While Norway was an autonomous kingdom, the question of English sovereignty is much more complex.[73] Foreign and native rulers had succeeded one another, often with multiple rulers and multiple ethnic fragmentations with diverse territorial boundaries. Despite the imposition of Danish law in pre-Conquest England, the Nordic settlements never extended much outside the so-called Danelaw, and the principles behind the rule were more in the line of cultural preservation and integration. The Anglo-Normans, however, were bent on conquest and dominion and sought to subdue even the most remote regions of the country through settlement, delegation of land, political manoeuvres and, last but not least, linguistic authority.[74] At the time of Marie de France's *Lanval* the English were thus subject to the rule of an Anglo-Norman king and court, albeit one not ruled by an absent empire, but by the invading force itself which maintained only indirect connections with the originating site of authority and power. The co-existence of French language, literature and social norms alongside the English language and customs alters the relationship between the two and hence affects authorial objectives and textual presentation.

---

[72] 'Marie de France and her Middle English Adapters', 127.
[73] The Norwegian royal history admittedly had its own share of complexities in the medieval period with contesting royal factions and intermittent shared kingship within Scandinavia, yet these are based on internal discords, rather than an invading force, and Nordic royal alliances through marriage and inheritance.
[74] While the intent of the Conquest was one of domination, many of the means used to gain control were both pacifying and integrating – such as inter-marriage and commercial relations – highlighting the qualities that made the Normans so successful in their exploits elsewhere in Europe (see Crane, 'Anglo-Norman Cultures in England', 36). The Norse origin of the Normans foregrounds the territorial and cultural movement of invasion, subjugation and assimilation taking place in northern Europe during the Middle Ages.

The writing of *Sir Launfal*, however, takes place at a time when those relations of dominion and authority are disintegrating. The English language is reappearing as a fashionable and literary language and the country has been at war with France since the middle of the century, creating a disjunction between the established earlier parameters of supremacy and subjugation.[75] As can be seen in *Sir Launfal*, the translated text undermines the authority of the original by destabilising the courtly ideology inherent to Marie de France's *Lanval*. The shift in function of the story and the ironic narratorial presentation revokes the assumed cultural authority of the original text. In *Lay le Freine*, the relocation of the tale to English (or Welsh) soil speaks similarly of the dissident nature, whether intentional or not, of the translation. The French exploitation of literary material across the Channel is foregrounded through the shifting of the location of the tale's origin from Brittany to the 'west cuntré', quite likely the Marches.[76] This interplay of linguistic authority and cultural transformations becomes more subtle in the case of Norway as there is no physical dominance by a foreign 'empire'. Translation becomes in this case a means of cultural reproduction rather than displacement owing to the cultural authority of the French and possible admiration by the Norwegian court. The precision in the Old Norse textual and thematic reproduction of the French *Lais* indicates the effort at accuracy in the transposition of the French material and alludes to the underlying objective of preserving and promoting the chivalric ideology embedded within the structure of the original text.

While the Norse translator attempted to reconstruct a foreign poem from a distinctly different poetic and linguistic tradition, the English adapter had no such need. The English were familiar with courtly literature through the influx of continental literary material and values that followed the Conquest. The multitude of literary themes, forms, and ideals that existed simultaneously within the multilingual territory of post-Conquest England afforded a diverse literary space quite removed from that of the rather uniform cultural domain of Norway. The conflict between 'native' and 'foreign', which had to be bridged in the Norse translations, therefore assumes another form in the context of England. While the Norse translator had to convey the unfamiliar system of values embedded within his source text, the familiarity of both language and cultural context by the English reading communities shifted the incentive

---

[75] For a discussion of the linguistic interrelations of English and Anglo-Norman and its co-existence with France in the fourteenth century see Rothwell, 'The Trilingual England of Geoffrey Chaucer'; Robert Bartlett, *The Making of Europe. Conquest, Colonization and Cultural Change 950–1350* (Princeton: Princeton University Press, 1994); Ardis Butterfield, *The Familiar Enemy: Chaucer, Language and Nation in the Hundred Years War* (Oxford: Oxford University Press, 2009); and Turville-Petre, *England the Nation*.

[76] For information on the Breton lays and their origins see *The Middle English Breton Lays*, ed. Laskaya and Salisbury; Mortimer J. Donovan, *The Breton Lay: A Guide to Varieties* (Notre Dame: University of Notre Dame Press, 1969); and Spearing, 'Marie de France and her Middle English Adapters'. For information on the ethnic and linguistic conflicts on the borders of Wales and England see Robert Bartlett, *The Hanged Man. A Story of Miracle, Memory, and Colonialism in the Middle Ages* (Princeton: Princeton University Press, 2004).

from a native rendition of a foreign text to the vernacularisation of an existing local text.[77] This change in textual motivation underlies both the flexibility with which the English adapters approached their sources and the implicit social implications of their texts.

The fusion between the French and the English literary cultures and languages thus removes the cultural disparity and diminishes the need for textual modification. Yet the transformations evident in the Middle English versions of the Anglo-Norman texts indicate that the reshaping of those texts within the English language entails their adaptation to separate codes and conventions. Similarly, the shift from the mainly aristocratic audience of *Lanval* to the middle-class audience of *Sir Launfal* requires the adaptation of courtly ideology to the conceptual realm and narrative predilection of its new reading community. Those alterations are brought about not only by linguistic changes, as a result of the move from one language to another, but by the entire cultural and ideological history embedded within the meaningful structures of that language. The aural quality, structural capacity and grammatical complexities of each language inevitably influence the extent to which rhythmical or acoustic characteristic and metrical forms are conveyed. They affect therefore by inference how the thematic content of a poem is transmitted.

Ruqaiya Hasan notes that the problem of comprehending a foreign tongue is 'not because the sounds and the wordings are unfamiliar, but more because the ways of meaning are not familiar – the manner in which the universe is made meaningful is not fully apprehended'.[78] Just as language is a code that requires familiarity with the underlying system for a successful act of communication, so too can culture be characterised as a semiotic system requiring the same familiarity with the code for the interpretation of cultural acts such as behaviour, manner and, ultimately, textual conventions. In the Norse text this can be seen in such minor details as the nightingale in *Laustiks lioð*. The symbolic function of the bird within the French poem loses its significance within the new Nordic context due to the lack of a *signified* within the cultural code of Nordic readers. Being unfamiliar with the bird, it has no specific connotation and would hence be meaningless as symbol within the text. The translator must translate the *function* of the bird within the text, and not only the image, to convey the symbolic nuances of the bird both as text and as a cultural sign.

Within the English context such disparity should be less evident, owing to the co-existence of the two cultures within the same geographic location, resulting, it would seem, in increased familiarity with the semiotic system

---

[77] Regardless of whether the intended public of the Breton lays discussed here were capable of understanding French or not, they were, by virtue of the co-existence of both Normans and English within the same location, accustomed to and cognisant of the various traditions present within England. Despite the substantial contact, both mercantile and political, between Norway and other nations, the manner of familiarity and integration must of necessity have differed quite profoundly.

[78] 'Ways of Saying: Ways of Meaning', in *The Semiotics of Culture and Language*, ed. Robin P. Fawcett, M. A. K. Halliday, Sydney M. Lamb, and Adam Makkai, vol. 1 (London: Frances Pinter, 1984), 105–62, at 108.

behind each language. The textual adaptations, however, demonstrate the fundamental uniqueness of each system and the interconnectedness of the specific linguistic code to certain cultural conceptualisations. The transfer from one system to the other thus necessitates not only formal and stylistic changes, owing to the basic grammatical and syntactical differences between languages, but more importantly occurs on the level of rhetorical presentation. By recreating an Anglo-Norman text in Middle English, the text takes on the collective textual and cultural memory of its creator and hence becomes profoundly localised and separate from the source it sought to replicate or replace. It is hence profoundly resistant to the dominating impulse of foreign control. The linguistic and formal transformations of the text undermine the notion of translation as a confirmation of privileged discourse. On the contrary, they draw attention to the intrinsic capacity of language to either resist or subsume foreign influence. Those transformations similarly emphasise the bearing the intended reading community has on the nature of authorial modifications as well as on the ultimate endurance of a translated text.[79] The Middle English versions of the Anglo-Norman poems therefore bear witness, along with the Old Norse texts, to the conceptual configurations fundamentally interconnected to the linguistic constitution of a society. Similarly the Norse and English translations reveal the inevitable cultural transformations that occur in the transposition of a text, written in a certain language and within a particular ideological framework, to a quite different linguistic and conceptual realm.

---

[79] It is of some significance in this context that *Strengleikar* does not seem to have had as great an impact upon Nordic audience, judging by the manuscript preservation and perpetuation, as some of the other translated texts, which might possibly be due to the unfamiliarity of the form and material. The *chansons de geste*, more ruthlessly masculine and heroic, and many later romances, similar in substance and presentation to the native *fornaldarsögur*, were for instance retranslated, recreated, and plundered for centuries afterwards. It is also of note that there are no existing Icelandic manuscript copies of the corpus as a whole, but individual *lais* seem to have had some influence in Iceland. The existence of an eighteenth-century manuscript containing *Gvímars saga*, derived from Marie de France's *Guigemar*, reveals the continued lifecycle of the *lais* beyond the thirteenth century (see Marianne E. Kalinke, 'Gvímars saga', Opuscula 7, Bibliotheca Arnamagnæana 34, Copenhagen: C. A. Reitzels boghandel, 1979, 106–39). *Tiodielis saga* is an Icelandic derivative version of *Bisclaretz ljóð*, the Norwegian translation of *Bisclavret* (see *Tiodielis saga*, ed. Tove Hovn Ohlsson, Reykjavík: Stofnun Árna Magnússonar í íslenskum fræðum, 2009). Elizabeth Ashman Rowe has furthermore suggested that *Helga þáttr Þórissonar* is under the influence of *Janual*, the Norwegian translation of *Lanval* (see 'Þorsteins þáttr uxafóts, Helga þáttr Þórissonar, and the Conversion Þættir', Scandinavian Studies 76 (2004), 459–74); Rosemary Power considers the *þáttr* to be influenced directly by the French *Lanval* (see 'Le Lai de Lanval and Helga þáttr Þórissonar', Opuscula 8, Bibliotheca Arnamagnæana, 38, Copenhagen: The Arnamagnæan Commission (1985), 158–61). It may be that once the function of the corpus of *lais* as a cultural capital was no longer relevant they had less of an immediate appeal within the Icelandic context of the fourteenth and later centuries. Individual *lais* may therefore have been copied or rewritten in a manner similar to the engagment with the *lais* by the English redactors.

CHAPTER TWO

Behavioural Transformations in the Old Norse Version of *La Chanson de Roland*

TEXTS ARE NOT CREATED IN A VACUUM but are fundamentally influenced by the historical and social conditions out of which they originate. Embedded within them, they contain an array of cultural signifiers that are more or less rooted in that social context. Some texts are more firmly grounded than others in the conditions out of which they arose, giving evidence of a particular political agenda, public preference, fashion or ideological questionings of an era, while others appear to us to transcend their temporal and contextual borders through their ability to respond to the concerns of later generations. Because of this perceived universality they remain vital beyond the boundaries of the civilisation that created them. Regardless of their capacity to reach beyond their time and place, however, texts are representative of a cultural context and require familiarity with that context for the comprehension of the culturally determined, integrative functions. This is of particular relevance to translations as they represent fundamentally the move from one linguistic realm to another, and consequently the transfer from one cultural sphere to another. I differentiate between cultural and geographical sphere here. In multilingual territories texts can exist in multiple languages without having to cross any territorial boundaries. The defining context is, however, intimately linked to the language in which the text is written and therefore of necessity shifts once the text is rewritten within its new linguistic context despite the possible co-existence of both versions within the same location.

While the implications of cultural adaptation in the translation process are generally recognised in modern translation theories, they have historically been overlooked in studies of medieval translation.[1] In these, the focus has

---

[1] In modern translation theories attention is generally devoted to the multiple cultural implications of the move of a text from one linguistic context to another rather than the perceived 'accuracy' with which a text is transferred. Gregory Rabassa approaches the problem of cultural context in translation on a linguistic level by analysing semantic differences between the corresponding signifiers in any given language in his article 'Words Cannot Express . . . The Translation of Cultures', in *Translation Horizons. Beyond the Boundaries of Translation Spectrum*, ed. Marilyn Gaddis Rose (Binghamton: State University of New York, 1996), 183–94. Lawrence Venuti similarly considers racial, ethnic and social implications of textual transfer between separate cultures in his article 'Translation as a Social Practice: or, The Violence of Translation', in the same volume, *Translation Horizons*, 195–214. André Lefevere and Susan Bassnett concentrate on the issues of context, history and convention in translation in the collection of essays, *Translation, History, and Culture* edited by them

traditionally been on the comparative literary quality of the translation with respect to the source and the relations of those translations to the source texts in linguistic and narrative proximity. Recent studies of medieval translation practices and theory are, however, increasingly shifting the focus to contextual comparative readings that recognise the value inherent in the translations themselves. Michelle R. Warren notes, for instance, the historically low status of translations within academic discourse and points out that 'translations offer an opportunity to redefine audiences, social relations, historical inheritance, and ethnic identities' in her article on Middle English translation.[2] Zrinka Stahuljak elaborates further on the epistemological function of translation, pointing out that the concept of translation reaches beyond the singular function of linguistic transference and suggesting that 'its metaphorization has come to connote translatability of historical, cultural and political contents and contexts'.[3] In fact, the way in which culturally contingent systems of meaning are transported between ideologically different societies is of profound value in the uncovering of behavioural patterns, particularly from civilisations of the past, where our only witnesses to the elements that make up the ideological and conceptual system are often precisely such artefacts as literary works.

The medieval period is inherently unstable, dynamic, evolving and, not least, intrinsically absent for the modern reader. David Lawton points out that any effort to reconstruct the medieval is contingent upon the fact that 'the "medieval" is itself culturally constructed – and so, for that matter is the framing category of "culture" itself'.[4] To look at culture as a semiotic system is to look at the ways in which the world is made comprehensible by a configuration of social, ideological and behavioural codes; upon these value systems are based and one can begin to decipher from them certain patterns that present themselves in the literary works and other objects born out of that culture. Just as language represents the system of meaning which supports and engenders the successful act of communication, so it is intimately interconnected with the social context out of which that specific discourse arose.

(London: Pinter Publishers, 1990), and in their later book *Constructing Cultures* (Clevedon: Multilingual Matters, 1998). In his article 'Translating Medieval European Poetry', Burton Raffel points out the difficulty of conveying medieval literature to a modern reader unfamiliar with the context out of which the original grew (in *The Craft of Translation*, ed. John Biguenet and Rainer Schulte, Chicago: The University of Chicago Press, 1989, 28–53). The focus is, however, on modern reception of medieval literature, not cultural differences within the medieval period itself.

[2] 'Translation', in *Oxford Twenty-First Century Approaches to Literature: Middle English*, ed. Paul Strohm (Oxford: Oxford University Press, 2007), 51–67, at 52.

[3] 'An Epistemology of Tension. Translation and Multiculturalism', *The Translator. Studies in Intercultural Communication* 10 (2004), 33–57, at 36. For studies of medieval translations in general see for instance The Medieval Translator series. For elaborations on the art of translation in the Middle Ages see for instance Rita Copeland, *Rhetoric, Hermeneutics, and Translation in the Middle Ages. Academic Traditions and Vernacular Texts* (Cambridge: Cambridge University Press, 1991); and Jeanette Beer, ed., *Medieval Translators and their Craft* (Kalamazoo: Medieval Institute Publications, 1989).

[4] 'Analytical Survey I: Literary History and Cultural Study', *New Medieval Literature* 1 (1997), 237–70, at 238.

In the process of translation, translators must negotiate not only the linguistic differences between the two languages, but also the contextualised symbolic system, both verbal and non-verbal, contained within his original. They must transfer the embedded cultural signifiers to make the text comprehensible to its new audience.

M. A. K. Halliday states that 'as speakers and listeners, we project the linguistic system on to the social system . . . interpreting verbal meanings as the expression of the meanings that are inherent in the culture'.[5] The interpretation of language can thus be described as a cultural act, and the translation process therefore depends on the successful reconstruction of those cultural meanings out of which the linguistic choices of the original text have been made. In translation theory this process is recognised as the translatability of a text – where, according to Mary Snell-Hornby, 'the extent to which a text is translatable varies with the *degree* to which it is embedded in its own specific culture'; the greater the distance that separates the cultural background of the source text and target text, both in terms of time and place, the greater the difficulty becomes of transporting the source text successfully to the target audience.[6] The transfer of an ideologically bound text to a community differing in its conceptual constructions thus calls for reconfigurations of those elements. This is so historically. As has been established in the previous chapter, such a process becomes apparent in the translations of Old French literary material in thirteenth-century Norway, where the social and psychological outlook of the Francophone authors and audiences often differs quite fundamentally from that of the receiving reading community.[7] The revisions of the French literary material expose the complex and sometimes contradictory medieval conceptualisations of text, literary creation and the function of translation. They also bear witness – in the conscious and unconscious modifications of the substance, form and representation of the texts – to the cultural configurations of the reading communities for whom the new texts were being translated.

Behavioural Patterns

This chapter seeks to explore the complexities of the transmission of behavioural patterns in translation through the textual analysis of the Old Norse

---

[5] 'Language as Code and Language as Behaviour', in *The Semiotics of Culture and Language*, ed. Robin P. Fawcett, M. A. K. Halliday, Sydney M. Lamb and Adam Makkai, vol. 1 (London: Frances Pinter, 1984), 3–36, at 9.

[6] *Translation Studies. An Integrated Approach* (Amsterdam: John Benjamins Publishing Company, 1995), 41.

[7] In this chapter Old French is used to designate the Langue d'Oïl of northern France, whose regional dialects, such as Picard, Anglo-Norman and Francien, are not distinguished, except where directly relevant. Despite their internal differences and the later disassociation between Anglo-Norman and the French cultural realm, these dialectic variations all draw on a common originating tongue that differs grammatically and semantically from both English and Norse. The terms 'France' and 'French' refer here to the common cultural heritage of the inhabitants of the kingdom of France.

version of *La Chanson de Roland*. More specifically it asks how the uniquely culturally determined elements of emotional or social values and psychological conceptualisations evident in the structure, characterisation and linguistic representation of the material are transported across linguistic and cultural borders. The *chanson de geste* tradition was profoundly connected to the sense of identity and past of the French people and drew its evocative force from the glorification of the French ancestors and, more importantly, the contemporary relevance of the battle between Christendom's defenders and infidels. In the voyage across the Channel and then further into northern terrains, the text had to be uprooted from its originating historic and epic context in order to be made relevant to Nordic readers. A closer look at the text will reveal the complexity of the adaptation process of culturally bound codes of conduct and behaviour.

The French medieval epic *La Chanson de Roland* has survived in several manuscripts in both assonanced and rhymed versions. The manuscript containing the oldest and best text, Bodleian Library, Oxford, MS Digby 23, is an assonanced redaction in Anglo-Norman that was copied in the twelfth century. While there are considerable discrepancies in the dating of the poem, critics now generally agree on the approximate date of 1100 for the assonanced version.[8] Jane Gilbert points out that the rhymed version is dated after 1180, hence almost a century after the assonanced version, and 'is thought to represent a *remaniement* or reworking in which the earlier, assonanced tradition was adapted to tastes, interests, and political imperatives of the late twelfth century.'[9] The rhymed version can therefore be described as a derivative version of the assonanced text, which itself stems from earlier oral and written sources. The Norse version thus forms part of a textual tradition of the Roland story that reveals the act of cultural adaptation not only across linguistic boundaries, but across temporal and communal ones as well.

The Old Norse version of the *Chanson de Roland*, *Rúnzivals þáttr*, forms a part of a compilation in prose of the history of Charlemagne entitled *Karlamagnús saga*, which draws on several different sources, most of which are Old French *chansons de geste*. Some of the originals that comprise the compilation are known to exist in French or Latin, while others are either lost or never existed at all, at least not in that form. *Rúnzivals þáttr* constitutes the eighth branch of *Karlamagnús saga*. The text is preserved in four Icelandic manuscripts, none of which are complete, and fragments of five more. The text is fairly similar in all the manuscripts and fragments, with only a few exceptions.[10] While *Karlamagnús saga* has only been preserved in

---

[8] See *La Chanson de Roland*, ed. and trans. Gerard J. Brault (University Park: The Pennsylvania State University Press, 1984), xviii.

[9] 'The *Chanson de Roland*', in *The Cambridge Companion to Medieval French Literature*, ed. Simon Gaunt and Sarah Kay (Cambridge: Cambridge University Press, 2008), 21–34, at 23.

[10] The edition of *Karlamagnús saga* used in this chapter draws on the four manuscripts: Vellum MS no. 180c fol. written in the second half of the fourteenth century; Vellum MS no. 180a fol. written in the fifteenth century; Paper MS no. 180d fol. written not long before 1700, which is practically complete; and Paper MS 531 4to written by síra Ketill Jörundsson (d. 1670), which contains the whole saga with only a few gaps. All four manuscripts are located

fourteenth- and fifteenth-century (or younger) manuscripts in Iceland, it is likely that the major part of the compilation was translated during the reign of King Hákon and transmitted from there to other Scandinavian countries. The compilation probably came about in two stages, with the earlier redaction being assembled from various Anglo-Norman sources of *chansons de geste*, including *La Chanson de Roland*, and possibly other literary material in the thirteenth century. The later version is believed to stem from 1290–1320, or even 1330–40, and comprises some elaborations of the earlier texts and additional branches.[11] The *Rúnzivals þáttr* belongs to the earlier redaction. While it is thus unclear how many of the changes occurring in the translation process can be attributed to the original translators and how much is due to later scribal revisions in Iceland, one can nevertheless assume a general commonality in the material's transformation and reception owing to the close connections and common background of the inhabitants. The *Rúnzivals þáttr* is based on a lost version of *La Chanson de Roland*, but shows extensive similarities with the Anglo-Norman copy in the Digby manuscript, which is used in this discussion for comparison. It can thus be surmised that the manuscript used by the Norwegian translator was an Anglo-Norman copy, perhaps not very different from the one preserved in the Digby manuscript, and that it was most likely transmitted to Norway via England.[12]

The Norse translator transforms the verse of his original into prose, resulting in significant changes in the formal presentation and tone, similar to the Norse version of Marie de France's *Lais*. The transfer from the metrical form of the French *Chanson de Roland* to the basic prose delivery of *Rúnzivals þáttr* indicates the necessary adaptations made by the Norwegian translator as the existing native metres, eddic and skaldic verse, were singularly unsuited for the assonanced poem.[13] There was, moreover, as has been said before,

---

in the Arnamagnæan collection in Copenhagen. Several manuscripts of *Karlamagnús saga* are mentioned in medieval inventories in various Icelandic monasteries (*Karlamagnus saga ok kappa hans*, ed. C. R. Unger, Christiania: H. J. Jensen, 1860; see also E. F. Halvorsen, *The Norse Version of the Chanson de Roland*, Bibliotheca Arnamagnæana 19, Copenhagen: Ejnar Munksgaard, 1959, 32–7).

[11] See Susanne Kramarz-Bein, 'Geschichtsdenken in Skandinavien in der Tradition der *Chansons de geste* am Beispiel der *Karlamagnús saga*', in *Arbeiten zur Skandinavistik. XII Arbeitstagung der Deutschsprachhigen Skandinavistik 16.–23. September 1995 in Greifswald*, ed. Walter Baumgartner and Hans Fix (Vienna: Fassbaender, 1996), 152–65. There has been a general consensus among critics that the compilation originally came about in Norway around 1250 and drew on a number of French and Latin texts. There have, however, been some disagreements as to the extent of this original compilation and that of the later reworkings. For the argument of different stages of translation see Paul Aebischer, *Les différents états de la Karlamagnús saga* (Berlin: Akademie Verlag, 1956).

[12] For a discussion of the preservation history of *La Chanson de Roland* as it relates to the Norse translation see E. F. Halvorsen, *The Norse Version of the Chanson de Roland*, 77–98.

[13] While there is evidence of native heroic tales (such as those preserved in the Icelandic *Eddas*) being popular in Norway in the twelfth century, as well as skaldic poetry being composed near the end of the century, they were either never written down, or the manuscripts containing such literature have been lost (Halvorsen, *The Norse Version of the Chanson de Roland*, 2–16).

an established tradition of vernacular prose in Scandinavia.[14] Yet despite the change in formal representation the translation adheres closely to the Digby text (sometimes almost line by line).[15] The close adherance to the original by the Norse translator of *La Chanson de Roland* reveals the *intended* act of transference of the material into its new linguistic form as opposed to a creative re-engagement with existing literary material as is evinced in the English texts and later Icelandic reworkings of the Norse translations. The shift in form accentuates the multiplicity of the translation process, where the material crosses not only linguistic, historical and cultural boundaries, but those of generic and formal conventions as well.

A comparison of the first lines of the French verse with those of the Old Norse text discloses an observance of the original to the point of verbal echoes despite the substitution of prose for metre:

> *Carles li reis*, nostre emperere magnes,
> *Set anz* tuz pleins ad estet *en Espaigne*.
> Tresqu'en la mer *cunquist la tere* altaigne,
> *N'i ad castel ki devant lui remaigne.*
> Mur *ne citet* n'i est remés a fraindre,
> *Fors Sarraguce, ki est en une muntaigne.*
> *Li reis Marsilie la tient, ki Deu nen aimet,*
> *Mahumet sert e Apollin recleimet*:
> Nes poet guarder gue mals ne l'i ateignet.   (1–9)

> [King Charles, our great emperor,
> Has been in Spain for seven long years.
> He has conquered that haughty land right to the sea.
> Not a fortress remains,
> No wall, no city, that he has not smashed,
> Except Saragossa, which is on a mountain.
> King Marsile holds it, he who does not love God.
> He serves Mohammed and prays to Apollo:
> He cannot prevent misfortune from befalling him
>   there.][16]

---

[14] As has been noted the *konungasögur* (sagas of kings) were written in Norse prose and intended for the courts, intimating that prose was an accepted and respected literary medium in Scandinavia.

[15] This shift in form common to all the Norse translations raises questions of the inherent changes that occur in the move from verse to prose. It also draws attention to cultural preferences for specific narrative presentations. Such deliberations are, however, beyond the scope of this chapter as they address aspects of textual representation and poetic and linguistic propensity, as well as questions of formal conventions within both Norse and French literary history that reach much further than the *chanson de geste* tradition or the translation practices in thirteenth-century Norway. For a discussion of the different modes of representation of the two forms, prose and verse, see for instance Jeffrey Kittay and Wlad Godzich, *The Emergence of Prose* (Minneapolis: University of Minnesota Press, 1987), particularly chapter 3, which elaborates on the signifying potential of prose versus verse.

[16] Quotations from the French text are taken from *La Chanson de Roland*, ed. Brault, and will hereafter be given with line numbers in parentheses in the text. The English translations are based on Brault's facing translation in the edition with some variations to illuminate points

Behavioural Transformations

This episode is related as follows in the Old Norse version:

Karlamagnús konungr var *7 vetr* alla samfasta *á Spanialandi*, ok *lagði undir sik alt* með sjá svá at *hvorki borg né kastali* var sá, *at eigi hefði hann undir sik lagt*, né heruð eða tún, *nema Saraguze*, er *stendr á fjalli einu. Þar réð fyrir Marsilius konungr* hinn heiðni, sá er *eigi elskaði guð*, heldr *trúði hann á Maumet ok Apollín*, en þeir munu svíkja hann.[17]

[King Charlemagne was in Spain for seven winters, and conquered everything along the sea so that there was neither a city nor castle that he had not conquered, neither estate nor farmstead, except Saragossa, which stands on a mountain. There reigned the heathen king Marsilius, he who did not love God, but rather trusted in Mohammed and Apollo, but they will betray him.][18]

The main semantic components of each verse – such as 'King Charlemagne' in the first verse and 'seven years' and 'Spain' in the second – are repeated in the Norse text with the syntactical structure adjusted to accommodate Norse grammar and the flow of the prose. The translator remains close to his original, recasting the content in its new linguistic form. There are only minor differences observable in the first lines, and these do not affect the transmission of the matter contained in the verses, but indicate the translator's propensity for reshaping his material to his new public.

The qualifier, 'nostre emperere magnes' (our great emperor) is omitted as the narrative voice shifts from an internal persona speaking to an implied French audience to an impersonal voice recounting legends from the past. The addition of 'heruð eða tún' (estate nor farmstead) likewise subtly adjusts the landscape to give the audience tangible visual images of familiar settings to supplement the representation of place. The cadence and rhythm of the original is obviously lost in the transition from the French assonanced verse to the Old Norse prose, and the emphasis seems to be on retelling the story rather than either recreating the sound and flow of the original, or embellishing the text with rhetorical flourish. The language is comparable to the narrative style of the *konungasögur* (sagas of kings), which differs significantly from the relatively formal linguistic presentation of the *chansons de geste*. The *konungasögur* flourished as a genre in the first half of the thirteenth century, thereby establishing a stylistic and rhetorical precedence for vernacular prose writing at the time of the translations.[19] Gabriele Röder uses E. F. Halvorsen's terminology of 'translator's prose'

---

of comparisons. The verbal echoes are italicised in both the French and the Norse citations for clarification.

[17] 'Af Rúnzivals bardaga', *Karlamagnus saga ok kappa hans*, ed. Unger, 484. The Old Norse version will hereafter be referred to as *Rúnzivals þáttr* and will be cited in the text with page numbers in parentheses.

[18] The English translations of the Norse quotations are my own and are meant to convey the sense of the Norse version, not the poetic quality. Constance Hieatt's English translation was consulted for concordances in each case (*Karlamagnús saga. The Saga of Charlemagne and his Heroes*, vol. 3, Toronto: Pontifical Institute of Medieval Studies, 1980).

[19] Ármann Jakobsson claims that *Morkinskinna*, which is thought to predate *Heimskringla*,

to designate the style of *Karlamagnús saga*, which is more colloquial and uses rhetorical devices less frequently than the 'court style', which is more ornate. She argues that the style apparent in the preserved texts bears close resemblance to that of the *konungasögur* and *Íslendingasögur* (sagas of Icelanders) and differs fundamentally from the formal language which has become the hallmark of the *chanson de geste* tradition.[20]

The logical and consequential structuring of episodes indicates the changes made by the translator to adapt his material to the literary expectations of the receiving public. The translator's disregard of such literary devices as epithets, *laisses similaires*, foreshadowing and soliloquies, employed by the French poem, shifts the focus from dramatic building towards an emotional climax to the action itself. Native Scandinavian literature customarily consisted of a series of episodes with rapid action and little attention given to the psychology or emotional life of its characters. Long monologues were non-existent and dialogues were short and to the point and meant to convey information with narratorial intervention and judgement kept to a minimum or avoided altogether. The apparently deliberate modifications made by the translator reveal an effort to make the foreign material conform to the existing native literary tradition, while at the same time maintaining the narrative and thematic content of the original and its structure.[21]

---

reveals an awareness of the rhetorical forms current in continental Europe, which indicates that the choice of style for both indigenous and translated texts reveals a conscious preference of narrative style rather than a lack of understanding or appreciation of the rhetorical forms current in Europe at the time (*Staður í nýjum heimi: konungasagan Morkinskinna*, Reykjavík: Háskólaútgáfan, 2002, 61–107). For a discussion of Icelandic literary production in a pan-European context see for instance Torfi H. Tulinius, 'The Self as Other. Iceland and Christian Europe in the Middle Ages', *Gripla* 20 (2009), 199–215, and Margaret Clunies Ross, 'Medieval Iceland and the European Middle Ages', in *International Scandinavian and Medieval Studies in Memory of Gerd Wolfgang Weber*, ed. Michael Dallapiazza, Olaf Hansen, Preben Meulengracht Sørensen and Yvonne S. Bonnetain (Trieste: Edizioni Parnaso, 2000), 111–20.

[20] 'Die *Chansons de geste* in der altnordischen *Karlamagnús saga*: Übersetzungen oder Adaptationen', in *The Medieval Translator. Traduire au moyen âge*, ed. Roger Ellis, René Tixier and Bernd Weitemeier, vol. 6 (Turnhout: Brepols, 1998), 134–58, at 138, and Halvorsen, *The Norse Version of the Chanson de Roland*, 10–12). It is unclear to what extent one can disassociate Icelandic writers from Norwegians at this point given that many Icelanders partook of the courtly life of Hákon's court and may have undertaken some of the translation activities. The Norse translations in general reveal varying degrees of stylistic and rhetorical embellishments and flourish, but seem to have favoured the plain straightforward prose that characterises the native saga style. The existence of the rhetorically and artistically complex skaldic poetry indicates that this preference does not indicate a lack of skills in rhetorical complexity in general, but signals rather a stylistic preference. Mats Mals suggests in a recent article that the choice of the plain style in translations may be a conscious rejection of what may have been perceived as an 'effeminate' language for a more masculine language ('The Notion of Effeminate Language in Old Norse Literature', *Learning and Understanding in the Old Norse World. Essays in Honour of Margaret Clunies Ross*, ed. Judy Quinn, Kate Heslop, and Tarrin Wills, Turnhout: Brepols, 2007, 305–20).

[21] For a detailed textual comparison of the French and the Old Norse version see Halvorsen, *The Norse Version of the Chanson de Roland*. Gabriele Röder's article cited above also contains an excellent overview of the various types of changes made by the Norse translator ('Die *Chansons de geste* in der altnordischen *Karlamagnús saga*').

In the translation dialogues are shortened and made more concise to move the story forward. The descriptive, repetitive and visual use of metre and vocabulary in the battle scenes in the French version is reduced, and the emphasis is on single battles with rapid action and brief interspersed dialogues. The narrative focus is shifted from the relations between the characters, their self-representation and emotional state to the *acts* of the characters and the way in which those actions propel the narration towards the inevitable impending death of Roland. In fact, the epic is brought to closure rather rapidly, omitting the episode with Bramimonde and the court proceedings – thus emphasising that the focal point of the translation is indeed the epic closure rather than its continuance, which in the French context, by contrast, is crucial for the interlinking of the heroic past and the contemporary present. This difference in focus signals narrative distance of the Norse reading community from the material, which represented a past that was distant and disconnected from the reader, both historically and culturally, and as such could be contained and described as a single, concluded narrative event. For its French audience, on the other hand, the Charlemagne cycle embodied a historical past that both defined and engaged the sense of contemporary cultural identity, and was therefore neither final nor containable. The epics symbolised the commemmorative heritage of the French, while they simultaneously engaged the economic, political or cultural conditions of its twelfth-century audiences. By 'commemmorative heritage' I do not intend to frame the *chansons de geste* as 'national' epics, a construction that reflects modern rather than medieval conceptions of the genre's function and meaning. Yet, the epics represented a literary means (as the sagas of Icelanders did in Iceland) of engaging and contending with contemporary cultural anxieties, communal identity and discourse by drawing on a commemmorative past (albeit reconstructed and fictitious).

The effort of cultural acclimatisation is apparent not only in changes in the formal presentation, but also on the level of rhetorical and textual presentation. Eugene Vance relates the discourse of Roland to changes in social conditions in twelfth-century France, signalling the interrelations between vernacular writing and cultural impulses.[22] Drawing on Vance's argument, I would argue that the signifying power of the *Chanson de Roland* lies as much in its representational capacity as it does in its narrative content. If one approaches the genre of the *chansons de geste* as discourse rather than form, the translator must find a discursive mode to represent the French epic in a manner conducive to its new audience's reception and comprehension.[23] He does so by omitting many of the rhetorical devices characteristic of the *chansons de geste*, such as repetition, amplification, anticipation and epithets

---

[22] *Mervelous Signals* (Lincoln: University of Nebraska Press, 1986), 120–3; see also chapter 3 on Roland.
[23] Vance relates discourse to style and hence to rhetorical representation that is separate from (although connected to) formal attributes. Since rhetorical conventions are historically determined; the discursive mode of a text is thus linked to the cultural conditions out of which the text stems.

as well as many of the descriptive passages that are inherently linked to the function of the *chansons de geste* within the originating context.

There is similarly a noticeable effort to adapt the French discourse to familiar native discursive patterns, as is evident in minor alterations in both thematic and linguistic representation.[24] During a dialogue between Roland and Oliver, close to the end of their final battle, Oliver remarks: 'Ja aves vos ambsdous les braz sanglanz' (See how bloody both your arms are!) and Roland responds: 'Colps i ai fait mult genz!' (I have struck many noble blows!) (1,711–12). In the Norse version the reply becomes: 'því valda stór högg ok þó mörg högg' (517) (literally: hard blows cause this, and yet many blows). The subjective 'I' of the original is replaced by an objective syntactical construction more characteristic of native writing. As a result the focus shifts from the agent, Roland, in the French text to the *action* in the Norse text, that is, the hard blows that are the cause of the bloody arms. The inclusion of 'genz' in the French original moreover suggests that the strikes are imbued with value and are therefore to be interpreted as righteous or virtuous strikes. The statement reveals a conviction that the blows have a moral significance that is intimately connected with the figure of Roland himself. The 'noble blows' struck by Roland thus foreground the underlying crusading spirit of the *Chanson de Roland* and underscore his role as a warrior of God.[25] The syntactical rearrangement in the Norse text, on the other hand, draws attention to the force of the blows, rather than their spiritual value. The focus is thus redirected from any underlying subtext of crusading ideology to an archetypal Nordic representation of masculine prowess and warrior spirit. While the passage in the *Rúnzivals þáttr* contains the essential message of the French text, that is, the blows struck by a heroic warrior, the subtle shift from 'colps i ai fait mult genz' to 'stór högg ok þó mörg högg' is one of cultural amplification. The translator (or scribe) has rephrased the original to call upon the collective memory of his audience of similar episodes in the native literary tradition.[26] The aim is to

---

[24] Given the temporal distance between the original translation and the writing of the extant manuscripts containing the text, many of those changes could be due to later efforts of Icelandic scribes to emulate saga writing. Recent comparative evidence of later Icelandic versions and older Norwegian fragments of Norse translations has, however, not necessarily substantiated closer adherence to the original by the extant Norwegian texts than the Icelandic versions. In her article '*Gvímars saga*', Kalinke demonstrates that the eighteenth-century Icelandic paper manuscript containing *Gvímars saga*, an Icelandic version of *Guigemar* most likely derived from the original Norse translation, often contains more accurate or more original readings than the thirteenth-century manuscript which preserves the unique version of *Guiamars lioð* (*Opuscula* 7, Bibliotheca Arnamagnæana 34, Copenhagen: C. A. Reitzels boghandel, 1979, 106–39). In view of the close connections between the two cultural realms such later amendments would not in any case detract from the general conception of cultural transformation being addressed here.

[25] While 'noble' may, of course, simply refer to Roland's aristocratic status, the context here would indicate that the blows are noble because they are struck to defend an ideal. They are, in fact, noble because of the underlying intent. For a discussion of the crusading ethos in *La Chanson de Roland* see for instance Sharon Kinoshita, *Medieval Boundaries. Rethinking Difference in Old French Literature* (Philadelphia: University of Pennsylvania Press, 2006), particularly 15–45.

[26] It should be noted here that Carol Clover has suggested that the Icelandic sagas, as formal

infuse the text with authenticity and, more importantly, a familiarity of values, characterisation and idiom.[27]

The difficulty of conveying the French text to a Nordic audience lies, however, not in the textual representation, which reveals simply the effort of adapting the foreign text to the familiar discourse of the native literature, but rather in the transmission of the ideological structures that differ from those of the receptive culture. Mary Snell-Hornby draws attention to what she calls 'perspective', where 'the reader of the source-language text is appealed to as a member of a particular cultural or social group, and where knowledge of or even a relationship to this culture is presupposed'.[28] Hornby conceives of the term 'perspective' as the 'viewpoint of the speaker, narrator or reader in terms of culture, attitude, time and place', which is, of necessity, shifted in the translation process.[29] The term therefore denotes a complexity in translation that is amplified by the degree to which the text is embedded within a particular cultural, historical or social context, and the degree to which the target reader is removed from that context. This distance therefore affects the way in which a translated works is received. The concept of differing perspectives denotes the intricacy of transmitting such implicit social or cultural messages to a reader either unfamiliar with the cultural standards of the source text, or from a different social and cultural context altogether.

Clifford Geertz additionally states that 'not only ideas, but emotions too, are cultural artifacts', foregrounding the relations between the depiction of emotions in literature and the ideological constructions that shape how, when and the way in which emotions are expressed.[30] It is, in fact, through behaviour that culturally determined concepts find their articulation, and the question of literary representation of behavioural patterns is thus profoundly relevant to the issue of translation.[31] In *La Chanson de Roland*, this culturally determined

---

constructions, are not separable from the larger European development of the thirteenth century, but in fact form part of it. She claims that the same literary forces that played an important role in the rise of imaginative prose forms in France also played an important role in the evolution of the prose saga in Scandinavia, despite the differences in temper and style (*The Medieval Saga*, Ithaca: Cornell University Press, 1982). This validates the constant reformulation of literary ideologies through cross-cultural encounters, even within a genre generally considered to be profoundly 'native' in both origin and execution. It similarly foregrounds the continual regeneration and intertextual negotiations of literary matter.

[27] For a general discussion of the parallels between *Karlamagnús saga* and native Scandinavian literature see Lars Lönnroth, 'Charlemagne, Hrólf kraki, Ólaf Tryggvason, Parallels in the Heroic Tradition', in *Les relations littéraires franco-scandinaves au moyen âge*, 29–52. Lönnroth argues that the form we have today of *Karlamagnús saga* is the result of scribal expansions in Iceland during the thirteenth and fourteenth centuries and that they therefore show extensive signs of influence from native writing.

[28] *Translation Studies* 51–3, at 53.

[29] Ibid. 51.

[30] *The Interpretation of Cultures* (New York: Basic Books, 2000), 81.

[31] For a discussion of emotion as a cultural construct see Geertz, *The Interpretation of Cultures*; Rom Harré, ed., *The Social Construction of Emotion* (Oxford: Blackwell, 1986); Rom Harré and W. Parrott, eds., *The Emotions, Social, Cultural and Biological Dimensions* (London: Sage Publications, 1996); Barbara H. Rosenwein, ed., *Anger's Past* (Ithaca: Cornell University Press, 1998); and her *Emotional Communities in the Early Middle Ages* (Ithaca:

representation becomes apparent in the portrayal of the characters and their relationships to each other. The weeping, lamenting and fainting of Roland at the sight of his dead comrades establishes within the French cultural context the close bond existing between the men. The verbal expression of that emotion confirms Roland's nobility, as the faculty for aristocratic male bonding is conveyed in the capacity for exalted emotions. Within a Nordic context, on the other hand, this would be relayed through the actions taken by the remaining individual to avenge and preserve the reputation of the fallen companion, rather than through the depiction of the internal sorrow felt at that loss.

In the process of transporting the story of Roland from the French cultural and literary context to its Nordic audience, the translator must either put those unconventional discursive traditions in a context comprehensible to the audience, or adjust them to the existing standards of behaviour, both cultural and literary. There are, within any given culture, established conventions as to how and when emotions are verbalised and displayed; the Norse translator therefore had to negotiate the cross-cultural differences between those conventions in a manner that would both allow the foreign text to maintain its exotic qualities, and take into account the disparate emotional codes of the receiving audience. My argument here is not that *La Chanson de Roland* differs necessarily from the native Scandinavian literature in its emotional force or dramatic undertone, but rather in the manner in which feelings and sentiments are expressed. Where the French epic exhibits emotion frequently, both in action and speech, it is rarely displayed in the Nordic literature and must rather be inferred from the context, characters' actions, or involuntary physical reactions.

In the Norse translation of *Chanson de Roland*, many of the episodes containing emotional outbursts, complaints, fainting or weeping are either abbreviated or left out altogether. In some instances the translator makes an effort to modify such behaviour by making it seem less emotional and rather born out of physical necessity, hence explaining what must have seemed 'unmanly', or in any case strange, behaviour to the Nordic audience unaccustomed to tears and laments by their literary heroes. Within the saga realm, the accusation of crying (with respect to men) was considered a tremendous insult to the masculine identity, as it was interpreted as an effeminization. The weeping continental hero must thus have been a rather startling discovery to the Nordic audience and one which necessitated some cultural shifting, both in the matter being translated and, in fact, in the conceptual realm of the audience itself. An example from one of the better-known Icelandic sagas reveals how the allegation of crying has severe ramifications within the narrative realm that will change the course of the story. In the feud between Otkell and Gunnarr in the first half of *Brennu-Njáls saga*, Skammkell insinuates that Gunnarr cried when Otkell accidentally rode him over and bloodied him with his spur: 'Þat myndi mælt, ef ótiginn maðr væri at grátit hefði'[32] (If he were

---

Cornell University Press, 2007).

[32] *Brennu-Njáls saga*, ed. Einar Ólafur Sveinsson (Reykjavík: Hið íslenzka fornritafélag, 1954), 135.

just an ordinary man, it would be said that he cried).[33] The insinuation is unequivocal and is intended as mockery. Runólfr's response, 'muntú þat eiga til at segja næst, er þit finnizk, at ór sé grátraust ór skapi hans' (135) (the next time you and Gunnarr meet you will have to admit that there is no trace of crying in his nature) (91), suggests, in a traditionally understated manner, that he may in fact have to pay dearly for the insinuation. When the words are relayed to Gunnarr his reaction is a clear statement of the offence implicit in the accusation:

> Gunnarr . . . tekr atgeirinn, ok sǫng i honum hátt, ok heyrði Rannveig, móðir hans. Hon gekk fram ok mælti: 'Reiðuligr ert þú nú, sonr minn, ok ekki sá ek þik slíkan fyrr.' Gunnarr gekk út ok stakk niðr atgeirinum ok varp sér í sǫðulinn ok ríðr braut. Rannveig gekk til stufu; þar var háreysti mikit. 'Hátt kveðið þér,' segir hon, 'en þó lét hæra atgeirrinn, er Gunnarr gekk út.' Kolskeggr heyrði ok mælti: 'Þat mun eigi engra tíðenda vita.' 'Þat er vel,' segir Hallgerðr; 'nú munu þeir reyna, hvárt hann gengr grátandi undan þeim.' (136)

> [Gunnar . . . took his halberd; it rang loudly, and his mother Rannveig heard it.
>   She came to him and spoke: 'You look angry, my son. I never saw you like this before.
>   Gunnar went out and thrust the halberd into the ground to vault into the saddle, and rode away. Rannveig went into the main room. There was a great din of voices there.
>   'You are talking loudly,' she said, 'but Gunnar's halberd was even louder when he went out.'
>   Kolskegg heard this and spoke: 'That means no small news.'
>   'Good,' said Hallgerd. 'Now they can find out whether Gunnar will go away from them crying.' (92)]

The text highlights the contrast between Gunnarr's reaction to the insinuation of crying and his general reluctance to respond with violence. It is of significance here that Gunnarr does not seem to react violently to the injury itself, but rather to the intimation of his having cried as a result of it. His mother notes that she has never seen him as angry before and Gunnarr's silence at her words relates more than any words would. The sounding of the halberd is an ominous sign of the impending killing, which Kolskeggr, his brother, immediately recognises. The repeated references to the accusation of crying throughout the section reveals the underlying motivational force of honour and the implicit threat to manhood. Gunnarr's words when he finds Otkell and his company that 'munuð þér nú ok reyna, hvárt ek græt nǫkkut fyrir yðr' (137) (you'll find out now if I'll do any crying for your) (92) firmly signals the underlying threat to Gunnarr's masculine identity, which can only be resolved by the death of one or the other.

A key example of such emotional amendments in the translation process is the poignant and evocative verse relating Roland's reaction to Oliver's death in the French version:

---

[33] *Njal's saga*, trans. Robert Cook (London: Penguin Books, 2001), 91.

> Li quens Rollant, quant il veit mort ses pers
> E Oliver, qu'il tant poeit amer,
> Tendrur en out, cumencet a plurer.
> En sun visage fut mult desculurer.
> Si grant doel out que mais ne pout ester,
> Voeillet o nun, a tere chet pasmet.
> Dist l'arcevesque: 'Tant mare fustes, ber!'
> (*Chanson* 2,215–21)
>
> [When Count Roland sees his peers dead
> And Oliver, whom he loved so well,
> He feels compassion, he begins to weep.
> His face lost all its color.
> He suffered such pain that he could no longer stand,
> Involuntarily he falls to the ground.
> The archbishop said: 'You have much grief, baron!']

The narrative perspective at the beginning of the passage is through the eyes of Roland and the focal point thus on the dead bodies of his companions, adding to the emotive thrust of the scene. The perspective shifts from his companions to Oliver, where it lingers; and the effect is underscored by the verbalisation of the love felt by Roland for his now dead friend. The climactic narrative moves from internal feelings of pity or tenderness to the external dramatisation of his sorrow through the tears shed and the pain felt by Roland, culminating in his collapse. At that point the narrative perspective shifts from Roland to the archbishop, through whom the audience is made to visualise the entire scene of the dead bodies, as well as the unconscious body of Roland himself. The focus is thus on the staging of the scene for maximum emotional impact and the dramatisation of the internal feelings experienced by the tragic figure of Roland.

In the Old Norse version the passage is reduced to a single sentence with Roland's 'ógleði' (sadness) being linked to his weakened state, culminating in the 'ómegin' (faint) that falls on him: 'Nú sá erkibyskup at Rollant hafði svá mikla úgleði, at hann lá í úmætti' (522) (The archbishop saw now that Roland suffered such grief that he had collapsed). The emotional weight of the passage is shifted with the effect coming rather from the *inside* as opposed to the actual description of the outburst of emotions of the French version.[34] The Norse translator moves the focal point to the archbishop and depicts the entire scene through his eyes, reducing the narratorial intrusion and giving

---

[34] It is of significance in this context that the sagas contain passages demonstrating similar internal emotional agitations, indicating the established conventions of representing emotion: 'Þórhalli Ásgrímssyni brá svá við, er honum var sagt, at Njáll, fóstri hans, var dauðr ok hann hafði inni brunnit, at hann þrútnaði allr ok blóðbogi stóð ór hvárritveggju hlustinni, ok varð eigi stoðvat, ok fell hann í óvit, ok þá stoðvaðisk' (Thorhall Asgrimsson was so shocked when he was told his foster-father Njal was dead and had been burned in his house, that his whole body swelled up and blood gushed from both ears, and it could not be stopped and he fell in a faint, and then it stopped) (*Brennu-Njáls saga*, ed. Einar Ólafur Sveinsson, 344–5, and *Njal's saga*, trans. Cook, 231; I have adjusted the English translation slightly).

the scene a sense of objectivity. Similarly, the climactic narrative movement from internal feeling to external representation of those feelings in the French text is omitted. In fact, the only word with sentimental value, 'ógleði', is presented as the archbishop's interpretation rather than a narratorial statement of Roland's state of mind. The impassive narrative mode is continued as the text relates the archbishops reaction to Roland's swoon: 'Þá tók hann hornit Olivant ok fór til vatns rennanda er þar var, en hann var svá ústyrkr af sárum ok blóðrás, at hann mátti hvergi komast, ok féll niðr, ok lét þá líf sitt ok fór til guðs' (522) (He then took the horn Oliphant and went to a running stream that was there. But he was so unsteady from his wounds and the blood loss that he could not get anywhere and fell down and gave up his life there and went to God). The text does not depict an emotional reaction by the archbishop to Roland's collapse. The focus is on his actions, the narrative components of the French text, depicting how he takes the horn and brings it to the water, where he subsequently collapses and dies as a result of his wounds and the loss of blood. The passage is devoid of emotive vocabulary and the attention remains on the essential facts.

In the Digby text, the passage marks the continued dramatic climax as it relates the death of all the peers, leaving Roland alone to die the heroic death and to be commemmorated in the epic:

> Li arcevesques, quant vit pasmer Rollant,
> Dunch out tel doel unkes mais n'out si grant.
> Tendit sa main, si ad pris l'olifan.
> En Rencesvals ad un ewe curant,
> Aler i volt, sin durrat a Rollant.
> Sun petit pas s'en turnet cancelant
> Il est si fieble gu'il ne poet en avant,
> N'en ad vertut, trop ad perdut del sanc.
> Einz que om alast un sul arpent de camp,
> Falt li le coer, si est chaeit avant.
> La sue mort l'i vait mult angoissant.   (2,222–32)

> [When the archbishop saw Roland faint,
> He suffered greater anguish than ever before.
> He stretched out his hand and took the oliphant.
> At Roncevaux there is a running stream,
> He wants to go there, he will give some water to Roland.
> He turns and goes away with short, faltering steps.
> He is so weak that he cannot go any farther,
> He has not the strength to, he has lost too much blood.
> In less time than it would take a man to cover a single acre,
> His heart fails him and he falls forward.
> His death is gripping him hard.]

The archbishop's great anguish motivates the effort to bring water to Roland, and thus infuses the passage with tragic undertones. The verbal construction 'aler i volt' (wants to go) indicates the desire to reach the stream, hinting that he may not reach it. The translation removes the implicit intentionality with a direct verb 'fór' (went), thereby removing the emotive force of the failed effort. The French narrative then decelerates and focuses on the minute details of the archbishop's actions; his desire to assist Roland, the turning to leave, the faltering steps resulting in the end in his collapse. The detailed description is a dramatic representation of the final moments of the archbishop, culminating in his death which is depicted as 'angoissant' (gripping him hard). The Norse translation, on the other hand, removes all emotional modifiers and strips the scene down to its rudimentary narrative elements (taking the horn, going to the stream, falling down from blood loss). His death is furthermore described in a passive manner as a departure from this life to the heavenly one, thereby negating the emotive intensity of the French text.

The death of the archbishop is then drawn out further in the French text by shifting the focal point to Roland so that the audience witnesses the last dying moments of the archbishop through the eyes of Roland. The focus is on the gruesome details of the bishop's 'anguishing' death, with his entrails spilling out and the brain oozing out, which is then contrasted with his 'blanches mains, les beles' (beautiful white hands), which he has crossed over his breast, to underscore his death as martyrdom.[35] While the Norse text relegates the symbolic imagery of the death of the Christian martyr by simply referring to his death as a passing to God, the French text enforces this symbolism through multiple subsequent references to a holy war and entreaties to God to grant him his blessing and ease his passing to Paradise.[36]

The depiction of the reaction of Charlemagne and his men to the news of the ambush and Roland's death is similarly curtailed through a reduction of the sentimentality and the shortening of the passage to make it more concise, less affected and more in tune with traditional Nordic views of honour and the obligation of revenge:

> Tiret sa barbe cum hom ki est iret,
> Plurent des oilz si baron chevaler.
> Encuntre tere se pasment .XX. millers,
> Naimes li dux en ad mult grant pitet.
> Il n'en i ad chevaler ne barun
> Que de pitet mult durement ne plurt.
> Plurent lur filz, lur freres, lur nevolz
> E lur amis e lur lige seignurs;
> Encuntre tere se pasment li plusur.
> Naimes li dux d'iço ad fait que proz,
> Tuz premereins l'ad dit l'empereür:
> ...
> 'Car chevalchez! Vengez ceste dulor!'   (2,414–28)
>
> [He tugs his beard like a man who is angry,
> His brave knights' eyes are brimming with tears.

---

[35] See lines 2,232–50, at 2,250.
[36] See lines 2,238–58.

> Twenty thousand fall to the ground in a swoon,
> Duke Naimes feels very great sorrow.
> There is not a knight nor a baron
> Who does not shed bitter tears of sorrow.
> They weep for their sons, their brothers, their nephews,
> Their friends and their liege lords;
> Most fall to the ground in a swoon.
> Duke Naimes did the wise thing,
> He was first to speak to the Emperor:
> ...
> 'Ride knights! Avenge this hurt!']

The Old Norse text condenses the description of the sorrow of the army by confining it to a single sentence applied to Charlemagne. The swooning of twenty thousand soldiers is reduced to Charlemagne falling off his horse for the sake of his 'ógleði' (sadness), again subtly transforming the *exposé* of the emotional tumult in the French version (falling to the ground in a swoon) to a natural and to some extent a physically explicable consequence of the sorrow felt by the emperor:

> Karlamagnús konungr sleit klæði sín ok skók skegg sitt ok féll af hesti sínum fyrir úgleði sakir. Nú var þar engi maðr er eigi feldi tár fyrir sakir sinna vina. Nemes hertugi hafði af því máli vel sem öllum öðrum, ok hann gékk nær konungi ok mælti: '. . . Nú væri þat drengiligra at hefna frænda sinna en at syrgja eftir dauða.' (525–6).

> [King Charlemagne tore his clothes and shook his beard and fell from his horse in his sorrow. There was no man there who did not shed tears for the loss of his friends . . . Duke Nemes did the right thing as in all other matters and he went to the king and said: '. . . Now it would be more honourable to avenge one's kinsmen than to mourn for the dead.']

The seemingly insignificant and minor adjustment at the end of the quoted passage epitomises the acclimatisation of the passage to the Nordic mentality of the receiving audience. Rather than simply urging the knights to retaliate for the harm, as the French text does, the translator adds the declaration that it would be 'drengiligra' (more honourable or brave) to avenge their brothers and friends than to sit and mourn those already dead. This notion of retaliatory action being a more appropriate masculine behaviour than the passive (presumably feminine) grieving of the dead is echoed in *Brennu-Njáls saga*, when Kári Sölmundarson tells of the burning of Njáll and his family after having escaped himself: 'Kári kvað annat karlmannligra en gráta þá dauða ok bað hann safna liði ok koma ǫllu til Holtsvaðs.' (Kari said there were more manly things to do than weep for the dead, and he asked him to gather men and bring them all to Holtsvad).[37] Both the verbal expressions *drengiligt* (honourable) and *frændr* (kinsmen), which are inserted by the translator, are representative of the cultural context of medieval Scandinavia (and appear frequently

---

[37] *Brennu-Njáls saga*, 339, and *Njal's saga*, trans. Cook, 227.

in the sagas); and the sentence as a whole both reflects and follows the typical Norse pattern of provocation preceding the traditional retribution for the killing of a family member.[38] The Norse translation thus shifts the expression of righteous anger in the French text to a formulaic ritual stemming from the pre-Christian Germanic mentality of honour and duty.[39]

Cultural Translation

Within both Scandinavian and Romance studies, the prevailing general conception of the Old Norse translations of the French *chansons de geste* and courtly material has traditionally been one of inferiority. They have suffered as the unequal and lesser literary tradition in comparison with the native genre of the sagas, and they have also suffered as the inferior and often inadequate counterpart of their French originals. Recent criticism has sought to negate this proclivity for dismissal and consider the translations as a corpus with its own internal coherence, structural integrity and intentions. This shift is part of a more general recognition of marginal genres, such as the native Icelandic romance, which has traditionally been conceived of as derivative (and hence of less interest than the presumed indigenous genres), much like the translations themselves.[40] Rather than analysing the translations based on the standards of a native genre, which are misleading in the evaluation of the translated material, or comparing them to their foreign originals irrespective of the impact the cultural context of the translators has had upon their structure, they should instead be studied on the basis of their internal coherence and as evidence of the cultural capacity for assimilation and adaptation of foreign material.

While it is true that much of the unique aural quality of the French *Chanson de Roland* is lost in the translation, owing to the transference from the metrical system to prose and the elimination of much of the characteristic rhetorical qualities which give the French poem its unique character, I disagree with E. F. Halvorsen's argument that many of the differences between the Old Norse and the French version are due to 'mistakes' in translation. Halvorsen refers to

---

[38] *Drengilegt* reflects the Norse notion of honourable and noble comportment, which is associated with both moral and ethical behavioural patterns (for example murder vs. justified killing, such as that due to an insult or brought about by the necessity of revenge) as well as the conceptualisation of 'manly' behaviour, for instance the duty of a man to behave in the appropriate manner (to take action rather than show emotion, for example). *Frændi* refers to a family member and can be used indiscriminately for a brother, or one connected to the family through bonds of marriage. In some cases it is also used for a close friend, often bound to the other by a pledge of honour.

[39] Much has been written on feuds and the concept of retaliation in the saga literature; see for instance Jesse Byock, *Feud in the Icelandic saga* (Berkeley: University of California Press, 1982).

[40] See for instance Geraldine Barnes, 'Romance in Iceland', in *Old Icelandic Literature and Society*, ed. Margaret Clunies Ross (Cambridge: Cambridge University Press, 2000), 266–86; Marianne E. Kalinke, *Bridal-Quest Romance in Medieval Iceland*, Islandica 46 (Ithaca: Cornell University Press, 1990); and Matthew James Driscoll, 'Þögnin mikla. Hugleiðingar um riddarasögur og stöðu þeirra í íslenskum bókmenntum', *Skáldskaparmál* 1 (1990), 157–68.

episodes describing battle scenes on horseback and argues that because of the translator's unfamiliarity with fighting with a lance on a horseback (since in thirteenth-century Scandinavia horses served as transport while men fought on foot with swords, spears and axes) he alters passages in his translation, resulting in misreadings and errors.[41] On the contrary, I would argue, along with Gabriele Röder, that such alterations mark a conscious modification by the translator for the sake of an *audience* unfamiliar with fighting on horseback.[42] The amendment thus becomes a deliberate component of the translation project and indicates again the effort of adjusting the text to its new cultural context through the transformation of cultural signifiers that otherwise would have been incomprehensible or misleading to the target audience:

> Sun cheval brochet, laiset curre a esforz,
> Vait le ferir li quens quanque il pout.
> L'escut li freint e l'osberc li desclot,
> Trenchet le piz, si li briset les os,
> Tute l'eschine li desevret del dos,
> Od sun espiet l'anme li getet fors,
> Enpeint le ben, fait li brandir le cors,
> Pleine sa hanste del cheval l'abat mort.   (1,197–204)

> [He spurs his horse, he lets him run full speed,
> The count goes to strike him with all his might.
> He smashes his shield and tears open his hauberk,
> Cuts into his breast and shatters his bones,
> He severs his spine from his back,
> He thrusts out his soul with his spear,
> He sticks it deeply into him, he impales his whole body,
> Running him through, he throws him dead from his
>   horse.]

The passage depicting Roland in battle striking with his lance is modified in the Old Norse version as follows: 'En Rollant ... reið í móti honum ákafliga ok hjó til hans með sverði sínu ok klauf í sundr skjöld hans ok brynju ok festi blóðrefil sinn í brjósti honum ok steypti honum dauðum af hesti sínum' (509) (Roland ... rode against him vehemently and struck him with his sword, and cut apart his shield and coat of mail: he plunged the point of his sword into his breast and cast him dead from his horse). Rather than sounding as Halvorsen would contend 'quite absurd', the passage would have provided the medieval Norse audience with a fairly vivid image of the battle, combining the established cultural conception of how fighting proceeds (that is, with a sword rather than a lance) with the foreign elements of the combat depicted in the French text.[43] The adjustment in fact displays a rather successful merging of

---

[41] *The Norse Version of the Chanson de Roland*, 129.
[42] 'Die *Chansons de geste* in der altnordischen *Karlamagnús saga*', 144.
[43] *The Norse Version of the Chanson de Roland*, 129. While fighting within the Norse cultural realm could take place with an array of weapons, from agricultural instruments to axes, the sword would be the most comparable weapon for a combat like the one described in the

the two cultural and literary realms.[44]

Halvorsen's argument that the translation is faulty or not accurate because of the translator's incompetence in the source language is based partially on misconceptions about medieval translation methods and objectives – where the goal was not to reproduce an 'accurate' version of the original, but rather to transmit the matter with varying degrees of faithfulness and no unconditional obligations of accuracy or truthfulness.[45] The text seems indeed to show a growing tendency toward such familiarisation of the source material as the translation progresses, with more omissions, transformations and insertions or replacement of Nordic-sounding expressions in dialogues. This could imply that the translator was growing more comfortable with his own creative share in the translation project. The material may have captured his imagination and the internal focus shifted from transcribing the French text to rendering the content in a manner inspired by his own literary and cultural background.

A comparison with the Old Norse version of Marie de France's *Lais*, *Strengleikar*, discussed in Chapter 1, is of interest with respect to textual transformation, the aim of translation and the impact of the expected public. The collection of French poems was translated during the same period in Norway and has been preserved in a Norwegian manuscript from the late thirteenth century, thus presenting an earlier version of a Norse translation. In the approach to translation, the collection shows marked similarities to *Karlamagnús saga*. It is noteworthy that both are compilations of individual French *chansons de geste*, on the one hand, and a collection of *lais* on the other, alluding perhaps to the seemingly Nordic propensity of gathering assorted but related material into compilations such as the *konungasögur*. The fact that hardly any of the poems contained within the collections have survived independently in a different form supports the notion that the translations were conceived of as compilations.[46]

French text and one that would befit an aristocratic environment. Swords are frequently the weapon of choice in literary depictions of duels (*hólmganga*) in Old Norse literature, indicating a narrative convention for swordfight, particularly between two opponents, rather than the custom of striking with a lance.

[44] Jonna Kjær argues, on the other hand, that the changes form part of a systematic effort to create a more 'courtoise' version of the French epic ('La réception scandinave de la littérature courtoise et l'exemple de la *Chanson de Roland* / Af Rúnzivals bardaga: Une épopée féodale transformée en roman courtois?', *Romania* 114 (1996), 50–69, at 67).

[45] The cultural adaptation of foreign linguistic structures and cultural customs is often misconstrued as linguistic ineptitude, as can be seen with the French battle cry 'munjoie', which is either omitted or changed in the translation, and which Halvorsen attributes to the translator's misunderstanding. Gabriele Röder has, however, demonstrated that the cry of war was indeed known since it is translated and explained in the first part of *Karlamagnús saga* ('Die *Chansons de geste* in der altnordischen *Karlamagnús saga*', 146–7).

[46] Paul Aebischer argues in his book, *Les différents états de la Karlamagnús saga*, that the first stage in the compilation was an introductory chapter about Charlemagne's early years based on a lost *Vie romancée de Charlemagne*, a chronicle drawing on various *chansons de geste* and dating from about 1200. Peter G. Foote also points out connections to the *Pseudo-Turpin Chronicle*, a legendary history in Latin that originates from the same traditions as the *Chanson de Roland*, which he claims was translated in Iceland in the early thirteenth century

The *Strengleikar* collection transforms the elegant verse form of Marie de France's *Lais* into prose and the pattern of condensation and omission resembles the translation mode observable in *Rúnzivals þáttr*.⁴⁷ Yet the linguistic presentations of the two Norse translations differ. While *Rúnzivals þáttr* shows distinct efforts to reduce the sentimentality of the original, *Strengleikar* retains many of the passages containing unfamiliar descriptions of courtly love behaviour, the anguish, swooning and sighing, thereby introducing 'foreign' terminology, such as *ástarangur* (love-sickness), *hugsjúkur* (melancholic) and *kurteiz* (courteous), into the Norse literary language.⁴⁸ The disparity between the two can be at least partially explained by the different material being translated. While the *Chanson de Roland* is a masculine poem celebrating the heroic death of the protagonist with ample violence and little or no female inspiration or influence, Marie de France's *Lais* celebrate and focus almost exclusively on the idea of courtly love, with minimal battle scenes, and are renowned for their uniquely feminine perspective. It stands to reason that the material of the *chansons* would seem more pertinent to the Nordic mentality and literary heritage and hence would assume some of the characteristics of similar native literature, whereas the matter of the *Lais* would have been utterly foreign, and was possibly translated accordingly to reveal to the audience the manners and customs of the courtly world hidden within the poems.

The disparity between the two French works ought to illustrate a greater or lesser adaptability to the target language and culture, as well as the diverse objectives behind the translation projects. The powerful and epic language of the *chanson de geste*, portraying the exclusive masculine world of battles and heroic deeds, contrasts noticeably with the courtly and playful tone of the *Lais*, accentuating the inherent difference in thematic presentation. The repetition of words or ideas within the poem along with the replication of sound patterns through the assonance within each *laisse* give the *Chanson de Roland* a solemn rhythmical quality that propels the song forward and substantiates the matter being recounted. The shorter couplets of Marie de France, on the other hand, give her poems a lighter touch and a sense of a

---

(*The Pseudo-Turpin Chronicle in Iceland*, London: London Mediæval Studies, 1959). It is likely though that the greater part of the collection was translated and assembled in Norway in the mid-thirteenth century, with later additional material possibly being interpolated or added into the existing collection (see Susanne Kramarz-Bein, 'Geschichtsdenken in Skandinavien in der Tradition der *Chansons de geste* am Beispiel der *Karlamagnús saga*', in *Arbeiten zur Skandinavistik. XII*, ed. Baumgartner and Fix; and Joanna Kjær, '*Karlamagnús saga*: la saga de Charlemagne', *Revue des langues romanes* 102, 1998: 7–24).

⁴⁷ Robert Cook and Mattias Tveitane point out in their edition of the poems that the fidelity varies between poems with many of earlier poems being translated quite accurately, while some of the later ones have been abridged somewhat more extensively (*Strengleikar. An Old Norse Translation of Twenty-one Old French Lais*, Oslo: Norsk historisk kjeldskrift-institutt, 1979, xxii–xxvii).

⁴⁸ The introduction of 'unfamiliar' vocabulary into Norse literature is, obviously, not limited to *Strengleikar*, nor do the words necessarily originate with that specific translation. *Tristrams saga* (a translation of Thomas's *Tristan*) contains, for instance, multiple examples of such usage. Those words are, nevertheless, ingrained in the language through their manifestation in such works as *Strengleikar*.

circular motion within each poem, enclosing the visual scenes which make up the symbolic substance. Whereas the rudimentary structures of the *Chanson de Roland* and the masculine world portrayed within the poem would have adapted well to the native Scandinavian literature, the lyrical quality as well as the courtly matter of the *Lais* would have contrasted profoundly with the traditional heroic ideals of the Nordic cultural mentality. The dissimilarity between the two Old Norse translations indicates the varying degrees of adaptability of foreign material to existing literary standards. While the Norse version of the *Lais* aspires to capture the poetic essence of the original, the linguistic emphasis in *Rúnzivals þáttr* is on dramatic momentum rather than symbolic imagery. The differences observable in the translated texts thus reiterate divergences in the content and the manner of representation of the French poems.[49]

It is of some significance in this context that *Strengleikar* seems to have been less popular and influential in Scandinavia, based on manuscript preservation and manifest influence within the literary tradition, than *Karlamagnús saga*, testifying perhaps to the consequences of audience expectations and cultural predilection for the durability of a translated text. While the semiotic system out of which the *Lais* originated was profoundly different from the existing narrative and cultural discourse of Scandinavian literary tradition, the heroic epic had its counterpart in Nordic legendary history and could thus be subsumed and given a familiar shape and form to facilitate the transfer of unfamiliar cultural elements. The negotiation of the separate semiotic systems of the French text and its Norse translation, evident in the diverse behavioural patterns that manifest the innate ideological principles, underscores elements that define the cultural conceptualising of self and social environment. By identifying such elements one can approach the text as a product of its culture and approach the 'medieval' through the location of those ideological signifiers that ultimately constitute a 'culture'.[50]

The adaptations evident in the otherwise close translation of *La Chanson de Roland* indicate the intimate interconnectedness between a language and its cultural constitution. The interpretation of discourse is therefore contingent not only upon the knowledge of the linguistic components of that language, but also upon the entire culturally determined semiotic system that underlies and enables its potential to convey meaning. The successful transposition of

---

[49] The *Gesta Danorum* of Saxo Grammaticus (1186–1218) reveals the contemporary cultural anxiety about the conflict between the ancient warrior ideals and the new influx of continental courtliness. The protagonist of the *Gesta* is torn between the realm of courtly ideals and values (diplomacy, lovemaking, attention to clothing etc.) and the traditional heroic ideals represented in the obligation of revenge (see C. Stephen Jaeger, *The Origins of Courtliness. Civilizing Trends and the Formation of Courtly Ideals 939–1210*, Philadelphia: University of Pennsylvania Press, 1985, 176–89).

[50] I use the word 'approach' here purposely, as any effort to describe the medieval is dependent upon modern perceptions of the past as contained, vanished and dissimilar, whereas any culture is, as is evident in this discussion by the adaptability of both the translated text and the reading community receiving it, in constant flux, dynamic and changing, and can thus neither be entirely contained nor depicted.

a text depends not only upon the linguistic transfer of the material, but more importantly upon the satisfactory negotiation between the structures that bear meaning within two cultures.

CHAPTER THREE

Narrative Transformations in the Old Norse and Middle English Versions of *Le Chevalier au Lion* (or *Yvain*)

THE SPREAD AND DIFFUSION OF THE ROMANCE GENRE throughout Western Europe signals one of the more significant cultural expansions in the Middle Ages. The fact that this development took place by means of books containing within them the tenets of courtly ideology makes it all the more unique. In the centuries following the rise of the French romance, the genre became known in both translations and original compositions throughout medieval Europe. The courtly ideology embedded within these works had an impact upon the social structures of the receiving communities in both manifest and hidden ways. The matter and form of the romance influenced the way in which authors and audiences came to view literature and its role within their social structures.

The significance of the French romance within medieval literary history has been amply recognised. The cultural encounter between native traditions and the new literary form being imported has, however, attracted less attention.[1] This is particularly relevant to medieval England, where Anglo-Norman and French romances were being reproduced in the native vernacular some centuries after their original appearance. Similarly, the extensive translations along with the subsequent copying of French courtly literature in Scandinavia have commonly been dismissed as inferior reproductions of an original genre. They have suffered from the comparison to native literary productions and

---

[1] I should like to note that this does not, however, apply to romance as a genre or to native productions of romance, whether in France or in England. Several outstanding volumes have appeared in recent years that deal with romance in its various forms. Geraldine Heng's book, *Empire of Magic*, for instance, offers a remarkable insight into the cultural origins of medieval romance as a genre (*Empire of Magic. Medieval Romance and the Politics of Cultural Fantasy*, New York: Columbia University Press, 2003). Helen Cooper and contributors to a volume edited by Corinne Saunders examine English romance in particular, one from a historical perspective and the other from a cultural perspective (Helen Cooper, *The English Romance in Time. Transforming Motifs from Geoffrey of Monmouth to the Death of Shakespeare*, Oxford: Oxford University Press, 2004, and Corinne Saunders, ed., *Cultural Encounters in the Medieval Romance of Medieval England*, Studies in Medieval Romance, Cambridge: D. S. Brewer, 2005). Many other critics have contributed to redefining the boundaries and ideologies of the romance genre, particularly in France and England. As this chapter deals with the tranmission of texts, rather than the production of romance, these will not be elaborated on further, but my indebtedness to these critics is hereby acknowledged.

have frequently been blamed for a degeneration of the Icelandic literary tradition. What has not been taken into account is the fact that the widespread copying of those imported texts alongside that of the native literature speaks volumes about the interest and literary habits of those reading communities. Rather than comparing the romance translations to the standards of a native genre, such as the sagas of Icelanders, which are based on completely different generic structures, authorial goals and cultural traditions, they should be analysed on the basis of their own internal coherence. In these terms they bear witness to the values, literary expectations and meaningful systems of the reading communities that received and preserved them.

The Middle English versions of the romances have likewise commonly been considered to be inferior replicas of their French counterparts, drawn by unskilled hands for a lower-class audience. While critics have begun to study the texts within the context of English cultural and literary traditions, the sense that their form and style reflect a decline in social environment nevertheless prevails.[2] It is generally assumed that the changes in the narrative structures of the English texts are due to the slide in social status of the reading communities and a lack of appreciation and understanding of the courtly ideals that motivated the creation of the romance in the first place. The purpose of this chapter is to reconsider the narrative configuration of the Old Norse and Middle English romance as evidence of narratological and cultural predilection by the reading communities that produced and preserved these works. The intention here is not to deny the likely differences in social hierarchy between the source and target audiences of the English texts, but rather to shift the focus from modern critical judgement of literary quality and skill to the conceptual framework that informed the literary decisions of the English authors.[3] The discussion of the Old Norse translations of the French romance will similarly take into account the complex transmission history of the texts in the analysis of the cultural context that informed the writerly choices in the translation. This will assist in exploring the different levels of textual modifications occurring in the translation and copying process. This chapter will thus explore the alterations that occur in the transmission of a text from its originating cultural context to a different cultural realm where audience expectations, literary traditions and symbolic connotations differ. The focus of the discussion will be the narrative transformations as

---

[2] See for instance Jocelyn Wogan-Browne, Nicholas Watson, Andrew Taylor and Ruth Evans, eds., *The Idea of the Vernacular. An Anthology of Middle English Literary Theory, 1280–1520* (University Park: The Pennsylvania State University Press, 1999); Murray J. Evans, *Rereading Middle English Romance. Manuscript Layout, Decoration, and the Rhetoric of Composite Structure* (Montreal: McGill-Queen's University Press, 1995); and Stephen Knight, 'The Social Function of Middle English Romance', in *Medieval Literature. Criticism, Ideology & History*, ed. David Aers (New York: St Martin's Press, 1986), 99–122.

[3] I use the words author, translator and redactor indiscriminately in this chapter to refer to the individuals that presumably composed the Old Norse and Middle English versions of Chrétien's *Yvain*. Given the precarious preservation issues with medieval texts, particularly vernacular English literature, this mode of address within the discussion makes allowance for the inevitable scribal errors and changes occurring in the manuscript transmission of any secular medieval text.

they appear in the Old Norse and Middle English translation of Chrétien de Troyes's *Yvain,* or *Le Chevalier au Lion.*

Literary Formation

By looking at culture as a semiotic system that finds its articulation through social behaviour one can discern the psychological structures that guide the judgements within that system.[4] Those ideologies are accordingly expressed through the communal structures of each society. Despite their inherently unstable and elusive nature, the symbolic units of that system can be observed within social discourse. By analysing the literary works of a given period one can discern some of the inscribed ideological constructions that governed their perception and understanding. As stated before, those constructions become particularly apparent in literary translations where the two diverse systems of source and target cultures must come together in a manner that conveys the unfamiliar semiotic structures in a comprehensible way to its new audience. The move from the linguistic structures of the source text to the conceptual realm contained within the system of meaning of its new language alters the impact and mode of the work itself. Similarly the shift in thematic emphasis indicates the changes in readerly values that have occurred in the transfer from one culture to another.

C. Stephen Jaeger maintains that the French romance genre is a direct expression of the social movement of courtesy aimed at the European feudal nobility in the twelfth century.[5] As a literary expression of a particular era it simultaneously described and prescribed the effort of infusing the ruling class with ideals of refinement and sensitivity perceived to be appropriate and beneficial to courtly life. The courtly romance was in fact the 'single most powerful factor in transmitting ideas of courtesy' in medieval French society and can therefore be seen not only as an indicator of social changes occurring during the time, but as means of producing and enforcing such social changes.[6] While the romance as a genre was heavily invested in the ideology of the courtly society that fashioned it, the popularity of the genre beyond its courtly realm indicates that it was not a static form directly dependent on the social conditions out of which it arose. It was in fact continually being reshaped and refashioned as new texts were created and old texts were transformed. The reception of the genre as form, as narrative content, and ultimately as an expression of a particular ideology can reveal how those aspects of the work were perceived by their new linguistic and cultural environment. Was

---

[4] For a discussion of culture as a semiotic system see Clifford Geertz, *The Interpretation of Cultures* (New York: Basic Books, 2000, originally published 1973). The interconnectedness between social performance and the semiotic coding of language is likewise explored in Robin P. Fawcett, M. A. K. Halliday, Sydney M. Lamb and Adam Makkai, eds., *The Semiotics of Culture and Language,* 2 vols. (London: Frances Pinter, 1984).
[5] *The Origins of Courtliness. Civilizing Trends and the Formation of Courtly Ideals 939–1210* (Philadelphia: University of Pennsylvania Press, 1985), 3.
[6] Ibid. 14.

the form itself viewed as fundamental to the comprehension of the romance as a generic text? Or was it the narrative matter that appealed to its receptive audiences more than the formal or poetic structures? And ultimately, how much impact did the originating social context of the courtly romance have in the perpetuation and spread of the genre?

This chapter will not provide an explicit answer to these questions, but it is worth keeping them in mind when approaching the translations as they tell us much about how those texts were viewed by the translators and what possible function they had within their new reading communities. We have seen in Chapter 1 how the English and Norse translators of Marie de France's *Lais* actively engaged with the underlying social worldview of the poems in a deliberate fashion to actively employ, or, conversely, to subvert that ideological subtext. Similarly, the Norse prose renderings of both the octosyllabic couplets of Marie de France's *Lais* and the assonanced metre of the *Chanson de Roland* indicate that the formal representation of the matter was in fact secondary to the narrative material it contained – at least to its Scandinavian adapters. This suggests that the narrative matter of a text and the ideological system out of which that text originates are intrinsically connected and that the form in which the material is presented is perhaps secondary to its power to convey meaning.

The innate correlation between narrative elements and the social and ideological structures represented by those elements is particularly relevant to the study of translations. As new linguistic renditions they capture in a sense the essential move in time and space between two separate and fundamentally different systems of meaning. This move is in turn made visible in the narrative reconfiguration of the text. The underlying system of values which informs the translation process thus alters the way in which a text is understood. While a text can be read in isolation (at least to a certain extent) from the context out of which it originated, the interpretation of it will depend upon the semiotic codes that address perceptions within the text's own culture. The aesthetic values as well as the socio-psychological system that shape readers' expectations thus influence the way in which the translated work is adjusted to conform to its new audience.[7] By analysing the narrative material as a pattern of semiotic codes capable of conveying multiple meanings, depending on the ways in which they are constructed and linked, one can perceive the underlying literary and cultural coding that has marked the Old Norse and Middle English translation of *Yvain*.

Matilda Tomaryn Bruckner reminds us that the 'self-reflexivity of romance

---

[7] Hans Robert Jauss designates this pre-existing communal literary experience 'horizons of expectations', whereby the reader is informed in his interpretation of any given work by the entirety of literary works read. His perception of works previously encountered, as well as of generic restrictions, is in turn influenced by the new literary experience (*Toward an Aesthetic of Reception*, trans. Timothy Bahti, Minneapolis: University of Minnesota Press, 1982). Brian Stock applies this notion of readers' expectations to medieval audiences in the form of 'textual communities', where, he claims, behavioural forms are altered by the 'process of absorption and reflection' resulting from the literary exposure (*Listening for the Text. On the Uses of the Past*, Baltimore: The Johns Hopkins University Press, 1990, 23).

form calls our attention to the way stories are put together in writing by authors who enjoin the reader to admire the work's shape, its *conjointure*, as a source of pleasure, but no less as source of meaning'.[8] This notion of literary formation is particularly relevant to the works of Chrétien de Troyes as he himself underscores the art of interlinking narrative matter to produce meaning in the prologue to *Erec et Enide*: 'et tret d'un conte d'avanture / une molt bele conjointure' (and from a tale of adventure he draws / a beautifully ordered composition).[9] The emphasis on the way in which the romance is constructed by the author himself calls attention to the narrative composition of *Yvain* as the means of conveying meaning and guidance to readers in their interpretation of the text.

Within theories of narrative grammar the basic unit of the narrative's structure is the episode, which through its positioning in relation to other episodes and within the framework of the story assumes meaning. Any alteration in the episodic structure, or in the interlinking of episodes, thus inevitably affects the reader's perception of the pattern of meaning.[10] Such narrative modifications are often overlooked as signs of unskilled redactors, who are presumed not to have understood the complexity of the original. Yet they are not necessarily unskilled, as is apparent in the facility with which many of the translators seem to have captured other aspects of the works they were translating. The alterations can, conversely, be seen as the authorial expression of an established rhetorical tradition and as such signal the pre-existing literary expectations of the translator and his targeted audience. They are therefore of great significance for the elucidation of the cultural traditions that guided the textual and narrative modifications of the translations.

Both the Old Norse and the Middle English translations of *Yvain* show surprising fidelity to the original. This apparent textual conformity to the source is, however, misleading as it diverts critical attention from the acts of conscious reshaping by the translators: any deviations that do occur are viewed as misunderstandings, a failure to reproduce the artistry of the source text by their translators. These deviations in fact signal very clear authorial divergences from the source, which, owing to their scarcity, may assume added significance. I shall present them in this chapter as evidence of deliberate authorial choices that signal a defined departure from the source text in terms of thematic or ideological orientation. This modified or altered thematic

---

[8] 'The Shape of Romance in Medieval France', in *The Cambridge Companion to Medieval Romance*, ed. Roberta L. Krueger (Cambridge: Cambridge University Press, 2000), 13–28, at 13.

[9] *Erec and Enide*, ed. and trans. Carleton W. Carroll (New York: Garland Publishing, 1987), lines 13–14.

[10] For information on episodic structuring as a means of conveying meaning see for instance A. J. Greimas, 'Narrative Grammar: Units and Levels', *Modern Language Notes* 86 (1971), 793–806. For a discussion of such narrative structures relating specifically to the romance genre see Peter Haidu, 'The Episode as Semiotic Module in Twelfth-Century Romance', *Poetics Today* 4 (1983), 655–81, and 'Romance: Realistic Genre or Historical Text?', in *The Craft of Fiction. Essays in Medieval Poetics*, ed. Leigh A. Arrathoon (Rochester: Solaris Press, 1984), 1–46.

direction in turn reveals the cultural and historical context into which the Norse and English translators were embedding their works.

Chrétien's *Yvain* was probably composed in the 1170s. It has been preserved in six complete manuscripts and five fragments.[11] The edition used in this chapter makes use of a single 'demonstrably good MS', the Paris Bibliothèque Nationale f.fr. 794 (the so-called 'Guiot manuscript'), dating from the early thirteenth century, as the basis for the text and translation.[12] The lack of a definitive edition, which would include all the different variants, obviously encumbers any direct linguistic comparisons between the French, Norse and English texts. Nevertheless, as the focus in this discussion is on the reception of these texts by the English and Norwegian (or Icelandic) reading communities, the fact that the edition is based on a single best-text manuscript copy should not greatly impede the argument.[13]

The unique copy of the Middle English *Ywain and Gawain* is preserved in MS Cotton Galba E.ix in the British Library. It is believed to have been composed in the first half of the fourteenth century, thus appearing some two hundred years after the writing of *Yvain*, and has only been preserved in this early-fifteenth-century manuscript. Nothing is known of the history of the manuscript until it came into the possession of Sir Robert Cotton (1571–1631).[14] The text is written in a northern dialect with some north-east

---

[11] *The Knight with the Lion, or Yvain (Le Chevalier au Lion)*, ed. and trans. William W. Kibler (New York: Garland Publishing, 1985), xvii–xxviii. Critics do not agree on the dating of the text, but the general tendency seems to be to place the composition of *Yvain* in the 1170s (Jean Frappier, *Etude sur Yvain ou Le Chevalier au Lion de Chrétien de Troyes*, Paris: Sedes, 1969; Anthime Fourrier, 'Encore la chronologie des oeuvres de Chrétien de Troyes', *Bulletin bibliographique de la Sociéte internationale Arthurienne* 2 (1950), 69–88). Tony Hunt argues, on the other hand, for the placement of the writing in the 1180s in his article 'Redating Chrestien de Troyes', *Bulletin bibliographique de la Société internationale Arthurienne* 30 (1978), 209–37. Jan Nelson, Carleton W. Carroll, and Douglas Kelly argue that the dating can be no more specific than between 1160 and 1190 (Chrétien de Troyes, *Yvain ou Le Chevalier au Lion*, ed. Jan Nelson, Carleton W. Carroll and Douglas Kelly, New York: Appleton-Century-Crofts, 1968, 2). W. Foerster narrows the date to between 1164 and 1173 in his early edition of the poem (Kristian von Troyes, *Yvain (Der Löwenritter)*, Halle: Verlag von Max Niemeyer, 1902, ix). The approximate dating to the 1170s will be assumed in this chapter, although the precise dating, that is, whether it is a decade earlier or later, does not have a significant impact on the arguments put forth here, as they focus on the *reception* of the text rather than the historical context of the original.

[12] *The Knight with the Lion*, xxviii–xxx.

[13] Kibler establishes in his edition the manuscript history and the basis on which he ascertains the superiority of the Guiot manuscript (ibid. xxviii–xxix).

[14] Friedman and Harrington date the writing of the poem to between 1325 and 1350. The hand responsible for Ywain and Gawain belongs, according to the editors, to the first quarter of the fifteenth century (*Ywain and Gawain*, ed. Albert B. Friedman and Norman T. Harrington, Early English Text Society 254, London: Oxford University Press, 1964, ix–xii, lvii–lviii). Mary Flowers Braswell states in her edition of *Sir Perceval of Galles* and *Ywain and Gawain* that the work was probably composed some fifty to one hundred years before being written down in this particular version that we have today, but that due to lack of topical references it is impossibly to date the composition any closer (*Sir Perceval of Galles and Ywain and Gawain*, ed. Mary Flowers Braswell, TEAMS Middle English Text Series, Kalamazoo: The Medieval Institute Publications 1995), 77.

Midland forms reflected in the rhyming, indicating that the author may have originated from that area.[15] The extant text is complete and runs to about four thousand lines, making it significantly shorter than Chrétien's six thousand eight hundred lines. The verses are arranged in four-stressed couplets, a popular metrical form in the fourteenth century.

The Old Norse version of Chrétien's *Yvain* was evidently translated in Norway in the thirteenth century as part of a collection of French courtly literature seemingly commissioned by King Hákon Hákonarson. The translator omits the parting words of his original, which declare Chrétien to be the author, and substitutes for it his own statement of origination: 'Ok lykr her sǫgu herra Ivent. er Hakon kongr gamli lett snua or franzeisu J norenu' (Here ends the saga of Sir Yvain which King Hakon the Old had translated from French into Norse).[16] The text has been preserved only in later Icelandic manuscripts, making the analysis of textual transmission somewhat more difficult owing to the unknown effect of scribal alterations in the process of copying in Iceland in the later centuries.[17] *Ívens saga* exists in fifteen manuscript copies, three of which are of textual significance:[18] Holm 6 4to (A) in the Royal Library in Stockholm, dating from the early fifteenth century; AM 489 4to (B) in Stofnun Árna Magnússonar (the Arnamagnæan Institute) in Iceland, written *c*. 1450; and Holm 46 fol. (C) in the Royal Library in Stockholm, dated 1690. A and B are the earliest extant versions of the text and are both written on vellum, while C is a paper manuscript. Eight additional paper manuscripts ranging from the mid-seventeenth century to the nineteenth century are derived from A. A single manuscript from the latter part of the seventeenth century is derived from B and there exist additionally three late abbreviated versions.[19]

B appears to be slightly superior to A, which is based on a defective original,

---

[15] Ibid. 77. Friedman and Harrington comment that it is likely that the scribe was more northern than the poet himself (*Ywain and Gawain*, xxxvi–xxxvii). For a description of the manuscript and possible provenance, see their edition, ix–xii and lvi–lvii, and *Sir Perceval of Galles and Ywain and Gawain*, ed. Braswell, 77–83.

[16] All quotations from the Old Norse text are taken from Foster W. Blaisdell's edition of *Ívens saga*, Editiones Arnamagnæanæ, Series B, vol. 18 (Copenhagen: C. A. Reitzels Boghandel, 1979), 147. The English translations of quotations are based on Blaisdell's translation of the text included in the edition (233). Some amendments have been made to the English translation to facilitate reading and comparison as Blaisdell's translation is intended solely as close control of the unnormalised Norse text. Quotations will hereafter be given with page numbers in parentheses for both the Norse text and the English translation.

[17] The epithet 'the Old' for King Hákon was, for instance, not used during his time, but was a later attribute used to distinguish his reign from that of his grandson, Hákon V (1299–1319). The reference to 'Hakon kongr gamli' (King Hakon the Old) would thus seem to diminish the authenticity of the ascription. It is quite possible, however, that the reference in the text was simply added by later Icelandic scribes as a means of signalling to the readers which king the text was referring to. There is no reason to doubt the ascription, as it conforms to such attributions in other texts known to have been translated in Norway during the thirteenth century. Similarly, the existence of a Swedish translation (*Herr Ivan*), ostensibly based (at least partly) upon the original Norse translation and executed between 1300 and 1312 for Eufemia, the wife of King Hákon V, would support the dating of the text.

[18] For a discussion of the manuscripts see Blaisdell's edition of *Ívens saga* (xvii–clv).

[19] Ibid. xi.

according to Blaisdell. A, however, is in a remarkably good condition compared to B, which is in a rather unfortunate state, with large parts of the codex lost or damaged.[20] Blaisdell also notes that the text of C is related in parts to A and that the scribe, Jón Vigfússon, changed from the lost vellum copy of Ormsbók to A somewhere along the way. There are nevertheless several deviations from A after the switch which may still derive from Ormsbók. The vellum manuscript may have been partially defective, explaining the use of A to fill in apparent gaps in the Ormsbók manuscript. It is, however, clear that he must have wanted specifically to use Ormsbók as he had access to the complete text in A and could have copied the text in its entirety from that copy had he wanted.[21] All three manuscripts are compilations of various romances, indicating their generic and thematic coherence within their Icelandic reading communities.

The manuscript context of the Norse text is important as it situates the text within a specific social framework of romance reception. Similarly, the internal differences between the texts of the various manuscript copies reveal the subtle changes that have occurred in the transmission of the text from its original French context through its translation at the Norwegian court in the thirteenth century and ultimately to its Icelandic reception in the fifteenth and subsequent centuries. As has been noted in Chapter 1, the translation of Marie de France's *Lais* formed a part of the institution and introduction of courtly literature at the Norwegian court. Assuming that *Yvain* was translated during the same period (and there is really no reason to believe it was not) it belongs to a group of French works that as a collection constituted a royal agenda of literary and ideological inauguration. The works of Chrétien de Troyes would have been ideally suited for this purpose as they represent within French literary history the epitome of the courtly romance as a genre. By the time that the Nordic translators were working, in the first half of the thirteenth century, Chrétien's works would have had an established reputation as the quintessential representation of courtly romance. While in France writers were moving beyond the restrictions and generic expectations to redefine and challenge the courtly ideology in such works as Jean Renart's *Romance of the Rose* (or *Guillaume de Dole*), the Norwegian court was discovering the magic of the courtly literature for the first time.[22] Three of Chrétien's works have been

---

[20] I was able to examine AM 489 4to at the Arnamagnæan Institute in Reykjavík, Iceland. Several folios are damaged and the vellum has deteriorated in parts to the point of disintegration. The text is worn and faded in parts and illegible. Where the text of B is damaged, Blaisdell uses MS British Library Add. 4857 from the late seventeenth century (which is derived from B) to fill in the gaps.

[21] The manuscript commonly referred to as Ormsbók ('Ormr Snorrason's book') was an Icelandic vellum manuscript from the mid-fourteenth century, which is now lost. It was, however, copied in parts by Jón Vigfússon, the scribe of C, and used by Swedish lexicographers in the seventeenth century (*Ívens saga*, ed. Blaisdell, lxxxix–xcvi).

[22] Sarah Kay notes that there is a discernible increase in ironic attitude towards courtly representation in romances postdating the writings of Chrétien de Troyes. This ironic stance becomes more pronounced in the late twelfth and early thirteenth centuries ('Courts, Clerks, and Courtly Love', in *The Cambridge Companion to Medieval Romance*, ed. Roberta L. Krueger, Cambridge: Cambridge University Press, 2000, 81–96, at 91).

preserved in Norse translations and it is possible that more of his works were translated, but for one reason or another have not come down to us.[23]

Courtly Ideals and Narrative Patterns

The conflict between love and the social code of chivalry, which underlies the entire narrative process of *Yvain*, signals one of the basic problems in the world of the romance: how to reconcile the concept of violence with the idea of noble love. C. Stephen Jaeger asserts that the great accomplishment of the courtly romance lies precisely in the 'harmonizing of those two codes . . . warrior valor and courtliness.'[24] The fundamental dichotomy between ancient warrior ideals and the ethical dictates of courtly behaviour is resolved in the figure of the knight, who remains 'an efficient engine of death and destruction in combat', while assuming the civilising form of the courtly lover once he is in the company of a lady.[25] This dichotomy is made highly visible in the figure of Yvain, where it is represented in the conflict between internal inclination and external codes of conduct. Norris J. Lacy notes that 'it is love which gives meaning to prowess' in *Yvain*, calling attention to the fact that the underlying motivation of Yvain's chivalry is love.[26] Yet it is not so much the emotional force of love that Chrétien seems interested in, but rather the way in which it relates to the meaningful structures presented in the work as a whole, most notably Yvain's passage from the self-centred pursuit of adventures to the altruistically motivated acts of honour at the end. The reader's attention is constantly diverted to the impulses underlying the adventures, rather than the adventures themselves.

In an insightful reading of the manuscript illuminations of *Yvain*, Sandra Hindman gives additional evidence in support of the notion that love, marriage and the courtly ideology indeed served as the motivational force in medieval interpretations of the text.[27] She notes that the manuscripts all share a common focus in the miniatures on the 'resplendent display of the more

---

[23] The three texts that exist in Norse translations are *Erec et Enide* (*Erex saga*), which shows extensive structural alterations from its original; *Li Contes de Graal* (*Parcevals saga*); and *Le Chevalier au Lion* or *Yvain* (*Ívens saga*, also sometimes spelled *Ívents saga*). The existence of these three works in Icelandic manuscripts makes for some interesting speculations as to why these were translated or preserved and what that may indicate in terms of audience predilection. Any conjectures on this topic would, however, be purely speculative as there is no way of knowing how many works may have been translated, how those texts were transmitted to begin with (that is, manuscript copies containing specific texts) and how and why those texts were conveyed to Iceland, where they were then copied and preserved. The fact that very little has been preserved in Norway of those early translations and that they exist mostly in late Icelandic manuscripts illustrates the precarious manuscript history of these works.
[24] *The Origins of Courtliness*, 196.
[25] Ibid. 196.
[26] *The Craft of Chrétien de Troyes: An Essay on Narrative Art* (Leiden: E. J. Brill, 1980), 30.
[27] *Sealed in Parchment. Rereading of Knighthood in the Illuminated Manuscripts of Chrétien de Troyes* (Chicago: University of Chicago Press, 1994).

public aspects of chivalry: costume and ceremony.'[28] Moreover, the various choices of scenes for illustrations in each manuscript signal the way in which the text might have been interpreted. The choice and arrangement of scenes within the manuscript is particularly relevant with respect to Yvain's marriage to Laudine, which despite taking place early in the narrative is not depicted until the end in the Paris manuscripts (used in this chapter). The fact that the illustration of the marriage is postponed until the end (and the fact that it is chosen at all for the miniature) intimates that for its French audience the intermittent passages of moral development may have been necessary for Yvain to truly gain Laudine's hand in marriage.

The development of the concept of love in the text is intimately related to the narrative configuration. It is generally acknowledged that the mastery of *Yvain* lies in its thematic and psychological representation, which is achieved through the use of specific narrative techniques.[29] The text moves between rapid narrative passages that relate events without situating them in a visual scene and scenes where the narrative flow is arrested to illuminate a certain topic, an event, or characterisation. Those static scenes serve to expand the narrative material through description, amplification or visualisation, and they draw out the characters by depicting their reactions and sentiments through their words and actions. Similarly the narratorial interruptions highlight the thematic direction of the text by directing the reader's attention to a certain topic that the narrator then deliberates upon.[30]

The opening lines of the story serve to demonstrate how the narrator shifts between recounting, narratorial philosophising, and static scenes:

> Artus, li boens rois de Bretaingne
> la cui proesce nos enseigne
> que nos soiens preu et cortois,
> a cele feste qui tant coste,

---

[28] Ibid. 51.
[29] The artistry of Chrétien's *Yvain* has been amply recognised and studied and will therefore not be addressed here except as it relates specifically to the two adaptations. For discussion of *Yvain*, or more generally of Chrétien's works, see for instance Douglas Kelly, 'Romance and the Vanity of Chretien de Troyes', in *Romance. Generic Transformation from Chrétien de Troyes to Cervantes*, ed. Kevin Brownlee and Marina Scordilis Brownlee (Hanover: University Press of New England, 1985), 74–90; Robert R. Edwards, 'Invention and Closure in Chrétien's *Yvain*', in his *Ratio and Invention. A Study of Medieval Lyric and Narrative* (Nashville: Vanderbilt University Press, 1989), 102–14; Hindman, *Sealed in Parchment*; Douglas Kelly, ed., *The Romances of Chrétien de Troyes. A Symposium* (Lexington: French Forum, Publishers, 1985); Karl D. Uitti (with Michelle A. Freeman), *Chrétien de Troyes Revisited* (New York: Twayne Publishers, 1995); Norris J. Lacy, Douglas Kelly and Keith Busby, eds., *The Legacy of Chrétien de Troyes*, 2 vols. (Amsterdam: Rodopi, 1987); Sarah Kay, *Courtly Contradictions. The Emergence of the Literary Object in the Twelfth Century* (Stanford: Stanford University Press, 2001); Norris J. Lacy, *The Craft of Chrétien de Troyes*; Joseph J. Duggan, *The Romances of Chrétien de Troyes* (New Haven: Yale University Press, 2001); and Norris J. Lacy and Joan Tasker Grimbert, eds., *A Companion to Chrétien de Troyes* (Cambridge: D. S. Brewer, 2005).
[30] Helaine Newstead discusses the use of narrative structure to foreground thematic direction and the correlation between plot, narrative techniques, and themes in *Yvain* in her article 'Narrative Techniques in Chrétien's *Yvain*', *Romance Philology* 30 (1977), 431–41.

qu'an doit clamer la Pantecoste.
Li rois fu a Carduel en Gales.
Aprés manier, parmi ces sales
cil chevalier s'atropelerent,
la ou dames les apelerent
ou dameiseles ou puceles.
Li un recontoient noveles,
li autre parloient d'Amors,
des angoisses et des dolors
et des granz biens qu'orent sovant
li deciple des son covant,
qui lors estoit molt dolz et buens;
mes or i a molt po des suens,
qu'a bien pres l'ont ja tuit lessiee;
s'an est Amors molt abessiee,
car cil qui soloient amer
se feisoient cortois clamer
et preu et large et enorable;
or est Amors tornee a fable
por ce que cil qui rien n'en santent
dïent qu'il aiment, mes il mantent,
et cil fable et mançonge an font
qui' s'an vantent et droit n'i ont. (1–28)[31]

[Arthur, the good king of Britain,
whose valor teaches us
to be brave and courteous,
held a court of truly royal splendor
at that precious feast
that is known as Pentecost.
The king was at Carduel in Wales.
After dining, the knights
gathered in the halls
at the invitation of
ladies, damsels, or maidens.
Some told of past adventures,
others spoke of Love:
of the anguish and sorrow,
but also of the great benefits often enjoyed
by the disciples of His order,
which in those days was sweet and flourishing;
but today very few serve Love,
for nearly all have now abandoned Him;

---

[31] Quotations from the French are taken from Kibler's edition and translation, *The Knight with the Lion, or Yvain (Le Chevalier au Lion)* (New York: Garland Publishing, 1985), and will hereafter be given with line numbers in parentheses following the quotation. The English translation is based on Kibler's facing translation with line numbers corresponding to the line numbers of the French text. Minor amendments have sometimes been made for comparative purposes.

> and Love is greatly abased,
> for those who loved in bygone days
> were known to be courtly
> and valiant and generous and honorable:
> now Love is a matter for pleasantries,
> because those who know nothing about it
> say that they love, but they lie, and those
> who boast of loving and have no right to do so
> make a lie and a mockery of Love.]

The passage begins *in medias res* with an omniscient narrator who recounts and situates the narrative in Wales at the court of King Arthur during Pentecost. The scene is set with the knights and the ladies gathering in the hall to speak of adventures and love. It is at this point that the narrator directly and explicitly comments upon both his literary realm and his contemporaries (and implicit readers). The narratorial emphasis on the corruption of Love in his time establishes the motivating force of the entire narrative. The reader is made to understand that he has lost the capacity for courtly and honourable love and that the process of regaining and re-establishing the reign of Love again will take centre stage in the story to come.

The narrator continues addressing the reader for a few lines and then turns back to the narrative until he has established his scene. While the king is asleep in his chamber, Yvain, along with a few fellow knights, are listening to a tale told by Calogrenant, at which point the queen arrives and the narrative shifts from indirect reporting to direct speech:

> Et Kex, qui molt fu ranponeus,
> fel et poignanz et venimeus,
> li dist: 'Par Deu, Qualogrenant,
> molt vos voi or preu et saillant.' (69–72)
>
> [And Kay, who was spiteful,
> wicked, sharp-tongued and abusive,
> said to him: 'By God, Calogrenant,
> I see how gallant and sharp you are.']

While the narrator describes the nature of Kex, his subsequent words serve to elaborate and expand on his portrait. What follows is in fact a lengthy scene depicted almost entirely through the actions and words of the characters themselves. Significantly, the tale of Calogrenant's adventure is told in direct speech, thus in effect establishing a scene within a scene and a secondary narrative layer. The nimble move between scene and narrative sections expands the emblematic pattern of the narrative realm as events and characters are made to materialise through the interlinking of the descriptive, rhetorical and episodic. In the Norse and English translations, however, the force of interlinking scenes and narratorial recounting shifts from the scenic to the narrative progression, thereby dismantling the intricate narrative framework established by Chrétien and hence destabilising the inherent patterns of meaning.

Such interlinking of episodes in the French text is fundamental to its thematic development. Lacy comments on the importance of interlacing, which organises the events into a 'symmetrical pattern', and so 'reflects and develops in a precise way the central theme of the roman'.[32] This central theme is directly connected to the moral maturity that Yvain must go through to regain Laudine's love. The three interlaced episodes where he has an obligation to a lady (his promise to Laudine, his duty to Lunete, and the undertaking on behalf of the younger sister) – each then diverted by intervening events – reveal Yvain's progress in learning to shoulder responsibilities befitting a knight and a courtly lover. The pairing of Yvain with Gauvain serves to foreground the contrast as Yvain comes to understand his duties through the progress of the story. Gauvain, on the other hand, remains static and absent, incapable of fulfilling promises made, such as those to Lunete and to his relatives, which Yvain must assume as Gauvain is nowhere to be found.[33] He is additionally responsible for Yvain breaking his promise to Laudine for the sake of selfish knightly exploits. His absence when Lunete is accused of treason is the reason she is nearly burned. The narrative configuration in the French text therefore echoes the thematic foundation of the story.

In *The Rise of the Romance*, Eugène Vinaver observes the role played by the narrative material of the romance in the interpretative process:

> The adventures which constitute the great cycles of romances thus become part of a carefully thought-out design of fantastic dimensions-of a narrative composition in which a coherence of the subtlest kind exists, though it is conveyed, not, as most modern readers would expect, through explanatory observations and discourses, but through the amplification and expansion of the matter itself.[34]

What might appear as arbitrary and incoherent digressions to the modern reader fulfil a function of interpretative amplification and orientation within the context of the romance genre itself. Critics now agree that the various adventures in the French *Yvain* are ordered as a sequence within the narrative structure. Julian Harris argues for a binary structure where the first part depicts how Yvain wins Laudine only to lose her again; the second part, however, displays a much less coherent narrative design of interwoven episodes intended to redeem and rebuild Yvain's moral character and reputation.[35] Harris sees Yvain's journey as a passage towards spiritual enlightenment, symbolically represented by his association with the lion.[36] Alfred Adler

---

[32] *The Craft of Chrétien de Troyes*, 94.
[33] Lacy proposes a reading of Gauvain as a negative double of Yvain. He functions both as a reminder of Yvain's offence and as a mirror to reflect his development in the text. He additionally notes that Chrétien uses the figure of Gauvain in the same manner in the *Chevalier de la Charrette* and the *Conte del Graal* (ibid. 94–8).
[34] *The Rise of the Romance* (Oxford: Oxford University Press, 1971), 76.
[35] 'The Rôle of the Lion in Chrétien de Troyes' *Yvain*', *Proceedings of the Modern Language Association of America* 64 (1949), 1143–63.
[36] Harris argues that both the poet and his medieval audience could not have overlooked the symbolic significance of Christ-like attributes attached to the lion in the Middle Ages. This

approaches the progress, on the other hand, as one of victory of meekness and self-knowledge over selfishness, resulting in the ultimate reward of Love.[37] Adler argues for a more complex, psychological progress that is ultimately connected with the overall narratorial concern with Love and how one loves properly. The practice of humility must be learned by Yvain before he is truly worthy of Laudine's love and that humility is gained through the narrative progress and the correlation of Yvain with both Gauvain and Esclados, Laudine's dead husband. Both interpretations are contingent upon the internal maturing of the protagonist himself and the various narrative episodes simultaneously instigate and depict this process.

While the Norse translation shows a remarkable fidelity to its source, the minor modifications at the level of narrative structure and rhetorical argumentation have a significant impact on the transmission of the original thematic context. The intrinsic link between *sens* and *matière* in Chrétien's *Yvain* makes any deviations from the thematic representation significant. A modification of the narrative substance or structure thus of necessity changes the implicit meaning. A comparison with the first lines of the French text cited above indicates how such minor amendments shift the thematic orientation of the translation to alter the meaningful essence while essentially retaining the narrative substance:

> Hin agæti kongr Artvrvs red firir Einglandi Sem morgum monnum er kunnikt hann var vm sidir kongr yfir Roma borg. hann <var> þeirra konga frægazstr er verith hafua þanuegh fra hafinu ok vinsælastzr annar enn Karlamagnus. hann hafdí þa rǫskuzstu Riddara er Jvoru kristninní. þat var einn tíma sem Jafnann ath hann hafdi stefnt til sinn ǫllum sinum vinum ok hellt mikla hatith áá pikís dogum er vær kǫllum huíta sunnu. ok sem kongrin sátt jsínu hasæti ok folkít var sem gladazst þa fell suo mikil þungi áá kongin. ath hann vard firir huathuetna fram ath ganga vtt jsítt herbergi ok sofa fara þetta vndruduzst

---

symbolic representation of the lion as redeemer underlines Yvain's journey of redemption. Recently critics have, however, attached a more complex significance to the figure of the lion. Eugene Vance points out that 'hybridized symbols were already current in the bestiaries of Chrétien's own time' and that the lion functions thus both symbolically and allegorically on multiple levels within the text (*From Topic to Tale. Logic and Narrativity in the Middle Ages*, Minneapolis: University of Minnesota Press, 1987, 85). The relationship established between Yvain and the lion is both personal and symbolic, where the 'differential relationship between human and animal' is erased as the lion exhibits the triumph over animal nature, while Yvain, on the other hand, regresses into an animalistic state in the forest (89). The lion as a symbol thus moves, according to Vance, between multiple different discourses, none of which is necessarily, or at least exclusively, religious. Norris J. Lacy similarly remarks that since the context of *Yvain* is not religious, but rather psychological and moral, the development of the lion in the work should be taken as symbolic for the moral ideal Yvain must reach (*The Craft of Chrétien de Troyes*, 17–19). Tony Hunt rejects any moral or spiritual interpretations of the lion, contending that Chrétien in fact blocked any such allegorical elucidation by the initial presentation, which he claims opposes such understanding of the animal ('The Lion and Yvain', in *The Legend of Arthur in the Middle Ages*, ed. P. B. Grout, R. A. Lodge, C. E. Pickford and E. K. C. Varty, Cambridge: D. S. Brewer, 1983, 86–98).

[37] Alfred Adler, 'Sovereignty in Chrétien's *Yvain*', *Proceedings of the Modern Language Association of America* 62 (1947), 281–305.

aller menn þui ath aldri fyr hafdí hann þetta giort. Drottníngín var hía honum jherbergínu enn fyrir suefnhus durum satu kongs Riddarar þessir. Lanceloth ok Sigamor herra Valuen Ivent ok Kæí. suo seem þeim leiddizst þar ath sittia. þa hlutudu þeir vm huer þeirra skyldí seggia ævæntyr. ok hlaut Kalebrant. hann hof upp eina sǫgu þa er honum var helldr til vanvirdingar enn sæmdar. þetta heyrdi drottnínginn ok gekk vtt til þeirra ok bad þa segía eventyrít suo ath hon heyrdí. Kalebrant sv(arar) fyrrí vildí ek þola mikil meinlæti enn nǫkkut ydr fra þessu segía. enn þo vil ek eigi angra ydr ok skal ek giora ydvart bod.   (3–6)[38]

[The excellent King Arthur ruled over England, as is known to many people. He later became king over Rome. He was the most famous of the kings who have been on this side of the ocean, and the most popular next to Charlemagne. He had the bravest knights in all Christendom. It happened once as was his habit that he had summoned to him all his friends and was holding a great feast at Pentecost, which we call Whitsuntide. And as the king was sitting on his throne and the people were as happy as possible, then there fell such heaviness upon the king that he had above all to go out to his quarters and sleep. All the people wondered at this, because he had never before done this. The queen was with him in his quarters, but in front of the bedroom door there were the following knights of the king: Lancelot and Sigamor, Sir Valven, Yvain and Kai. As they got tired of sitting there they drew lots about which one of them should tell an adventure and Kalebrant drew the lot. He began a certain story which was rather to his disgrace than to his honor. The queen heard this and went out to them and asked him to tell the story so that she would hear. Kalebrant answered: 'Rather would I suffer a great distress than tell you anything about this, but nevertheless I do not wish to anger you and I shall do your bidding.' (151–2)]

The most obvious change is the rearrangement of Chrétien's octosyllabic verse into prose, which, as we have seen, was a common feature of the Norse renderings of French poetry. The first line retains all the necessary verbal correlations of its source, but the dramatic emphasis of the syntactic positioning of 'Artus' is significantly diminished by shifting it from its initial positioning, which gives it its force in the French verse, to the explanative positioning in the Norse prose. The translator (or scribe) then omits the following lines 'la cui proesce nos enseigne / que nos soiens preu et cortois' (whose valor teaches us / to be brave and courteous). The focus is thereby shifted from any didactic function of chivalry to the story itself. The addition of Rome and Charlemagne is likely to have served to indicate to Nordic readers, unfamiliar perhaps with the legacy of Arthur's court, the greatness of his kingdom and hence the significance of his knights. The surprising inclusion of Lancelot in the group of knights might similarly have functioned to connect the story of a rather unknown Yvain with better known figures from the literary realm of Arthurian adventures. This presumes of course that the story of Lancelot

---

[38] The quotation is based on the A copy, but neither B nor C shows any significant deviations from the text here, concurring overall with the A text, apart from some spelling and minor verbal differences.

was known to the Nordic audiences, either through Chrétien's *Le Chevalier de la Charrette*, which has not been preserved in a Norse translation, or other similar works.

There are two further examples of acculturation evident in the passage that are reminiscent of the mode of adapting and explaining unfamiliar concepts and ideas to its Nordic readers seen in the translations of both the *Lais* and *La Chanson de Roland*. These involve the minor addition of 'er vær kǫllum huíta sunnu' (which we call Whitsuntide) to explain the reference to Pentecost and, secondly, the representation of Arthur's drowsiness. The French text states that the king arose early from the table and went to his room to sleep or rest and that he 'si demora tant delez [la reïne] / qu'il s'oblia et endormi' (and he tarried so long at [the queen's] side / that he forgot himself and fell asleep) (51–2). In the Norse version this minor scene is skilfully adjusted to incorporate a Nordic motif familiar from native folklore while retaining the essential events as depicted in the French text.[39] Rather than simply stating that the king arose and went to his room, the Norse redactor makes an unexplained 'heaviness' fall upon him while sitting in the throne: 'þa fell suo mikil þungi áá kongin' (then there fell such heaviness upon the king). The scene recalls episodes akin to those found in Icelandic sagas where such heaviness or drowsiness suddenly coming upon men compels them to lie down and sleep at otherwise inappropriate moments.[40] Such occurrences often function as premonitions of events to come. It is likely that the motifs were familiar to audiences prior to their appearance in the sagas as they stem from folklore or beliefs that were a part of the cultural fabric of the Icelandic people, and quite possibly the Norwegian people as well given their close cultural connections and heritage at the time.

The most drastic alteration and the one which most significantly alters the thematic conceptualisation of the French text is, however, the omission of the scene at the court with the knights and the ladies gathering to exchange stories of adventure and love and the accompanying narratorial commentary upon the past and present nature and role of Love. In Chrétien's *Yvain* the scene is very much in accord with the image of courtly splendour, and it is completely eliminated in the Norse text, which states simply that 'folkít var sem gladazst' (the people were as happy as possible). There is no mention of knights or

---

[39] As with any such changes it is impossible to know how much can be ascribed to the translator and how much is attributable to later Icelandic scribes. Regardless of whether it was in fact the thirteenth-century translator who modified his source, or a fifteenth-century scribe who saw an opportunity to insert a familiar motif, such modifications show a systematic effort of adaptation to a cultural context different from that of the source text.

[40] In *Brennu-Njáls saga* (*Njal's saga*) Gunnarr feels a drowsiness descend upon him as he rides with his company, forcing him to stop and lie down. As he sleeps he dreams of an impending ambush: 'Gunnarr ríðr austr yfir Þjórsá. En er hann var kominn skammt frá ánni, syfjaði hann mjǫk, ok bað hann þá æja; þeir gerðu svá. Hann sofnaði fast ok lét illa í svefni' (He rode east across the Thjorsa river, and when he was only a short way beyond the river he became very sleepy. He asked his companions to stop and they did so. He fell into a deep sleep but slept restlessly) (*Brennu-Njáls saga*, ed. Einar Ólafur Sveinsson, Reykjavík: Hið íslenzka fornritafélag, 1954, 155; and *Njal's saga*, trans. Robert Cook, London: Penguin Books, 2001, 104).

ladies and, most importantly, no reference to love, which is the incentive for the narrator's commentary on the topic of Love in the French text. The entire elaboration on Love is omitted, which shifts the thematic foundation of the story from the dilemma of knightly duties of love and honour to that of the adventure and hence the narrative process itself. This minor omission of a few lines therefore drastically alters the underlying thematic orientation and destabilises the entire framework of meaning of the text itself.

The passage above is representative of the general modifications made by the Norse translator to his French original. The narrative pace is increased and there is an overall reduction in direct speech with many of the dialogues and monologues in *Yvain* either omitted entirely, curtailed severely or reported in an indirect narrative mode. There is a distinct effort at abstaining from narratorial interferences, and the scenes are both less descriptive and less elaborate. The translator moves between direct translation and paraphrasing of his source text, thereby disrupting Chrétien's elaborate structure of interlaced scenes and narration. The passage depicting the encounter between Yvain and Esclados and the subsequent burial and mourning of his death by Laudine provides a good example, but is too long to quote here.[41] The text evinces its faithfulness to its source in verbal echoes of the French verse lines, yet it simultaneously exhibits the effort at reducing description and increasing narrative speed by selectively paraphrasing other parts: 'Et maintenant vanta et plut / et fist tel tans com fair dut' (At once it began to blow and rain / and storm just as it was supposed to') (805–6) is rendered accurately in the Norse prose as 'ok giordízst þegar mikil vindr ok vatz fall ok slikr stormr sem vant var' (25) (at once there arose a fierce wind and torrents of rain and such a storm as was usual) (162). Yvain's long internal monologue, as he is consumed with love for Laudine, is, however, omitted and the scene of Íven falling in love with the Lady is paraphrased in a few lines with much-reduced emotional investment.[42] By altering the original conception of narrative units, the translator is able to enforce his own structure upon the adopted material, thereby shifting the focus to what one assumes must have been of interest to him (or his intended public), that is, the adventures and tribulations of Íven the knight. The philosophical subtext of Chrétien is transformed as the focus moves from the moral and psychological tenets of Love and knightly duties to the action and events of the story.

Geraldine Barnes suggests that the modifications to the Norse romances show a specific pattern which can be attributed to the original Norwegian translators and are not due to later scribal amendments or mistakes.[43] Marianne E. Kalinke rejects this notion, claiming that the courtly romance was intended as entertainment in the Francophone courts and that it served the same purpose among its Nordic audience and would thus not have needed to

---

[41] See pp. 24–39 in the Norse text and lines 800–1,592 in the French.
[42] See pp. 37–9 in the Norse text and lines 1360–1,592 in the French.
[43] Barnes bases her argument on the comparison between texts preserved in both Icelandic and Norwegian manuscripts ('The Riddarasögur: A Medieval Exercise in Translation', *Saga-Book of the Viking Society* 19 (1977), 403–41).

undergo any systematic structural changes.[44] Kalinke believes that the original translation of *Yvain* transmitted the source text both more accurately and in more detail than the examples we have today would indicate, and that the reductions apparent in the extant manuscripts are the result of scribal attrition and cannot be attributed to the translator himself.[45]

While Kalinke's argument is plausible, the fact remains that the text as we have it today shows distinct structural modifications. It is clear that there are some scribal alterations evident in the existing manuscript copies, but they do not indicate radical narrative reconstructions of the text by the Icelandic scribes, but rather suggest that the Norse translator modified his source text and that later scribes accentuated these existing adjustments by further omissions or shifts in thematic emphasis. In fact, these modifications are in accordance with those observed in other texts belonging to the same period. Thus the Norse translations of Marie de France's *Lais*, which exist in a much earlier Norwegian manuscript, show similar patterns of alteration.[46] These narrative modifications thus reveal a distinct move away from the originating context of Chrétien's courtly audience and the focus in the French text on the ideological dilemmas faced by the merger of the two contradictory concepts of knightly heroism and courtly submissiveness. The Norse text instead captures a world of mystery that is full of excitement and adventure and depicts foreign knights battling exotic beasts for the love of their ladies. As such it introduced the Norwegian court to the world of courtly ideals of refinement of manners, noble comportments and knightly adventures. It simultaneously provided for the dramatic developments of Yvain's knightly encounters, yet without the philosophical context of Love so central to the courtly ideology of its French aristocratic audiences.

Thematic Agenda and Rhetorical Reconstruction

While Chrétien's *Yvain* originates in the social context of the 'civilising' movement of courtly life, the Middle English text, like the Norse, speaks of the different communal concerns being addressed. Written some two hundred years

---

[44] *King Arthur North-by-Northwest. The 'matière de Bretagne' in Old Norse-Icelandic Romances*, Bibliotheca Arnamagnæana 37 (Copenhagen: C. A. Reitzels boghandel, 1981).
[45] Her argument here is based on a comparative reading of the three manuscript groups with a view to textual corruption. According to her both A and B stem from the same lost manuscript copy, while C represents a different branch going back to Ormsbók. Both of these branches go back to an archetype which she believes must have been written before 1400 (ibid. 64–8).
[46] The existence of the eighteenth-century manuscript containing the text of *Gvímars saga*, an Icelandic version of the Norse *Guimars ljóð* preserved in the Norwegian De la Gardie manuscript, allows for the comparison of the two texts to establish possible textual corruption by later Icelandic scribes. Given that the Icelandic text at times preserves, according to Kalinke, the content and structure of the text better than the Norwegian copy, which must have been written down relatively soon after its original conception (*c*.1270), it is apparent that these changes occurred possibly as early as the thirteenth century and in Norway (see *King Arthur North-by-Northwest* 49–52; and '*Gvímars saga*', *Opuscula* 6, Bibliotheca Arnamagnæana 34, Copenhagen: C. A. Reitzels boghandel, 1979, 106–39).

later, possibly in the north-east Midlands, it is bound to have had a different meaning among its English audience.[47] Despite the significant reduction of the original text it is evident that the author of the Middle English version must have had the French original at hand. The alterations are thus likely to reflect deliberate authorial decisions (as far as these can be ascertained) rather than being the result of the faulty memory of a minstrel recreating a text heard rather than read.[48] The textual modifications must then signal the presumed narratological predilections of the reading community to which the Middle English redactor addressed his new text. Whether or not the audience was familiar with the story of the Knight with the Lion, the omissions, abridgements and revisions signal the adaptations, both structural and thematic, that the text underwent as it was transformed from its twelfth century French elite milieu into its new Middle English form.

Critics generally assume that the majority of the alterations can be explained by the effort to adapt the story to its new and less sophisticated audience. Friedman and Harrington state in their edition of the text that the 'poem is clearly the work of a minstrel catering for the sober, realistic audience of a provincial baron's hall, an audience whose sensibilities and sympathies were not adjusted to Chrétien's elaborate and subtle representations of courtly love or to high-flown chivalric sentiment.'[49] Keith Busby ascribes the changes to a shift in gender orientation of the audience, claiming that the faster pace and disregard for psychological subtleties indicates a less aristocratic and moreover a male-oriented reading public.[50] Dieter Mehl likewise notes that the changes show that the 'English adapter wrote for a completely different audience from that of Chrétien, an audience not very interested in ideals of knighthood and *amour courtois*.'[51] All of the critics mentioned above presume a certain type of audience based on the reconfigurations of the French text. However, we know very little about the actual historical audience of the text.[52] MS Cotton Galba E.ix is an anthology of miscellaneous English verse, seemingly executed at some

---

[47] For information on English romance in the fourteenth century and its historical condition see for instance Rosalind Field, 'Romance in England, 1066–1400', in *The Cambridge History of Medieval English Literature*, ed. David Wallace (Cambridge: Cambridge University Press, 1999), 152–76.

[48] Dieter Mehl remarks that 'the particularly careful text makes it very unlikely that oral transmission was involved, and the manuscript, obviously a very faithful copy, gives the impression of having been composed by a professional and at some expense' (*The Middle English Romances of the Thirteenth and Fourteenth Century*, New York: Barnes & Noble, 1969, 180).

[49] *Ywain and Gawain*, xvii.

[50] 'Chrétien de Troyes English'd', *Neophilologus* 71 (1987), 596–613, at 603.

[51] *The Middle English Romances of the Thirteenth and Fourteenth Centuries*, 181.

[52] I draw here on Anne Middleton's distinction between audience and public for the differentiation between the evidence of actual historical audiences and the presumed public the translator must have had in mind when composing his work ('The Audience and Public of *Piers Plowman*', in *Middle English Alliterative Poetry and its Literary Background*, ed. David Lawton, Cambridge: D. S. Brewer, 1982, 101–23). Most of the deductions in this chapter rest on the textual evidence of the perceived public and what those manifestations of the implicit reader tell us about the influences at work in the reshaping of the text in Middle English.

expense.[53] We know next to nothing about its ownership, or the transmission of the text. In fact, were it not for the preservation of the text in this single manuscript we would have no evidence of its existence in Middle English form. What we do know is that the historical audience in all probability belonged to the north-east Midlands region and that the owner of the manuscript might have had it professionally composed and bound and that he was apparently interested in owning a collection of English verse.[54]

While one cannot say for certain whether or not the audience was indeed able to comprehend or grasp the finer artistic points of Chrétien's work, it is obvious that they obtained their literary satisfaction not from those aspects of the work, but from something entirely different. The fact that numerous English translations and copies of Anglo-Norman or French texts exist shows that they derived certain pleasures, whether artistic or otherwise, from those texts. The public the text appears to be addressing reveals, however, a distinct shift in narrative concerns and interests. As with the Norse translation, the English version of *Yvain* bears witness to the subtle modifications occurring in the transmission of the text – despite its apparent adherence to its source – which signal specific narrative preferences and thematic interests by their redactors and their perceived public.

That the author of the Middle English text was working from a manuscript copy containing the French text is apparent in the multiple passages of close or literal translation as well as in the identical narrative process of the tale.[55] A short example from the beginning of the story should suffice to indicate the close rendering of the French verse:

> Par mon chief, fet mes sire Yvains,
> vos estes mes cosins germains;
> si nos devons molt entr'amer;
> mes de ce vos puis fol clamer
> quant vos tant le m'avez celé.
> ...
> Bien pert que c'est aprés mangier,
> fet Kex, qui teire ne se pot:
> plus a paroles an plain pot
> de vin qu'an un mui de cervoise. (579–92)

---

[53] For information on the manuscript see Gisela Guddat-Figge, *Catalogue of Manuscripts Containing Middle English Romances* (Munich: Wilhelm Fink Verlag, 1976), 173–6.
[54] Guddat-Figge notes that the manuscript we have today is likely to have consisted of three separate manuscripts that were, however, bound together in a collection at an early date (ibid. 175). The careful execution of the manuscript intimates that it was composed at some expense.
[55] Based on a detailed textual comparison of *Ywain and Gawain* and the extant French versions, Gustav Schleich argues that variant readings indicate that none of the existing manuscript copies could have served as the original text. While the English text bears close affinity to a group of manuscripts designated by him the ß-family, Schleich finds plausible evidence that the manuscript copy used by the English translator was closer to the original version of Chrétien's romance than any of the French texts existing today (*Über das Verhältnis der mittelenglischen Romanze Ywain and Gawain zu ihrer altfranzösischen Quelle*, Berlin: R. Gaertners Verlagsbuchhandlung, 1889, 18–19).

['By God!,' said Sir Yvain,
'you are my first cousin
and there should be much love between us.
But you are a fool
that you have kept this from me so long.'
...
'Ah well, it's after dinner,'
said Kay who could never be quiet.
'There are more words in a pot
of wine than in a barrel of beer.']

In the Middle English text the same passage reads as follows:

'Now sekerly,' said Sir Ywayne,
'þou ert my cosyn jermayne;
Trew luf suld be us bytwene,
Als sold bytwyx breþer bene.
Þou ert a fole at þou ne had are
Tald me of þis ferly fare.'
...
And þan als smartly sayd Syr Kay
(He karpet to þam wordes grete):
'It es sene now es efter mete!
Mare boste es in a pot of wyne
Þan in a karcas of Saynt Martyne.'   (457–70)[56]

The translator renders his source text faithfully, down to verbal echoes such as 'vos puis fol clamer' (you are a fool) and 'Þou ert a fole', as well as 'plus a paroles an plain pot de vin' (There are more words in a pot full of wine) and 'Mare boste es in a pot of wyne'. Not only does the translator pay great attention to verbal detail here, but he is aware of the more implicit function of the French proverb in the last two lines. Brenda B. Hosington notes that the translator, while changing the second referent of Chrétien's line, renders the sense accurately and maintains all the essential features of the proverb as used by Chrétien; 'binary structure, couplet form, conciseness, and comparison'.[57] This shows that not only was the English redactor quite capable of understanding verbal nuances in his source text, but he was also capable of elaborating on the wordplay. Incidentally, the Norse translator

---

[56] *Ywain and Gawain*, ed. Friedman and Harrington, 13. Quotations from the Middle English text are taken from Friedman and Harrington's edition and will hereafter be given with line numbers in parenthesis in the text.

[57] Hosington notes that Chrétien already alters the existing French proverb from 'plus a paroles en un petit pot de vin qu'en mult de fein (haystack)', thereby intensifying the original meaning. She believes that by substituting St Martin's body for the French 'mui de cervoise' (literally: hogshead of beer), the translator was in fact alluding to other French proverbs that associate St Martin with drunkenness ('Proverb Translation as Linguistic and Cultural Transfer in Some Middle English Versions of Old French Romances', in *The Medieval Translator. Traduire au moyen âge*, ed. Roger Ellis and René Tixier, vol. 5, Turnhout: Brepols, 1996, 170–86, at 174).

reveals here his close relation to both the French and English texts as he not only accurately relates the scene, but directly echoes some of the same verbal details as the English translation:

> Gud veítt kuath herra Ivent *þu ert mínn skyldr frændí* ok þu giordir eigi vel er *þu leyndir mik þessu* ok þui jata ek ef gud vill ath ek skal hefna þínnar sviuírdíngar. þa sv(arar) Kæi. Nu megum vær heyra Ivent ath þu ert uel metr *þu hefir fleiri ord enn fullr potr víns*. (20, my italics)

> ['God knows,' Sir Yvain said, *'you are my close kinsman*, and you did not do well that *you concealed this from me*. That I promise, if God is willing, that I shall avenge your disgrace.' Then Kai answered: 'Now we can hear Yvain, that you are quite full. *You have more words than a pot full of wine*.' (160, my italics)]

As in the Norse text, the English redactor does not mention his source other than by the customary references to the 'boke' in which he claims he read the tale (3,209, 3,671). The short postscript in the French text referring to the author by his name is similarly excluded in the English version: 'Del Chevalier au Lyeon fine / Chrestïens son romans ensi' (6,820–1) (Thus Chrétien brings to a close / his romance of the Knight with the Lion). The English redactor adds in its place his own postscript in the traditional manner of English minstrel endings:

> Of þam na mare have I herd tell
> Nowþer in rumance ne in spell.
> Bot Jhesu Criste for his grete grace
> In hevyn-blis grante us a place
> To bide in, if his wills be.
> Amen, amen, par charite.   (4,028–33)

It is obvious, however, that despite the textual proximity, the English redactor abridges and condenses his source. The abridgements are of a systematic nature and have often been categorised as omissions of descriptive, spatial and temporal details; reduction in attention to love and courtly etiquette; and a lack of psychological depth in characterisation, which so clearly defines Chrétien's romance.[58] The pattern of omission thus follows remarkably close to that of the Norse translator, which similarly omits scenes that slow down or impede the narrative movement and turns attention from the philosophical and psychological subtext to the episodic structure of the text. The change from the meticulous and attentive narrative process of Chrétien's poem to the compact and rapid narrative sequencing evident in both the English and the Norse texts reveals the fundamental shift that has occurred in the function of the source text and their translations.

---

[58] For a discussion of the pattern of abbreviation and a detailed comparative reading of the French and Middle English texts see for instance *Ywain and Gawain*, ed. Friedman and Harrington, xvi–xxxiv; Schleich, *Über das Verhältnis der mittelenglischen Romanze Ywain and Gawain zu ihrer altfranzösischen Quelle*; and Busby, 'Chrétien de Troyes English'd'.

A closer look at the first lines in *Ywain and Gawain* reveals, as in the case of the Norse translation, specific deviations that synthesise the shift in thematic orientation:

> Almyghti God þat made mankyn,
> He schilde his servandes out of syn
> And mayntene þam with might and mayne,
> þat herkens Ywaine and Gawayne;
> þai war knightes of þe tabyl rownde,
> þarfore listens a lytel stownde.
>
> Arthure, þe Kyng of Yngland,
> þat wan al Wales with his hand
> And al Scotland, als sayes þe buke,
> And mani mo, if men wil luke,
> Of al knightes he bare þe pryse.
> In werld was none so war ne wise;
> Trew he was in alkyn thing.
> Als it byfel to swilk a kyng,
> He made a feste, þe soth to say,
> Opon þe Witsononday
> Att Kerdyf þat [es] in Wales,
> And efter mete þare in þe hales
> Ful grete and gay was þe assemble
> Of lordes and ladies of þat cuntre,
> And als of knyghtes war and wyse
> And damisels of mykel pryse.
> Ilkane with oþer made grete gamin
> And grete solace als þai war samin.
> Fast þai carped and curtaysly
> Of dedes of armes and of veneri
> And of gude knightes þat lyfed þen.
> And how men might þam kyndely ken
> By doghtines of þaire gude ded
> On ilke syde, wharesum þai ȝede;
> For þai was stif in ilka stowre,
> And þarfore gat þai grete honowre.
> þai told of more trewth þam bitw[e]ne
> þan now omang men here es sene,
> For trowth and luf es al bylaft;
> Men uses now anoþer craft.   (1–36)

The English translator has inserted an invocation reminiscent of English minstrel romances, addressing the audience and asking them to 'listens a lytel stownde', before turning to Chrétien's text and the court of King Arthur. He omits the very same didactic lines at the beginning of the poem, referring to Arthur's valour, as the Norse translator does, suggesting that the objective of the translation is not to instruct the reader in the arts of chivalric behaviour, but something else entirely. Then, again in the manner of the Scandinavian translator, he adds his own culturally relevant titbit that not only did Arthur rule over England (Britain in the French text), but 'al Scotland, as sayes þe buke, / and mani mo, if men wil luke'.

It is, however, the second addition, which occurs before returning back to Chrétien's scene at Arthur's court, which reveals the subtle yet distinct reorientation of the poem. The translator states that Arthur was 'trew' in everything, a statement absent in the French text. This reference to 'trew' or 'trowth' is repeated five more times in the opening lines before depicting the king departing for his bedchambers. The addition by the English redactor of the following lines in fact amounts to a declaration of thematic agenda:

> With worde men makes it trew and stabil,
> Bot in þaire faith es noght bot fabil;
> With þe mowth men makes it hale,
> Bot trew trowth es nane in þe tale. (37–40)

This narratorial concentration on 'trowth' and how 'with worde men makes it trew' redirects the thematic subtext of the French text indicating that the English redactor had a different objective in mind when he adapted his French source. Gayle K. Hamilton suggests that the pattern of abbreviation and modifications in the English text in fact reveals a new *sens*, one that differs from its source, and hence indicates the authorial intent behind those alterations.[59] According to her the shift in focus from the narrator's complaints about the lack of true love in the French text to the lack of 'trowth' in the English poem signals a thematic reorganisation that dictates the structure and meaning of the text. The function of the various adventures and Ywain's relationship with both Alundyne and Gawain is thus to manipulate the various aspects of knightly behaviour to establish a proper conception of 'trowthe' as it pertains to both societal and personal relationships.[60] In fact, the English redactor omits the narratorial digression in the French text on the conceptualisation of Love, just as the Norse translator had done before. This suggests that despite the relative closeness of the English translation to its source, both in narrative structure and thematic development, the subtle verbal substitutions and the shift in textual focus distinctly alters the meaning of the text.

The various episodes thus serve, both in the French and the English text, to augment the ideological substance of the text. Except that ideological substance has shifted direction in the translation process. It is, however, built into the narrative as well as into the rhetorical framework of the text in both the French and the English versions. Robert R. Edwards points out that in

---

[59] 'The Breaking of the Troth in *Ywain and Gawain*', *Mediaevalia* 2 (1976), 111–35. Tony Hunt similarly notes a distinct shift in thematic focus to the primacy of 'trowthe' in the English poem, indicating that the English translator restructured his poem to illustrate the theme of this tale ('Beginnings, Middles, and Ends: Some Interpretative Problems in Chrétien's *Yvain* and its Medieval Adaptations', in *The Craft of Fiction*, ed. Leigh A. Arrathoon, Rochester: Solaris Press, 1984, 83–117, particularly 90–2).

[60] *Trowthe* is, of course, associated with Gawain (as in *Sir Gawain and the Green Knight*), which complicates the text's conceptualisation of *trew* behaviour and knightly values, particularly as it pertains to the representation of Ywain and his relationship with Gawain.

Chrétien's *Yvain* the 'thematic amplification of the poem is matched by an amplification of language'.[61] The rhetorical effect of interlace, embellishment and versification suffuses the thematic substance with added significance. Chrétien thus seeks to express his *sens* not only through the elaboration of the *matière* itself, but through the very linguistic, metrical and structural conceptualisation of this material. Douglas Kelly additionally notes that

> the development, as amplification or abbreviation, is the artful expression and interpretation of the context in the 'place', and, thus, the effective communication of both *matiere* and *san*. The mastery of the formal constraints by the *brisure du couplet* as well as supple use of rhyme reduced the consciousness of listening to verse, allowing the public to concentrate on what the verse said, on its *matiere* and *san*.[62]

Any alteration of the rhetorical invention of the poem thus of necessity affects its *sens*.

The change from verse to prose in the Norse translation drastically alters the rhetorical force of the versification, rhyme and metrical arrangement of Chrétien's material. As Marianne Kalinke has shown, the Nordic translator was, however, by no means impervious to the connections of the rhetorical construction and the narrative material of his original. Kalinke illustrates how the Nordic redactors of the French romances made use of alliteration to intensify action or dialogue, thereby signalling the relation between the material and formal representation.[63] The poignant passage depicting Yvain's despair at having lost Laudine's love is rendered in the Norse text through the use of such rhetorical devices. In fact, Íven's lament 'constitutes the most compact and rhythmic concentration of alliterative pairs in the entire saga':[64]

> Til huers skal ek lífa vesal madr var ek suo v geymín. huat skal | ek vtann drepa mik sialfr. Ek hefí tynt huggan minní ok fagnadi ok um snuít af sialfs míns glæp virdíng minní ok vent tign minní jtyníng yndí mítt J angurssemí. lif mítt J leidíndi. hiarta mítt J huggsott. vnnustu mína J <o>vín. frelsi mitt J fridleysí. e(da) huí duel ek ath drepa mik.   (103–4, my bold)

> [For what purpose shall I live, wretched man that I was so heedless! What shall I do but kill myself. I have lost my consolation and joy, and destroyed through my own crime my reputation and lost my honor. [I have changed] my happiness into sorrow, my life into misery, my heart into sickness, my love into enemy, my freedom into despair. Why do I delay in killing myself!   (201)]

The alliterative pairing compensates for the emotional force of the poetic rendering of the lament in Chrétien's work and gives the passage a sense of

---

[61] *Ratio and Invention*, 106.
[62] 'The Art of Description', in *The Legacy of Chrétien de Troyes*, ed. Norris J. Lacy, Douglas Kelly, and Keith Busby, vol. 1 (Amsterdam: Rodopi, 1987), 191–221, at 193.
[63] *King Arthur North-by-Northwest*, 158.
[64] Ibid. 165.

rhythmical cogency that is uncharacteristic of Nordic prose.[65] While the dramatic emphasis with Chrétien often lies in the narrative monologues and characters' soliloquies, that are usually either drastically reduced or omitted altogether in the Norse translation, the translator is not only conscious of the changes he has made to his material, but in fact makes an effort to compensate for the rhetorical force of the French verse through his own poetic and narrative techniques.

One can observe similar efforts at rhetorical and poetic reconstruction of the material in the English translation as well. The poetic emphasis shifts from the narratorial soliloquies of the French text, which form the dramatic peak in *Yvain*, to the interlinking of the narrative units in the English text. The subtle yet poetic force of Chrétien's rhetoric in those introspective dialogues marks them as the focal point for textual impact. By curtailing or eliminating those passages altogether the English author destabilises the rhetorical framework of his original, thereby shifting the attention to the events themselves.

The encounter between Ywain and the lion, for instance, forms a narrative unit where the main semiotic components are the figure of the knight (Ywain), the lion and the dragon. While the lion symbolises Yvain's growth towards the ideal of knighthood in the French text, the English translator adapts its symbolic function to his own narrative agenda. This becomes perhaps most obvious in the semantic merger of the two in *Yvain*, where the lion quite literally vanishes from the narrative once Yvain has come into his own as a true knight. The English redactor, however, seems to feel that the fate of the lion needs to be explained along with that of the other major protagonists.[66] He declares at the very end that not only did Sir Ywain and his wife live in joy

---

[65] The Nordic romances share certain stylistic features that differentiate them from the style common to native Scandinavian literature. These consist of longer and more complex sentence structures, the use of word pairs and alliteration to emphasise dramatic or emotionally charged scenes, and the use of metaphors and exclamations to render the poetic sense of their originals. This style draws on the learned tradition of Latinity for its syntactic and rhetorical structures and is most pronounced in *Tristrams saga* (translation of Thomas's *Tristan*) which is commonly believed to have been one of the first of the French courtly materials to have been translated (see Paul Schach, 'Some Observations on the Translations of Friar Robert', in *Les relations littéraires franco-scandinaves au moyen âge*, Paris: Société d'édition 'Les belles lettres', 1975, 117–36; Böðvar Guðmundsson, Sverrir Tómasson, Torfi H. Tulinius and Vésteinn Ólason, eds., *Íslensk bókmenntasaga*, vol. 2, Reykjavik: Mál og menning, 1993, 200–6; and Peter Hallberg, 'Norröna riddarasogur. Några språkdrag', *Arkiv för nordisk filologi* 86 (1971), 114–38).

[66] Juliette de Caluwé-Dor comments on the differences in the animal representations between the French and English texts and proposes that they may be due to the English redactor combining elements from Celtic oral traditions with the French original. She notes that the English lion resembles more a faithful dog than Chrétien's 'faithful vassal', and that both the English and the Welsh version of the tale include lions in the wild herds in the woods (the French and Icelandic texts do not), indicating perhaps some secondary influences in the textual transmission of the tale ('Yvain's Lion Again: A Comparative Analysis of its Personality and Function in the Welsh, French and English Versions', in *An Arthurian Tapestry. Essays in Memory of Lewis Thorpe*, ed. Kenneth Varty, Glasgow: University of Glasgow, 1981, 229–38). The fact that the English translator changes the puzzling fire-spitting serpent in the French text to a dragon, along with the other behavioural changes in the lion, supports the notion of an active engagement by the author with his material.

and bliss, but 'so did Lunet and þe liown' (4025), thereby placing the lion at the narrative level of Lunete. She is in fact, as the lion was to Ywain, the corresponding faithful companion of Alundyne.

The signification of the union between the lion and the knight is foregrounded through formal and linguistic accentuation:

> Grete fawning made he to þe knyght.
> Down on þe grund he set him oft,
> His forþerfete he held oloft,
> And thanked þe knyght als he kowth,
> Al if he myght noght speke with mowth;
> So wele þe lyon of him lete,
> Ful law he lay and likked his fete.
> When Syr Ywayne þat sight gan se,
> Of þe beste him thoght pete,
> And on his way forth gan he ride;
> Þe lyown folowd by hys syde.
> In þe forest al þat day
> Þe lyoun mekely foloud ay,
> And never for wele ne for wa
> Wald he part Sir Ywayn fra. (2,002–16)

The ensuing affiliation between Ywain and the lion underscored by the use of the words 'ride' and 'by his side' and 'never for wele ne for *wa* / Wald he part Sir Ywayn *fra*' to form the rhyming pattern of the verse lines (2,012–15).[67] During those transitions the use of alliteration is often more pronounced, signalling perhaps the narrative significance of the events. In the example quoted above the last two lines are further linked by means of the alliterating effect of the words 'wele', 'wa' and 'wald', thus subtly suffusing those lines with narrative force. This is comparable to the way in which the Norse translator uses alliteration to draw attention to a particular action, or to support emotional dialogue, suggesting perhaps a common northern narrative tradition of using linguistic emphasis, such as alliteration, to reinforce and heighten aural impact.[68]

The alliterative pattern becomes even more pronounced in the description of the combat between Sir Ywain and Sir Gawain, where it serves to highlight the dramatic peak of the story through aural intensification. The battle is of significance both as narrative climax and as the thematic representation of

---

[67] Obviously the available diction, metric form and rhyming pattern will to a large extent dictate the choice and placements of words within the line. Such changes in stanzaic construction and linking of words in metrical patterns, however, of necessity influence how a poem is perceived, particularly when read out loud.

[68] Given the intermingling of Norse and English inhabitants (particularly in the northern and north-eastern regions of England) through colonisation and later through commerce, it is quite plausible to suggest that they were exposed to each other's narrative traditions, particularly oral poetry. The rhythmic structuring through alliterative repetition of sounds would enhance the impact of such delivery, regardless of the listeners' capacity to actually understand the language in which it was delivered.

the conflict between the representative figures of the two opposing concepts of 'trowth' and 'untrew':

> Bot in þat time bitid it swa,
> Þat aiþer of þam wald oþer sla.
> Þai drow **sw**erdes and **sw**ang obout,
> To **d**ele **d**ynts had þai no **d**out.
> Þaire **sh**eldes war **sh**iferd and helms rifen,
> Ful **st**alworth **st**rakes war þare gifen.
> Bath on **b**ak and **b**restes þare
> **W**ar bath **w**ounded **w**onder-sare. (3,535–42, my bold)

The disparity in linguistic presentation between the French and English texts demonstrates not only the inherent differences between the two vernaculars, but also how the poetic capacity of each language is used to convey the content in a manner that simultaneously contains and expounds its potential to convey meaning. The structural changes support this effort of reconstructing the meaningful elements of the text to adapt them to the new reading community.

Narrative Conventions and Semiotic Representation

While the thematic development of the story is thus the same in the French poem and the translations, the effect is different. By reducing the narratorial commentary and Chrétien's elaboration on the theme of love and knightly courtesy, the English and Norse redactors create a rapid-paced sequence of adventures, which is determined by dramatic tension and movement rather than by philosophical or psychological development. The concise narrative structure of the French text is composed around the spiritual, or perhaps more aptly the social development of the protagonist. This process in turn serves a philosophical or psychological agenda. The inherently contradictory principles of courtly society can thus be explored within the unconstricted realm of literary representation. Any alterations to the narrative pattern thus destabilise this inherent, dialectic relationship between the literary depiction of courtly society and the actualities of its aristocratic French readers.

While the English text demonstrates a definite pattern of narrative reorientation, the Norse text is somewhat ambiguous in its motivation. The text in fact foregrounds sometimes both the elements which make it unfamiliar (by retaining passages containing uniquely chivalric behaviour patterns, such as Íven's lament) and those which correspond more to familiar structures of existing native literatures and lore (such as depersonalising the narrative voice and removing internal depiction of characters). This textual incongruity could be the result of a disparity in the translator's intent and later scribal motivations. If *Yvain* was in fact translated as a part of a concerted effort by the Norwegian monarchy of importing and instituting courtly values in his court, as chapter one suggests, the inclusion of passages depicting courtly behaviour within the context of familiar literary representation would make sense.[69] This original impulse would then have become irrelevant as those stories were adapted by Icelandic reading communities in the later centuries, where the intent was no longer to reproduce the courtly essence, but rather to portray an exotic world of knights, their love affairs, and their adventures. Those texts would thus be marked by a duality of purpose emerging over time.

The English text shows, however, marked signs of a determined refashioning of the French text within the conceptual realm of English literary traditions. This is apparent within the narrative and symbolic reconfiguration as well as on the level of character representation. Rather than focusing on the moral enlightenment of a single character, the author of *Ywain and Gawain* explores various social conceptualisations by stringing together recognisable semantic units, which by nature of their relation to each other and to the characters, assume signification. Ywain is moved through the narrative fabric in an effort to foreground the various principles he stands for within the social context of the literary realm. In fact, he does not progress as a character himself, instead his figure assumes signification through the narrative progress not as an individual, but as a semiotic representation.

The focus is shifted from characters as individuals to their *function* within the narrative realm. It is no longer the internal dilemmas and spiritual process of the characters that are of importance, but rather their place within the contextual framework. The characters draw their substance from their positioning within the narrative and the symbolic connotations that are drawn from the interlacing of character's actions and the consequences of those actions. In Chrétien's *Yvain* the final passage depicting the reconciliation between Yvain and Laudine indicates the internal maturation that has occurred:

> Mes sire Yvains ot et antant
> que ses afeires si bien prant
> qu'il avre sa pes et s'acorde,
> et dit: 'Dame, misericorde
> doit an de pehceor avoir.
> Conparé aim on nonsavoir,
> et je le voel bien conparer.
> Folie me fist demorer,
> si m'an rant corpable et forfet
> Et molt grant hardemant ai fet
> qant devant vos osai venire;
> mes s'or me volez retenir,
> jamés ne vos forferai rien.' (6,783–95)
>
> [My lord Yvain heard and understood
> that his cause was proceeding so well
> that he'd have his peace and reconciliation;

---

[69] While Chapter 1 deals specifically with the importance of Marie de France's *Lais* in connection with the particular translation agenda at the court of King Hákon Hákonarson, the theory applies generally to the French courtly material translated during the period at the instigation of the king, and hence also to Chrétien's *Yvain*.

> he said: 'My lady, one should
> have mercy on a sinner.
> I have paid dearly for my foolishness,
> and I am glad to have paid.
> Folly caused me to stay away,
> and I acknowledge my guilt and wrong.
> And I realize that I am very bold
> to dare to come before you now
> but if you would care to keep me,
> I'll never do you wrong again.']

The passage denotes a process of acknowledgement and recognition of previous errors ('Folie me fist demorer, / si m'an rant corpable et forfet') (Folly caused me to stay away, / and I acknowledge my guilt and wrong) and the determination to do better in the future ('jamés ne vos forferai rien') (I'll never do you wrong again). The reconciliation and the successful resolution of the dilemma of Love are in fact contingent upon Yvain's penitence and promise to not violate the tenets of Love again.

The English text in essence depicts the same scene of Ywain requesting mercy for his past mistakes, except it does not indicate this process of *internal* growth as does the French text. Ywain has made a mistake, but it is the mistake of going back on his word, not that of an immature misconception of his duties towards his lady or his obligations as a knight:

> 'Madame,' he said, 'I have miswroght,
> And þat I have ful dere boght.
> Grete foly I did, þe soth to say,
> When þat I past my terme-day.'   (3,995–8)

Ywain does not acknowledge his 'corpable et forfet' (guilt and wrong) and prior misconceptions as in the French text, but rather explicitly states that what he did wrong was to 'past my terme-day' and for that he has had to pay. This statement draws attention to the narratorial concern with 'trowthe' signalled at the beginning of the text. The failure to keep his word is, as a matter of fact, foregrounded as the underlying cause of the offence, rather than the fact that he betrayed his beloved as in the French text.

In the English text the focus has thus shifted from the psychological maturing of the protagonist (needed for him to become worthy of Love and of the reputation as 'the Knight with the Lion'), to the narratorial depiction of the social obligations of giving one's word. The characters do not signify in themselves, but function as vessels of potential meaning that assume significance as the reader proceeds through the narrative. It is of interest here that the Norse text depicts a similar shift in this passage from a generalised notion of psychological maturity to the single aspect of being true to your word: 'Fru miskunn beidaz misverkar. Ek hefí dyrt keyptt heimsku mína ok v vizsku þui gef ek mik sekíann ydr jvalld. ok ef þu vil nu taka vid mer. þa skal ek alldri optar misgíora vid þigg' (147) (My lady, forgiveness is begged for misdeeds. I have paid dearly for my folly and foolishness. Therefore I give myself, as guilty, into your power. If you are willing now to receive me, then I shall never again do wrong toward you) (233).[70] By removing the internal complexities of the characters the audience's attention is diverted from the elaboration of individualistic psychological insight to generalised traits of gendered and socially prescribed behavioural patterns. Ywain is cast in a role that is immediately recognisable and can therefore be used to represent the narratorial concerns of the author.

Such use of character in narrative representation becomes particularly evident in the scene portraying the wooing and marriage of Ywain and Alundyne. While with Chrétien the emphasis lies in the moral dilemma of honour and love, the passage serves a different function within the English text. When Laudine first appears in Chrétien's text as the grieving widow, she displays her grief both verbally and physically. She screams and cries, pulls her hair and claws at her body between falling repeatedly in a swoon. The French poem then devotes some thirty-seven lines to her haunting declaration of grief and sorrow:

> Por ce tel duel par demenoit
> la dame, qu'ele forssenoit,
> et crioit come fors del san:
> «Ha! Dex, don ne trovera l'an
> l'omecide, le traïtor,
> qui m'a ocis mon boen seignor?
> ...
> Certes, se tu fusses mortex,
> n'osasses mon seignor atendre
> qu'a lui ne se pooit nus prendre.»
> Ensi la dame se debat,
> ensi tot par li se conbat,
> ensi tot par li se confont
> et, avoec lui, ses genz refont
> si grant duel que greignor ne pueent.   (1,203–47)

> [Because of this the lady was so
> griefstricken that she quite lost her mind,
> and cried out as if she were mad:
> 'Ah! my God! will they never find him
> the murderer, the traitor,
> who has killed my good husband
> ...
> Indeed, if you had been a mortal man,
> you would never have dared attack my husband,

---

[70] The C copy of the Norse text has an interesting variation of this scene, where no words are exchanged and Íven simply falls on his knees before his lady, who raises him up, and they embrace, signalling their reconciliation: 'Enn er Ivent finnur fruna lagdist hann fyrir fætur henne enn mærinn reisti hann upp ok falla þau i fadma ok hefvur nü Ivent feing<it> sïna list ok fagnad' (147) (When Yvain met the lady, he lay down at her feet, but the girl raised him up, and they fell into an embrace. Now Yvain had gotten his desire and joy) (233).

for no one could capture him.'
Thus the lady argues within herself;
thus she struggled alone
thus she confounded herself;
and along with her, her people too lamented so
that it was impossible to grieve more.]

In the English version, however, the lament is omitted. The reader observes how 'sho wrang hir fingers, outbrast þe blode; / For mekyl wa sho was nere wode. / Hir fayre hare scho al todrogh, / And ful oft fel sho down in swogh' (821–4).[71] The elaborate depiction of her maddening sorrow is reduced and the intensity is decreased. The focal point in the English text becomes in fact the *vision* of the lady, which will consequently kindle Ywain's love, as opposed to the self-representation of Laudine expressing her own internal emotions.

As in the French text, the initial impact is visual. Only after the depiction of the lady does the narrative perspective move to Ywain himself, who to begin with only *hears* her. While the focalisation in the French text is unclear (i.e. who is observing her and from where), the English text is quite specific on the point:

> Þan Sir Ywayn herd þe cry
> And þe dole of þat fayre lady,
> For more sorow myght nane have,
> Þan sho had when he went to grave.
> Prestes and monkes on þaire wyse
> Ful solempnly did þe servyse.
> Als Lunet þare stode in þe thrang,
> Until Sir Ywayne thoght hir lang;
> ...
> He said, 'Leman, I pray þe,
> If it any wise may be,
> Þat I might luke a litel throw
> Out at sum hole or sum window,
> For wonder fayn,' he sayd, 'wald I
> Have a sight of þe lady.' (833–52)

In the French text Laudine passes through the room along with the funeral procession and her husband's body, whereas the Middle English text narrows the viewpoint by shifting the attention to Ywain, who observes *her* through a window.[72] While Chrétien's dramatic setting is thus concentrated on Laudine

---

[71] Gustav Schleich in fact finds this lacuna in the Middle English translation suspicious and argues that it corroborates his theory of scribal mistakes. The exclusion is not due to its English author, according to Schleich, but is rather the fault of later copyists, who mangled the otherwise accurate translation (*Ywain and Gawain*, ed. Gustav Schleich, Oppeln: E. Franck's Buchhandlung, 1887, lx–xliv). Norman T. Harrington refutes this claim in a later essay, where he provides evidence confirming the narrative coherence of the English text ('The Problem of the Lacunae in Ywain and Gawain', *Journal of English and Germanic Philology* 69 (1970), 659–65, especially 660–2).
[72] While Yvain watches Laudine through a window in the French text as well it occurs later

as the vocalising subject that dominates the scene, Alundyne is objectified in the English version through both the visual focalisation and the elimination of her speech. By excluding Laudine's monologue and reducing the emotional imagery, the emphasis thus shifts from the internal turmoil of Laudine to the external manifestations of conventional feminine bereavement. Similarly, the elaboration of the physical and psychological wounds inflicted by 'Love' in *Yvain* (1,359–1,508) is curtailed to a simple declaration that 'luf, þat es so mekil of mayne, / sare had wownded Sir Ywayne' (871–2). The focus is thereby directed away from the ideological notion of 'Love' to its narrative function within the story.

The attention is shifted from the fallacies of Love (represented as an abstract and philosophical concept) to the realities of social and marital duties. Alundyne needs a husband to defend the spring (a social necessity that would have made perfect sense within its contemporary context) and Ywain as a courtly knight must conquer his beloved (similarly a requisite for the validation of masculinity and knightly valour). Both elements reflect the communal concerns of medieval society regarding gender roles and social order and hierarchy. The cultural anxiety generated by the notion of an autonomous and unattached widow, particularly one in possession of land and power, is solved in a practical manner by quickly wedding her to the victorious knight.

Keith Busby notes that there is a 'general switch of attention from women to men and a reduction in the submissiveness of men to women' in the English text.[73] He attributes this switch to the conservative and hierarchical structures of a male-oriented society – both in terms of the intended reading public of the text and the societal structures portrayed within the Middle English romances in general. The existing patriarchal constitution is thus confirmed in the text and the fact that there might be something ethically questionable about Alundyne marrying her husband's slayer so shortly after his death is dismissed by the practical needs of establishing and maintaining social order:

> Þai wate ful wele þat he es ded,
> Þat was lord here in þis stede.
> None es so wight wapins to welde
> Ne þat so boldly mai us belde,
> And wemen may maintene no stowre,
> Þai most nedes have a governowre.
> Þarefor mi lady most nede
> Be weded hastily for drede.   (1,217–24)

in the narrative and is preceded by the progression with the bleeding corpse of her husband presumably either through the room he is in, or in his vicinity (as the body bleeds as a sign of the presence of its killer). The focal point is vague, leaving it unclear where precisely Yvain is situated in relation to Laudine.

[73] 'Chrétien de Troyes English'd', 603. Derek Pearsall similarly observes a difference in the relationship between Yvain and Laudine and that of their English counterparts (see *Old English and Middle English Poetry*, London: Routledge and Kegan Paul, 1977, 146).

The narrative makes use of the generalised figures of the lady and the knight to reconfirm and validate existing social structures. The interaction of the various characters and their modes of operation within each situation thus address questions of social and cultural relevance for the audience. The conflicting ideas of marital duties, knightly obligations and emotional devotion are explored in the text through the destabilisation and the subsequent reconstruction of social order.[74]

Once Ywain breaks his promise to Alundyne and overstays his given period of knightly freedom the established social structures collapse. Ywain's descent into insanity, represented by his exodus from civilisation into the wilderness (the symbolic representation of social disorder and lack of civilising structures), draws attention to the volatile balance of social harmony. The intermittent passages serve to re-establish the social code through an exploration of masculine identity and the meaning of true valour. Built-in social coding and ethical questions can thus be explored by the mere representation of character behaviour within certain situations. Notions of masculine identity, knightly ideals and justifiable emotions are examined as the various situations call for appropriate reactions determined by pre-existing codes of conduct. Cultural dichotomies such as the relation between knightly bravery and Christian humility are explored as Ywain battles for himself, for his love and ultimately for the greater good of the community.

The characters can be perceived as figurative guides to the built-in pattern of meaning by focusing on them as narrative units that serve the purpose of pulling together the various narrative threads to form a cohesive and meaningful whole. This mode of conveying meaning would most likely have been both familiar and immediately relevant to its English audience. To take an example apparently at furthest remove, one of the more popular texts written in the English vernacular in the fourteenth century, *Piers Plowman*, in fact conveys meaning not through the psychological complexity and depth of its protagonist, but precisely through his placement within and process through the narrative.[75] The figure of Will is indeed not so much a character as a narrative sign that draws its signification from the figurative engagements with the symbolic rubric of the narrative matter. Each act thus becomes meaningful both as a literal event and as an allegorical allusion to medieval spiritual and social world-view. While the text of *Ywain and Gawain* is engaged with

---

[74] John Finlayson's analysis of the romance is based on this contradictory relationship between the ideals of love and prowess. He argues that the various adventures serve the purpose of moving from a personal glorification to a definition of true chivalry symbolised in the humility of the Knight of the Lion ('*Ywain and Gawain* and the Meaning of Adventure', *Anglia* 87 (1969), 312–37).

[75] The text of *Piers Plowman* has been preserved in fifty-six manuscripts and fragments and multiple early printed editions, witnessing to its popularity among medieval readers. The earliest version of the text (the A-text) is presumed to have been in circulation in the 1360s, thus placing it within decades of the writing of *Ywain and Gawain* (see William Langland, *The Vision of Piers Plowman*, ed. A. V. C. Schmidt, London: The Everyman Library, 1995, and Kathryn Kerby-Fulton, '*Piers Plowman*', in *The Cambridge History of Medieval English Literature*, ed. David Wallace, Cambridge: Cambridge University Press, 1999, 513–38).

secular concerns, rather than religious disputation, such hermeneutic practices of gathering meaning from symbolic connections within the narrative material would have been immediately familiar to its audience.

Many of the major medieval English texts function indeed through such interlacing of narrative units to form a meaningful symbolic whole, as opposed to focusing on the interior and psychological workings of an individual. Even in *Sir Gawain and the Green Knight,* which perhaps more than any of the English romances appears to depict the progress of internal growth of its protagonist, the process of spiritual maturing is not so much internal as it is an external development involving multiple narrative levels and symbolic representation. While Sir Gawain learns humility and has to confront his own weakness at the end, he remains nonetheless fundamentally the same throughout the story. The final shift in perception and the shattering of the magical illusion of the Green Knight takes place at the level of narrative, and in the end it is the reader rather than the character who has come to a greater understanding.[76] The apparently arbitrary sequencing of adventures of *Ywain and Gawain* thus becomes meaningful not so much in the development of the philosophical notion of *amour courtois* and knightly ideals, but rather in the interlinking of narrative movement and events to a network of meanings.[77] The reorientation from individuality to social order thus dictates the modifications occurring in the process of the textual transmission of the source text.

The Old Norse text shows a similar tendency to reduce the depiction of the internal emotional realm of its characters. Monologues are omitted or greatly reduced and there is an overall effort at minimising emotional display. As a result of this shift in focus from the internal to the external, the characters' words and reactions often seem somewhat unmotivated and incoherent. In the effort to adapt their behaviour to the Nordic mentality, the fundamental aspect of their function within Chrétien's work is lost. When Laudine (referred to simply as the lady) first appears on the scene in the Norse translation, the external acts of bereavement are portrayed: 'Enn eftir líkinu geck ein fru suo faugur at j allri ueraulldu matti eigi finnazst hennar noti hun syrgdi ok æpti sinn harm stundum fell hun j ouít' (35–6) (After the body there went a lady so fair that in the entire world her equal could not be found. She mourned and cried out her sorrow. At times she fell in a faint) (168).[78] The internal

---

[76] *Sir Gawain and the Green Knight, Pearl, Cleanness, Patience,* ed. J. J. Anderson (London: The Everyman Library, 1996), 167–278.

[77] John Finlayson draws attention to this 'dramatic rather than explicit revelation of *sens*' where 'themes are expressed in action rather than through the narrator's comments' and notes that 'most English narratives of the fourteenth century seem to work in this oblique fashion' ('*Ywain and Gawain* and the Meaning of Adventure', 314). David E. Faris also explores the structure of romance narrative as means of engaging the audience's imaginative response in his article 'The Art of Adventure in the Middle English Romance: *Ywain and Gawain, Eger and Grime*', *Studia Neophilologica* 53 (1981), 91–100.

[78] The C text has a slightly different version, preserving some of the description of Laudine's appearance, which has been omitted in the B text (there is a lacuna here in the manuscript containing the A text): 'hon var skrydd skynandi skickiu, hon var þa biort sem dagss brun, enn hennar litur sem at samtemprat væri það snió huita gras lilium ok hin rauda rösa enn harid sem gull borit Augu hennar voru skynande sem carbünculi þeir steinar sem sva heita,

motivation for the excessive display of sorrow is, however, greatly reduced and the focus shifts from personal grief to the idealised notion of feminine mourning. The image of bereavement is then interlinked to the narrative concern with bravery and cowardice by the words spoken by the grieving lady:

> Su uirduliga fru sprack naliga af harmi ok mælti ef þu hínn uondí suikarí ert her jnni at mínn bonda hefir drepít þa gack | fram til mín ef þuert eigi huglaus suo at ek mega taka a þer suo framt sem ek ueti attu hefir [damage in MS] s[ui] kum þuiat j ollum heimenum eigi uar hans iafningí at uaskleik ok at gerfi ok uopn. (36)[79]
>
> [But that worthy lady nearly burst from sorrow and spoke: 'If you, that evil deceiver, are inside here, who has killed my husband, then come forward to me, If you are not cowardly, so that I might get my hands on you, to the extent that I know that you have [damage in MS – presumably referring back to the slaying of her husband, i.e. 'killed him with'] deceit, because in all the world there was not his equal in bravery and ability.' (168)]

While this rhetoric is present in the French text, it is subservient to the ideal of courtly Love and valour, whereas here it takes centre stage as the underlying force of both her grief and her accusation. These are the only words out of the entire lament the translator (or the scribe) has retained and they refer directly to the conceptualisation of bravery and cowardice and make no mention of the internal turmoil and emotional upheaval so prominent in the French text. There is a distinct move away from the personalisation of Laudine to a generalisation of her figure as the typified 'lady in mourning'. This indicates a difference in literary preoccupation in the Nordic reading communities where the subtleties of courtly love were perhaps less relevant than the dictates of appropriate behaviour with respect to honour and masculine obligations.

Ultimately, the shift in narrative focus from the internal development of the ideal knight to the actions and events to which he is subjected shows the movement away from the interplay of love and chivalry of the French text

---

hennar mottull var af bisso allur skynandi ok oll hennar klædi voru gulli buinn þat bæta þotte, ok þottu þo svort hia hennar birte' (37) (She was adorned with a shining cloak. She was then bright as daybreak, and her color as if the snow-white plant, the lily, and the red rose were mingled together, and her hair like beaten gold. Her eyes were shining like carbunculi – those stones which are so named. Her mantle was of byssus, all shining, and her clothes were adorned with gold – where it was thought to improve them – and yet they seemed black beside her brightness) (169). Such discrepancies in manuscript copies indicate that the extant texts reflect layers of modifications, where one text has preserved original features that have been lost in other copies, which have nevertheless retained other aspects more accurately.

[79] Again the C text differs from the B version, but in this instance it is in omission. The entire lament in the French text is omitted without even the accusation of cowardice being retained. The lady remains completely silent. Íven sees her image through the window and the text simply states that she 'syrgdi sinn bönda miok hormuliga, enn stundum fiell hon i övit' (37) (mourned her husband very sorrowfully and at times she fell in a faint) (169). The statement is then followed by the description of her appearance. Both texts accord, however, in their pattern of modification in the absence of internal depiction of emotion and a shift in focus from the depiction of the lady as an independent personality to her function as figurative and representative within the narrative pattern.

to the more socially-oriented focus of both the English and the Norse texts. By generalising the characters they are made immediately familiar to the audience, allowing for the attribution of signification from their place within the narrative structure rather than from their individuality. The nuances of courtly etiquette and the intricacies of chivalric behaviour and manner of twelfth-century France were perhaps of less interest to its fourteenth century English author. The number of romances being produced in England at the time indicates, however, that there was no lack of interest in the courtly genre and that it was indeed being steadily copied, emulated and recreated. The differences in textual orientation between the French texts and their English translations can be explained by underlying differences in literary tradition and cultural perception of the target audience. The predilection for fast-paced narrative would thus be indicative of a cultural preference that is not necessarily (or solely) based on literary sophistication or social status, but is deep-rooted in the social conditions and literary heritage out of which the author obtained his training and knowledge.

The Norse text displays a more complex issue of cultural transformation, perhaps owing to the fact that the extant texts exhibit varying layers of cultural and historical influences. The initial translations may have contained more of the original elements of courtly values while showing some of the signs of cultural adjustment in sentiment, narrative pace and gender-dictated values common to all the Norse translations. Later Icelandic scribes would then have adjusted the texts to their own conceptualisations of audience predilection or cultural values. This would explain the discrepancies between the manuscript copies in the depiction of Laudine, for instance. Both the B and C texts (there is a lacuna in the A text) reveal a reduction in sentimentality and portrayal of the inner workings of Laudine. Each manuscript copy, however, retains a portion of the French text that is missing in the other, giving the account a specific and unique narratorial direction.

While the story is thus true to its source in thematic development in both the English and Norse translations, it becomes something very different in the hands of the translators. The texts are not only transformed linguistically and formally, but their entire cultural function has changed. The rhetorical reconstruction of the French text to foreground the conceptualisation of 'trowthe' and knightly honour in the English text shows a destabilisation of the original courtly function of the source text. Similarly, the sometimes contradictory modifications of narrative structure in the Norse texts indicate the multiple layers of authorial influences in the transmission process that have guided the reconstruction of the story. Ultimately, both the Norse and English translations reveal a distinct movement away from a focus on the individual in Chrétien's work to a concern with social order and the role played by appropriate behavioural models in achieving and maintaining such communal coherence. The transposition of the romance has thus resulted in a shift from the French story of *amour courtois* and chivalric idealism to the fast-paced and narrative-oriented English and Norse accounts that demonstrate less interest in the courtly ideology than the way in which the narrative *matière* can be used to foreground the authors' own cultural concerns.

CHAPTER FOUR

Female Sovereignty and Male Authority in the Old Norse and Middle English Versions of *Partonopeu de Blois*

THE ROLE OF *Partonopeu de Blois* in the formation and dissemination of the romance genre in medieval Europe has often been overlooked. This much-translated romance clearly appealed to a wide range of readers over several centuries. It exists in Old French, Middle English, High German, Low German, Dutch, Old Norse, Old Danish, Spanish, Catalan and Italian. The French poem, an anonymous twelfth-century romance that draws on the Cupid and Psyche myth as well as Celtic folklore, is extant in seven complete (or near complete) manuscripts as well as two fragments and an excerpt.[1]

The romance has been preserved in two different versions. To version I belongs the French verse romance along with translations into Middle English, High German, Low German, Dutch and a loose adaptation in Italian. It begins in France and relates the royal descent of Partonopeu going back to Troy.[2] It then tells how, during a hunt with his uncle, the king of France, Partonopeu finds himself lost in a forest. He arrives at a seashore, where a magical ship guided by unseen hands carries him to an equally magical city. Partonopeu is served dinner in a great and splendid hall by invisible servants and later retires to bed. He is then joined by a mysterious lady, who implores him to leave. He begs for her mercy and is in the end allowed to remain. This is followed by a seduction scene, after which she reveals her identity as Melior, the queen of Constantinople, and announces that she has brought about his arrival in her city as her future husband. Partonopeu is to remain with her, invisible to her court, until the day they can wed.[3] The only condition is that he cannot see her until then. They stay together at night and during the day Partonopeu amuses himself in her lands.

---

[1] *Partonopeu de Blois. A French Romance of the Twelfth Century*, ed. Joseph Gildea (Villanova: Villanova University Press, 1967), viii. For a discussion of the manuscript tradition of the French text see Penny C. Simons, 'A Romance Revisited: Reopening the Question of the Manuscript Tradition of *Partonopeus de Blois*', *Romania* 115 (1997), 368–405.
[2] The narrative progress of all the versions discussed in this chapter is outlined in the Appendix, which contains summaries of the texts, revealing the main differences and concordances between the various versions.
[3] There are some minor discrepancies between the various versions, such as the length of time determined for the waiting period (two and a half years in the French text, one and a half years in the English), but overall they concur in the structure of the narrative process outlined here.

113

After a year has passed Partonopeu requests leave to go back to France. Melior grants him leave, but reminds him of his promise to her. Partonopeu finds his homelands besieged by Saracen armies and offers his services to the French. He battles the pagan king Sornegur and wins back the lands. His mother is distressed to find out about the love affair and the strange condition set by his beloved and believes he has been enchanted by the devil. She induces her son to betroth himself to the king's niece by means of a magic drink. The spell is broken when the maiden mentions his old love and Partonopeu returns to Melior, who forgives him his infraction. After some time Partonopeu wishes to return to France. Melior warns him against his mother, but grants him leave again. His mother turns to the bishop for help and he persuades Partonopeu to bring a lantern to their bedchamber to ensure that his lover is indeed no devil. Partonopeu returns to Melior and during the night he raises the lantern, thereby exposing her beauty and breaking the spell. Partonopeu, as a result of his betrayal, is now visible to the inhabitants of the castle. Melior is despondent at the breach of his promise and at the loss of her powers of necromancy, and banishes Partonopeu from her city despite the pleas of her sister Urrake.

Partonopeu returns to Blois heartbroken and desperate. He falls ill and returns to the forest with a young pagan squire, whom he baptises. He abandons the squire and awaits his death. He is then found by Urrake, who convinces him that Melior has sent her. She nurses him back to health with the help of a young maiden, Persewis. Urrake returns to Melior and scolds her for her cruelty to Partonopeu. There she learns that Melior, who grieves for the loss of her love, is to be married to the winner of a tournament. Urrake then conceives of a plan to bring them back together. Partonopeu is girded by Melior in preparation for the tournament, without her recognising him. On his way to the tournament, Partonopeu is lost in a storm and finds himself taken captive by a cruel lord by the name of Armans on an island. Partonopeu persuades Armans's wife to let him go and proceeds to the tournament, where he is joined by a knight, Gaudin, who becomes his companion. Partonopeu distinguishes himself at the three-day-long tournament and in the end is declared winner, and he and Melior are therefore finally united in marriage.[4]

---

[4] The mythological folktale of Cupid and Psyche agrees with version I in fundamental narrative structure inasmuch as the text (as it is elaborated by Apuleius) begins with the description of Psyche (the narrative equivalent of Partonopeu) and then relates how she is brought to the palace of Cupid, who, unknown to her, makes her his wife. He extracts a promise from her not to try to see him; she remains in the palace among invisible (although audible) servants, and the couple spend the nights together. Psyche is ultimately convinced by her jealous sisters to bring a lantern to the bedchamber, thereby causing Cupid to expel her from his palace. Psyche wanders around seeking her husband and is punished severely by Venus. Eventually Cupid regrets his dismissal of her and they are reunited (Apuleius, *Cupid and Psyche*, ed. E. J. Kenney, Cambridge: Cambridge University Press, 1990). The roles of the lovers are reversed in the romance, with a female sovereign taking the place of the masculine deity seducing the mortal woman. The close parallels to the narrative elements of the folktale indicate that the material must have been known, in some form, to the author of *Partonopeu de Blois*. Whether he was familiar with the version depicted by Apuleius in his *Metamorphoses* remains, however, uncertain at this point. For information on the connection between the text and the Cupid and Psyche tradition see for instance Thomas H. Brown, 'The

Version II includes a fragment of a Middle English text, an Old Norse prose version, a Danish translation, a Spanish prose version and a Catalan translation of the Spanish text. It begins in Greece with Melior as the protagonist. She inherits the kingdom of Constantinople from her father. She then sends messengers around the world to find a suitable husband and only after she has chosen Partonope does the hunting scene take place. In fact, the reader does not learn about Partonope until this point. He is then brought, as in version I, by ship to Melior's magical kingdom, where he encounters her in her bed. The ensuing events follow in the main the narrative structure outlined above. Partonope breaks his promise and is banished from Melior's kingdom, until he wins her back at the tournament and they are wedded.

Despite the apparent popularity among medieval audiences, the romance has so far received little critical notice. It is only within the last decade that critics have started taking note of the French romance and its significance within French literary history.[5] In 1953 S. P. Uri wrote an article lamenting the lack of critical attention devoted to what he believed to be 'one of the best loved romances in the Middle Ages and for a long time after', stating that the romance of *Partonopeu de Blois* 'seems nearly forgotten in the 20th century'.[6] Much of this neglect can be attributed to a lack of modern editions of the text. The Old French version was published by A. C. M. Robert and G.-A. Crapelet in 1834, and it was not until 1967 that a new edition was produced by Joseph Gildea.[7] New critical research on the historical and political subtext of the French text as well as intertextual connections to other major medieval writers has generated a renewed interest and appreciation for the romance as an example of both generic flexibility and complex narrative layering.[8] The Old

---

Relationship between *Partonopeus de Blois* and the Cupid and Psyche Tradition', *Brigham Young University Studies* 5 (1963), 193–202, and Lise Præstgaard Andersen, '*Partalopa saga*, homologue scandinave d'*Eros et Psyché*', *Revue des langues romanes* 102 (1998), 57–64.

[5] Much of this renewed critical interest has been in connection with an electronic edition of the French *Partonopeu de Blois* at the University of Sheffield, as well as articles generated by the editors and an international conference held at Sheffield in 2003 on 'Partonopeus in Europe'. A collection of the papers delivered at the conference was published in a special issue of *Mediaevalia* 25.2 (2004).

[6] 'Some Remarks on *Partonopeus de Blois*', *Neophilologus* 37 (1953), 83–98, at 83–4. Uri's article is a sweeping commentary on the sources of the romance and historical evidence, some of which is, however, outdated or simply wrong.

[7] *Partonopeus de Blois*, ed. A. C. M. Robert and G.-A. Crapelet, 2 vols (Paris: G-A. Crapelet, 1834), and *Partonopeu de Blois*, ed. Gildea.

[8] See for instance Penny Simons and Penny Eley, 'The Prologue to *Partonopeus de Blois*: Text, Context and Subtext', *French Studies* 49 (1995), 1–16, and 'A Subtext and its Subversion: The Variant Endings to *Partonopeus de Blois*', *Neophilologus* 82 (1998), 181–97; Penny Eley, Catherine Henley, Mario Longtin and Penny Simons, '*Cristal et Clarie* and a Lost Manuscript of *Partonopeus de Blois*', *Romania* 121 (2003), 329–47; Roberta L. Krueger, 'The Author's Voice: Narrators, Audiences, and the Problem of Interpretation', in *The Legacy of Chrétien de Troyes*, ed. Norris J. Lacy, Douglas Kelly and Keith Busby, vol. 1 (Amsterdam: Rodopi, 1987), 115–40; Roberta L. Krueger, 'Textuality and Performance in *Partonopeu de Blois*', *Assays* 3 (1985), 57–72; and Peter S. Noble, '*Partonopeu de Blois* and Chrétien de Troyes', in *Studies in Honor of Hans-Erich Keller*, ed. Rupert T. Pickens (Kalamazoo: Medieval Institute Publications, 1993), 195–211.

Norse and Middle English texts have, on the other hand, failed to benefit from this critical revival. They still suffer from the modern privileging of the source text over its foreign offspring and the tendency to base aesthetic judgement on the fidelity or deviation from that source. The focus on 'accuracy' in the translation process, however, negates the prevalent medieval perception of the nature of translation and textual transmission. The notion of textual fidelity was in fact foreign to a mindset that viewed vernacular texts and stories not as singular and fixed entities, but rather as collective material to draw on in the creative process. Such approaches also overlook the profound impact of cultural and historical context in the reception and transmission of texts, and disregard the signs of cultural reception imprinted upon those texts in their movement across linguistic and national boundaries.

In this chapter I shall examine patterns of textual transmission and cultural reception by analysing the Old Norse text, the two Middle English versions and the French text together. The purpose is to illuminate the cultural impressions that lie behind the textual modifications and the different narrative patterns of these works. The cross-cultural comparison serves to draw attention to differences in character portrayal, narratorial positioning and ideological representation. Such evidence is of value in mapping the social and cultural conceptions of the various reading communities for which the texts were created and within which they survived. It similarly assists in illuminating the complicated relations between the various versions and the significance of such intertextual connections for modern comprehension of medieval literary culture. My focus here will be on a comparative reading of the two Middle English versions with the Nordic one. The aim is to draw attention to the significance of the various versions of the Partonope story for the exploration and understanding of the cultural transformation of narrative material across medieval Europe.

Patterns of Transmission

The existence of two different variations of the story is of considerable importance when tracing patterns of transmission. Such mapping of narrative dissemination is made particularly difficult by the fact that the romance exists in French in only one of these versions. Critics generally assume that there were two versions of the French text in circulation and that one or the other was subsequently transmitted across Europe to be translated there into the various vernaculars. A. Trampe Bödtker surmised that the version beginning in Greece was probably a revised version of the one beginning in France, which would hence have been the earlier one.[9] He then supposed that this

---

[9] He moreover maintained that the new adaptation was based on a manuscript related to one of the extant French manuscripts, Bibl. Nat. MS Fr. 368 (*Parténopeus de Blois. Étude comparative des versions islandaise et danoise*, Christiania: J. Dybwad, 1904, 55). Eugen Kölbing believed, on the other hand, that the version beginning with Melior was the original one and closer to Apuleius' myth. He considered the Trojan genealogy to be a later addition and that the philosophical and moral deliberations were inserted into this revised version

now lost continental version branched into two groups, one containing the Spanish and Catalan translations, and the other a lost Anglo-Norman version from which the English fragment was derived as well as a purportedly lost Norwegian translation, which Bödtker took to be the source of both the Norse (Icelandic) and Danish versions.[10] In the most recent edition of the Norse text, however, Lise Præstgaard Andersen rejects Bödtker's proposed stemma and the notion of a lost Norwegian text. She argues that there is nothing about the 'language and style of Partal[opa saga] that particularly suggests a 13th-century Norwegian source'.[11] Andersen finds no philological evidence of a previous Norwegian translation, nor are there any indicators that the romance ever existed in Norway.[12]

The romance is in fact quite different, both in style and in linguistic presentation, from the courtly material known to have been translated in thirteenth-century Norway. This difference signals either dramatic modifications by Icelandic scribes, or, alternatively, that the romance was indeed translated almost a century later than has commonly been assumed and in a different social setting altogether. It is of note here that Icelandic scribes were diligent in copying and editing Norwegian translations, often to the extent that the resulting texts differed rather extensively from their Norwegian originals. The creative reworking of a Norwegian text of *Partalopa saga* cannot be excluded, even though there is no trace of such a text. The survival of a native Icelandic version of the Tristan legend (*Saga af Tristram ok Ísodd*) alongside the original Norwegian translation (*Saga af Tristram ok Ísönd*) shows that writers drew on and reshaped existing literary material for their own purposes. It is clear, however, that in this case the native version is a completely reworked version of the legend seemingly in the manner of a satire and as such differs from *Partalopa saga*.[13]

('Über die verschiedenen Gestaltungen der Partonopeus-Sage', *Germanistische Studien*, Supplement zur *Germania* 2 (1875), 55–114, see particularly 103–6). Anthime Fourrier, along with Bödtker, rejected the primary relationship of the version beginning in Greece to the one beginning in France (*Le courant réaliste dans le roman courtois en France au moyen-âge*, Paris: Nizet, 1960, 317). All three critics presuppose the existence of two or more versions of the Partonope story in French at some point.

[10] *Parténopeus de Blois. Étude comparative des versions islandaise et danoise*, 47. Kölbing reaches similar conclusions as to the origin of the extant Icelandic version in his essay 'Über die verschiedenen Gestaltungen der Partonopeus-Sage', 74–6.

[11] *Partalopa saga*, ed. Lise Præstgaard Andersen, Editiones Arnamagnæanæ, Series B, vol. 28 (Copenhagen: C. A. Reitzels Forlag, 1983), xxi.

[12] A Norwegian origin can usually be established on the basis of palaeographical, internal or linguistic evidence for many of the romances. A small fragment from the beginning of the fourteenth century has, for instance, survived of the Norwegian translation *Flóres saga ok Blankiflúr* (from the Old French *Floire et Blancheflor*), which exists otherwise solely in Icelandic manuscripts from the fifteenth century. Both this romance and *Ívens saga* were the sources of Swedish translations in the fourteenth century, similarly indicating the existence of a Norwegian source (see *Partalopa saga*, ed. Andersen, xix–xxii).

[13] For information on the two Norse versions of the Tristan legend see for instance Paul Schach, 'The "Saga af Tristram ok Ísodd": Summary or Satire?', *Modern Language Quarterly* 21 (1960), 336–52, and Sverrir Tómasson, 'Hvenær var Tristrams sögu snúið?', *Grípla* 2 (1977), 47–78.

Bödkter's presumption of a thirteenth-century Norwegian original is based on a preconceived notion that, since most of the extant romances are known to have been translated as part of a larger programme of introducing French courtly literature into Norway during the reign of King Hákon Hákonarson, there is no reason to think that independent translation activity took place in Iceland in the subsequent centuries. Given the vigorous literary activity in fourteenth-century Iceland it is, however, not unlikely that literary patrons would have taken an interest in a text, procured perhaps during time spent abroad, with a storyline that would have appealed to Icelandic audiences. Andersen instead proposes a lost French archetype as the source for the Icelandic and Danish translations and the English fragment, which she furthermore places in the first half of the fourteenth century.[14] Based on her supposition, the version beginning in Greece would thus have come into being about a century and a half after the original story was written down in France.

There is, however, no evidence that this alternative version ever existed in France. The number of manuscripts preserved of the French *Partonopeu de Blois* testifies to its esteem among medieval audiences, and it could be surmised that at least some fragment would have been preserved containing the other version. Its absence, despite this otherwise excellent record of textual preservation, might indicate that this alternative version came into being during or as a result of the translation process itself, outside France.[15] Recent theories connecting the text to social and political events of the 1170s would support the idea of later rewriting, incorporating textual modifications to meet the expectations of new reading communities, or merely the preferences of redactors.[16] This modified version would then itself have been disseminated.[17] The fact that both versions exist in English makes England a prime candidate for this process of textual refashioning. As stated before, there is philological evidence that many of the French texts translated in

---

[14] Andersen bases her theory on a lost vellum manuscript dated c.1350–60, which is known to have included a text of *Partalopa saga*. This manuscript, traditionally referred to as Ormsbók, thus provides the *terminus ante quem* for the presumed lost archetype (*Partalopa saga*, xxi).

[15] Then again given the precarious preservation of medieval manuscripts, the multitude of manuscripts containing the first version could, of course, simply imply the popularity of that version over the other.

[16] There are two current theories on the dating of the romance. The general consensus has hitherto been that it was written around 1180–5 and that it was largely inspired by the works of Chrétien de Troyes (see for instance Fourrier, *Le courant réaliste dans le roman courtois en France au moyen-âge*, 392–411). Recent critical work on the romance has, however, uncovered some internal evidence that would place its writing a decade earlier (see Simons and Eley, 'The Prologue to *Partonopeus de Blois*', and Penny Eley and Penny Simons, '*Partonopeus de Blois* and Chrétien de Troyes: A Re-assessment', *Romania* 117, 1999, 316–41). Penny Eley and Penny Simons link the narrative presentation to the social context and political events of the 1170s as a means of establishing the point of origin of this particular version of the story. The critical debate over the dating of the French romance is as yet unresolved.

[17] The third option is that the change from *ordo artificialis* to *ordo naturalis* was made independently in the various subgroups. They would then not necessarily be related. The likelihood of such independent reconfiguration of the text is, however, fairly remote, given the consistency in the narrative order between the texts belonging to version II.

Norway came from England. Anglo-Norman spelling of proper names, as opposed to continental forms, indicates that the transmission of manuscripts took place across England rather than France in the thirteenth century. Norwegian translations of courtly material were brought to Iceland already in the third decade of the thirteenth century and there are indications that this process may have begun as early as the twelfth century.[18] Given the creative liberty with which English redactors approached their French sources, the notion that the text underwent the narrative reconfiguration in England is by no means an unlikely option. Further examination of the version beginning in Greece – hereafter termed the 'short version' to differentiate it from the 'longer' French version – and a comparative analysis of the various texts belonging to that group are necessary in order to establish possible textual interrelations or to trace potential manuscript transfer.[19] Such an examination goes beyond the scope of this chapter.[20]

The Old Norse version is preserved in no fewer than thirty-one manuscripts, ten of which are of text-critical significance.[21] *Partalopa saga* has, moreover, survived in two separate redactions, which are nonetheless clearly derived from the same original translation. A comparative reading with other extant versions of the text indicates, furthermore, that they both preserve features that must have formed part of the original translation, but were for some reason or another omitted in the other redaction.[22] Most of the extant manuscripts fall under the category of what Andersen terms the A group, with only a single complete manuscript representing what she terms the B group. Andersen uses AM 533 4to (A1) in the Arnamagnæan Collection in Copenhagen, which dates from the mid-fifteenth century or later, as the base manuscript, indicating deviations and variant readings through JS 27 fol. (A3) in the Landsbókasafn-Háskólabókasafn in Reykjavik, dated 1662–7, along with examples from other A-group manuscripts in the footnotes. The B group is represented by Papp. fol. nr. 46 (B1) in the Royal Library in Stockholm, the only existing manuscript containing this specific redaction of the saga, which is dated to the second half of the fourteenth century and thus presents the

---

[18] Guðrún Nordal, Sverrir Tómasson and Vésteinn Ólason, eds., *Íslensk bókmenntasaga*, vol. 1 (Reykjavik: Mál og menning, 1992), 181–4, 203.
[19] For the sake of simplicity the two versions will hereafter be referred to as the longer version (beginning in France) and the shorter version (beginning in Greece), in view of the general difference in length between the two variant versions. Both the Norse text and English fragment (which contain the version beginning in Greece) are significantly shorter than their French and English counterparts (which preserve the version that begins in France).
[20] For a discussion of the transmission patterns and interconnections between the various texts see the forthcoming edition of *Partonope of Blois*, ed. David Lawton and Sif Rikhardsdottir, TEAMS Middle English Text Series (Kalamazoo: The Medieval Institute).
[21] For a listing and description of both primary and secondary manuscripts and their interrelation see *Partalopa saga*, ed. Andersen, xxvi–xcv.
[22] Each redaction has preserved textual details that can be found in the extant French text, indicating that they are likely to have formed part of the presumed original translation. It must thus be assumed that the French version the Norse text is based on contained those details, or, alternatively, that the translator had access to both versions. This again needs further comparative research of all the extant texts of the short version.

earliest extant version of the text.[23] I will be making use of both A1 and B1 in the discussion – the variations of the other A manuscripts being such as not to affect textual interpretation – and will hereafter refer to them simply as the A and B text for clarity.

The English manuscripts present an even more complex issue. The so-called longer Middle English version, which is a close translation of the French *Partonopeu de Blois*, survives in five manuscripts, of which only one is complete. Two of the remaining manuscripts are defective at the beginning and the end and two are only fragments. MS Add. 35288 in the British Library, dating from the late fifteenth century, is the only complete manuscript and is used as the base manuscript by Bödtker in his 1912 edition of *Partonope of Blois*.[24] MS University College 188 in the Bodleian Library, dating from the mid-fifteenth century, consists of 7,096 lines (as opposed to the 12,000+ lines of Add. 35288); it contains the oldest as well as the best text, and is likely to come closest to representing the original text. Bodleian Rawl. Poet. 14 is slightly later than University College 188 and somewhat longer, but is closely related to that text despite its overall lesser quality.[25] There are additionally two fragments in a fifteenth-century hand, MS Lat. Misc. B.17 (about 200 lines) and MS Eng. Poet. C.3 (about 158 lines), both in the Bodleian Library. All the extant manuscripts, except notably Add. 35288, are defective at the beginning and the end. Eng. Poet. C.3 comes closest to the end, breaking off at line 12,093, only 102 lines before Add. 35288 ends. None, however, begins before line 1,608, which is where University College 188 begins. The missing leaves at the beginning of all of the extant manuscripts except Add. 35288 are of considerable significance and will be discussed later.

The Middle English version corresponding to the Icelandic text exists only as a fragment of 308 lines in a vellum manuscript from 1450–60, and is currently in the private collection of Toshiyuki Takamiya (*olim* MS Penrose 10, *olim* Vale Royal MS, *olim* Delamere MS). Bödtker reprinted the text from an earlier 1873 edition for the Roxburghe Club in his edition.[26] The manuscript has been in private ownership since it was edited in the late nineteenth century and has not been re-edited since.[27] The text begins with Melior, confirming

---

[23] The text in Stockholm papp. fol. nr. 46 is believed to derive from the Ormsbók manuscript, which is thought to have been destroyed in a fire in 1697. Swedish lexicographical works from the seventeenth century similarly refer to Ormsbók as a source and contain entries that correspond to the extant text of the B redaction (ibid. xlvii–lxv).

[24] *The Middle-English Versions of Partonope of Blois*, ed. A. Trampe Bödtker, Early English Text Society, Extra Series 109 (Millwood: Kraus Reprint, 1981).

[25] For information on the English manuscripts see *The Middle-English Versions of Partonope of Blois*, vi–viii, and Gisela Guddat-Figge, *Catalogue of Manuscripts Containing Middle English Romances* (Munich: Wilhelm Fink Verlag, 1976), 164–5, 279, 281, 295–6, 299. I have examined all the manuscripts in question and any discussion of the manuscripts themselves will thus be based on these examinations.

[26] *A Fragment of 'Partonope of Blois', from a Manuscript at Vale Royal in the Possession of Lord Delamere*, ed. R. C. N[ichols] (London: Nichols and Sons, 1873).

[27] Bödtker states in his edition that all attempts at seeing the manuscript were unsuccessful and reprints R. C. Nichols's nineteenth-century edition of the text. The current owner, Toshiuyki Takamiya, has kindly provided access to the fragment and a re-edited version

that it belongs to the second grouping of the Partonope story, the so-called shorter version. It relates the events up to Melior's instructions to Partonope, at which point (line 276), seemingly in the middle and with no apparent break, it leaps forward to the third day of the tournament (corresponding to line 10,811 in the other version) where it continues for an additional thirty-one lines before breaking off.[28] The French, English and Norse manuscripts therefore form groups that overlap and interact with each other in a complex manner that foregrounds the underlying intricate pattern of textual transmission.

Female Sovereignty and the Concept of Manhood

As in the English fragment, the Norse text begins with the presentation of Marmoria (the Norse rendering of Melior). The narrative focus is thus from the beginning on her persona and the story is conveyed through her rather than through Partalopi (Partonopeu). The story follows the same narrative thread as the other versions. Her father dies, leaving her as heir to his empire. She sends messengers to find the most suitable husband and then departs by means of her magical skills to see him for herself. The hunting scene then takes place, followed by the seduction. The significant difference here is in the representation of both Marmoria and Partalopi. This is signalled right at the beginning in the way in which Marmoria is depicted. The text relates how her father dies when she is fifteen years old 'en hon var þa meykongvr yfir ǫllv rikinv' (A 2)[29] (and she was then maiden-king over the whole kingdom) (130).[30] The short English version, which corresponds here to the Norse text in narrative progress, simply states that after her father's passing she was then 'quene of that londe' (48).[31] The reference to Marmoria as *meykongur* (maiden-king) rather than the more commonly used designator *drottning* (queen), corresponding to 'quene' in the English text, is directly related to

---

will appear in the forthcoming edition of *Partonope of Blois*, ed. David Lawton and Sif Rikhardsdottir. For information on the fragment see Guddat-Figge, *Catalogue of Manuscripts Containing Middle English Romances*, 112–13.

[28] The perplexing continuity of the text despite the apparent narrative lacuna is discussed in the forthcoming edition of *Partonope of Blois* along with deliberations on the probable means of manuscript transmission and possible reading communities of the short versus the long version.

[29] Quotations from the Old Norse version will be taken from Andersen's edition of *Partalopa saga*, along with page numbers provided in parentheses within the text. Given the often considerable textual discrepancies between the A and B manuscript groups, the manuscript group will be identified along with the page numbers and when necessary both will be quoted.

[30] The English translations of the Icelandic text are based on Blaisdell's translation, which follows the Icelandic text in Andersen's edition. Only minor changes have been made where needed for comparative purposes or clarification. Page numbers will hereafter be given in parentheses in the text. The translation will obviously be based on the A or B group depending on which is being quoted.

[31] Quotations from the English texts will be taken from Bödtker's edition of *Partonope of Blois*, along with the line numbers in parentheses following the quotation. When citing from the longer version the relevant manuscript will be identified if necessary, otherwise, for the sake of simplicity, quotations will be from the base text in Bödtker's edition, British Library Add. 35288.

Icelandic culture and folk traditions.³² The motif of the female ruler who does not wish to marry and rejects her suitors is developed in other native romances and is unique to Icelandic literature.³³ The exploration of the motif in Icelandic literature signals an apparent communal concern with women of high status and their potentially inferior suitors and the social need for marriage. It similarly reveals the literary engagement with the concept of female independence. The Icelandic redactor appropriates the image of a female in a dominating political position in his source text and recasts it within the context of his own literary and cultural realm. The context of meaning for the Icelandic audience is thus established and the reference to Marmoria as 'maiden-king' instantly associates her both with other heroines familiar from native literature and lore and with the ideological concept of the dominant feminine ruler.³⁴ It signals therefore the integration of the text into the existing cultural and literary tradition.By drawing on vocabulary ingrained in Icelandic society and literature the text establishes significant connotations that would have had an instantaneous meaning within their new reading communities, but which were not merely absent, but in fact non-existent in the original cultural context. This is further emphasised in the text as Marmoria deliberates over the choice her envoys have made for her:

> En því gerdi hon þetta at hon villdi ǫngvann mann lata vera sier rikara ef hon mætti rada ok sa hon þat sem var at sa mvndi keisari verda yfir allri Grecia er hennar feingi ok sa mvndi rikari verda en hon ok þotti henni þat mikil minkan at heita sidan keis<ar>ina þar er advr het hon meykongvr yfir P(artalopa) ok morgvm ǫdrvm hǫfdingivm. Sidan for hon aptvr til Mikla gardz ok gerdi sier þat ihvg at hon skylldi leyniliga med þessv mali fara ok fa hann þo allt at einv hon red nv riki sinv vel ok sæmilega ok let svo fyrir vinvm sinvm at hon villdi ǫngvm manni giptazt þeim er þar vissi hon deili æ þviat eingin var þar sa svo reyndur at riddaraskip at svo væri yfir ǫdrvm riddvrvm sem hon var yfir ǫllvm jvngfrvm þetta þotti ǫllvm satt er hon sagdi her vm. (8–9)

[She did this, because she wanted to let no man be more powerful than herself, if she could have her way. She perceived that he who married her would become emperor of all of Greece and would be more powerful than she.

---

³² The B redaction omits this reference to Marmoria's status as maiden-king and simply states that she was the heir after her father died: 'Enn sva bar til fyrr enn hon var gefvinn at fadir hennar andadist, enn sidann kongurinn var fra fallinn, þótti einginn arfvi sannari til landa ok kongdoms enn Marmorja dottur hans' (B 2) (But thus it happened before she was given in marriage that her father died, and after the king had passed away, no heir seemed more proper for the lands and kingdom than Marmoria, his daughter) (130). She is, however, referred to as 'maiden-king' at a later point in the text (8).

³³ The motif of the 'maiden-king' appears in several Icelandic romances, among them *Clari saga, Sigurðar saga þögla, Nitida saga, Viktors saga ok Blávus, Sigrgarðs saga frækna* and *Dínus saga drambláta*. For further information about the maiden-king tradition see Marianne E. Kalinke, *Bridal-Quest Romance in Medieval Iceland*, Islandica 46 (Ithaca: Cornell University Press, 1990).

³⁴ For a discussion of the ideological conflict regarding gender roles and social positioning in the maiden-king tradition see Sif Ríkharðsdóttir, 'Meykóngahefðin í riddarasögum: hugmyndafræðileg átök um kynhlutverk og þjóðfélagsstöðu', *Skírnir* 184 (2010), 410–33.

That seemed to her a great abasement to be called afterward empress where before she was called maiden-king over Partolopi and many other chieftains. After that she went back to Constantinople and took it into her head that she should secretly deal with this matter and get him nevertheless. She now ruled her kingdom well and honorably and pretended thus to her friends that she did not wish to marry any man of those she knew, because there was not one there so proven in knighthood that he would be so above other knights as she was above all noble maidens. What she said seemed true to all. (134–5)]

This passage shows a substantial departure from the source material, which has no such reflections on female status and power. The text depicts her as a ruling monarch, quite literally appropriating a male position signalled by the use of the masculine noun *kongur* (king) over the more grammatically and socially correct mode of address of *drottning* (queen). More important, however, is the fact that Marmoria clearly has no intention of marrying at all. This early statement of (albeit royal) female independence is a significant deviation from both the French and the English versions, where her intent to marry is clearly stated and it is only a question of postponement of the nuptials.[35] Marmoria is hesitant because she is concerned to 'let *no man* be more powerful than herself'. By giving her hand in marriage she effectively relinquishes the control she has hitherto commanded as she must give up her position as 'king' to her husband and take the secondary seat of 'queen' herself. And the text surprisingly supports this declaration of female sovereignty by stating that she ruled her kingdom 'well and honorably'.

The figure of Partalopi himself has also undergone some major transformations in the transmission from the original French depiction of a child ('l'enfant') to the Nordic ideal of a masculine hero. In the hunting episode, where both the French and English Partonope find themselves lost in the forest, fearful and hungry, the Icelandic Partalopi appears in no way to be distressed by his predicament. As the French Partonopeu loses his way in the woods, the text portrays a forlorn and frightened youngster who has been removed from the security of his civilised environment and placed in a mysterious and treacherous wilderness. The text in fact paints a remarkably realistic picture of a child who is tired, hungry and fearful, as one would assume children to be: 'Il a peor et faim et soi' (657) (He is afraid, hungry, and thirsty).[36] In the long English version Partonope is similarly referred to as 'chylde' and he finds himself, like his French counterpart, lost in the woods and suffering from hunger and fear: "'Allas," he thoghte, "what may I do? / For colde and honger I am fulle wo. / A-ferde also nowe of my lyffe'" (658–60).

In the Norse text there is not a single mention of him expressing or experiencing fear, nor are there any invocations to God to save him, as in the other texts: 'Il plore et crie a Deu merci' (*Partonopeu* 681) (He wept and cried out

---

[35] See for instance line 1,396 and onward in the French text and line 1,676 in the longer English version.

[36] Quotations from the French text are taken from *Partonopeu de Blois*, ed. Gildea, with line numbers given in parentheses in the text. English translations are all mine and are intended for comparative purposes, not as poetic renderings of the French verse.

to God to have mercy) and in the English: 'Helpe me lorde Gode *and* eke seynte Sythe' (661). There is additionally an absolute absence of tearful laments or crying. The image of the hero wandering through the forest forlorn and weeping would have been culturally inappropriate and, moreover, incomprehensible to a Nordic audience accustomed to radically different standards of masculine behaviour.[37] The experience is rather described as one of wonder, which is supported by positive adjectives such as 'lovely' and 'delightful' giving an impression quite the opposite of the French text, where the reader is made to sympathise with the fearful Partonopeu as he wanders alone in the wilderness:

> Er hann hafdi leingi ridit kom hann vm sidir asægnipv eina þar var storliga favrt at sitia ok lystilikt hann hliop þar af hesti sinvm ok sa ahafit vt ok ætladi þar at sitia til þess er hann feingi nǫckvra vitran af þeirri villv er yfir hann var komin. (A 11–12)

> [When he had ridden a long time he came at last to a coastal cliff. There it was very lovely to sit and delightful. He jumped from his horse there and looked out at the sea and intended to sit there until he got some revelation about that delusion which had come over him. (136).]

While the courtly topos of the young sensitive knight was familiar to Icelandic audiences from other translated romances (such as Chrétien de Troyes's *Yvain* and the Tristan legend), it was understood to represent a foreign heroic mentality and was therefore not directly transferable. Such representation in fact directly opposed the Nordic convention of masculine heroic behaviour and attitude, which was rooted in early Germanic ideological structures. This intrinsic transformation of Partonopeu's character thus shows the adjustments made for the sake of an audience accustomed to the more reticent and manly protagonists of the Icelandic sagas.

Partalopi's bravery is furthermore underlined by several other minor textual changes. Once he arrives in the magic city, Partalopi enters a splendid palace, where he is provided with food by invisible servants, as in the other texts. As night approaches he is led by lighted torches to bed. Rather than being led directly to the bedchamber, however, the Nordic Partalopi proceeds through three halls, each filled with a number of beds, which serve to emphasise both his courage and the precarious situation in which he finds himself.[38] Ultimately, once he comes to Marmoria's chamber he declares, in a very Nordic manner indeed, that he will defend himself against whoever is the owner of the bed: 'þviat þat mvndi talad þa er ek var heima med fedvr minvm at ek

---

[37] As mentioned before, crying was not considered socially appropriate and most certainly not for men in medieval Scandinavia. The accusation of a man crying was in fact justifiably avenged with death. Such behaviour would thus not have been acceptable within the social fabric of masculine heroic mentality of the Icelandic audiences.

[38] The A text lists first a hall with five hundred beds, a second one with three hundred beds, and a third hall apparently intended for kings and dukes, after which Partalopi comes to the small room with a single bed, which he believes must belong to the chieftain of the city (20–4). The B text similarly lists three preceding halls only the number of beds differs slightly.

mvndi eigi vpp standa or þeirri hvilv er ek væri jkominn fyrir einvm riddara ok nv skal ek gera þvi framar at ek skal nv veria fyrir .x. þott til komi' (24–5) (because that would be said, when I was at home with my father, that I would not get up from that bed which I had gotten into because of one knight. Now I shall act thus all the more, that I shall now defend it against ten) (143–4). The portrayal of Partalopi thus indicates the cultural appropriation that has occurred in the adaptation of the French (or English) text to its new literary environment.

The seduction scene which follows differs radically from both the French text and the long English version. In both these texts, Partonopeu is lying in bed in the dark when he is all of a sudden joined by an unknown body, which the text reveals to be that of a woman. She directly orders him out of her bed, which is then followed by the alternate pleading of Partonopeu and her commands for him to leave – culminating in the seduction itself (or rape). While the Norse text shows the same fundamental narrative structure as the other two, the tone is quite different. Upon discovering the woman in bed with him, Partalopi 'lagdi sinar hendvr vm hals henni ok mælti eingi madvr kemvr sa her er þik taki af mer' (27) (placed his arms around her neck and spoke: 'No one will come here who could take you from me') (145). This immediate declaration of ownership and physical dominion of her body is an assertion of his masculine prowess, intended both for Marmoria, who as previously noted will succumb to no man that she feels is not her equal, as well as for the audience. Marmoria instantly retorts with her own affirmation of power: 'veiztv at riki mitt stendvr yfir kongvm ok hertvgvm ok jorlvm ok jafnvel yfir fodvr þinvm ok þvi er þer þat ofmikil diorfvng at taka bervm hondvm áá minvm likama' (28) (Do you know that my power extends over kings and dukes and earls and likewise over your father, and for that reason it is a too daring feat on your part to put your bare arms on my body) (146).

What follows is a verbal battle of wills – a linguistic foreplay in a sense – that serves to establish their respective autonomies and reinforce the physical valour of Partalopi needed for her to accept him:

> Hon sv(aradi) gack brvtt skiott jminv ordlofi ella skaltv lata lifit jstad. P(artalopi) sv(aradi) fyrr skaltv lata meydominn en ek lifit ok ecki hrædvmzt ek Riddara þina ok betra þicker mer at lata lif mitt jþinne sæng en riddarar þinir kalli mik hvglavsann enn giorla veit ek jvngfrv at med ydarri list kom ek hingad en þo mvn ek eigi vpp gefa þetta hvs fyrir riddorvm þinvm medan ek ma veriazt hon mælti diarfvr mvntv vera jFraklandi heima er þv ert slikvr her jGriklandi en likligt þickir mer at þat mvni satt vera at hingat hefir sagt verid af þer. . . . nv skempta þav sier þa nott eptir þvi sem þeim likadi ok sofnvdv sidan jfogrv fadmlage ok godv. (29–33)

[She answered: 'Go away quickly with my permission, or you shall lose your life at once.'

Partalopi answered: 'Sooner shall you lose your virginity than I my life. I do not fear your knights, and it seems better to me to lose my life in your bed, than that your knights call me cowardly. I know well, lady, that I came here through your magic art, but nevertheless I shall not give up this room before your knights while I can defend myself.'

She spoke: 'You must be daring at home in France, when you are such a one here in Greece. It seems to me likely that what has been told of you must be true.' . . .

Now they entertained each other that night according to what pleased them and fell asleep afterwards in a lovely and good embrace. (146–8)]

The French Partonopeu wins Melior over by begging her mercy and by Melior's resulting pity, whereas the Icelandic Partalopi is accepted by Marmoria for the sole reason that he evinces his *lack* of fear. The actual sexual act is here the direct result of Partalopi's successful substantiation of his worthiness through dialogue and is granted by Marmoria herself. There is thus a substantial shift in the power relations and the delegation of authority apparent in the Norse adaptation that reveals significant differences in the social conceptualisations of gender structures. This shift becomes evident when one looks at the corresponding mode of representation in the other versions. There these interrelations signify radically different ideals of female and male interactions.

A closer look at the English fragment, which contains the same version of the story, will help to elucidate such divergences in cultural representation. While the Icelandic version and the short Middle English text belong to the same branch of the romance transmission, it is clear that the Icelandic text is not based on the surviving English fragment. A comparative reading of the first few lines, which relate the same events, shows substantial textual discrepancies that discount any direct correlation or textual dependence between the two texts:

> Whilum ther was a noble kynge,
> That was dowghtty holden in dede.
> Atte iustys an ate turnementtynge
> Hee bare hym weelle upon a stede.
> He was curteys in alle thynge,
> And whit lewte his land dede leede.
> He hadde thane two dowghttris yinge,
> . . .
> Melior was thee Eldere maydenys name,
> That wonder fayire was on to see,
> And as a wight moost worthily in wane.
> Vrake was kleped here suster free. (Short 1–16)

The beginning lines in the Icelandic text are as follows:

> Svo er sagt at fyrir Mykla gardi red sa keisari er Saragvs het hans dottir het Marmoria er allra kvenna var vænst þeirra er j þann tima vorv j heime hon var ok svo godvr klerkvr at eingi fekzt henni jafngodvr j ǫllv Griklandi hon kynni svo vel stiǫrnv bok at hon matti þvi til leidar koma sem sv list ma efla. (A 1–2)

[Thus it is told, that over Constantinople there ruled the emperor whose name was Saragus. His daughter's name was Marmoria and she was the loveliest of all the women who at that time were in the world. She was also such a good scholar that no one could be found as good as she in all Greece. She knew the book of astrology so well that she could bring about that which that art can accomplish. (130)]

The Icelandic text has transformed the verse of the original into prose, which, as we have seen in the preceding chapters, was common practice in Old Norse translations of Old French poetry. The Icelandic version is also much abridged, signalling the tendency of medieval Nordic translators to eliminate unnecessary descriptions and narratorial intrusions which would slow down the account in order to create a fast-paced narrative focused on the interrelation and movement of events.[39] More importantly, however, the Norse text refers to Melior's father, the emperor, by name and indicates the territory over which he rules and which Melior subsequently inherits. The English text gives no indications of the eastern origin of Melior, or of the location of her domain, thus eliminating the cultural and political allusions associated with the love affair in the other versions. Here her father is simply a 'noble kynge' that rules over an undefined kingdom. Melior is thus notably no longer the ruler of Constantinople, but merely the yet unwed heiress of a king.

This reorientation of the location of the story dramatically changes both the audience's conception of Melior and the implications of her relationship with Partonope. If the audience for which the fragment was intended had been unfamiliar with the story one would assume that the reference to a 'noble kynge' would have created mental associations of local and familiar kingdoms, hence an English one (or possibly European), rather than Constantinople.[40] The fact that the Old Norse text gives both her name and that of her father along with the location of his empire indicates that the translator must have had access to a manuscript (or manuscripts) containing that information.[41]

[39] The general pattern of modification in the transposition of French courtly matter into Norse is discussed in detail in the preceding chapters and will not be elaborated on here. It suffices to state that they all show to a greater or lesser degree a tendency to shorten and reduce the material, and to focus on the movement of the narrative as opposed to the visual imagery, philosophical deliberations or idealisation of tropes such as love, which so often characterise the French texts.

[40] In the longer version the narrator (posing as translator) interrupts his account to declare that: 'For y am comawndyt of my souereyne / Thys story to drawe fulle *and* playne, / *Be-cawse yt was ful vnkowthe* and *lytel knowe*, / Frome frenche ynne-to yngelysche, that bet*er* nowe / Hyt my3th be to euer-y wy3the' (2335–2340, my italics). It is of course quite possible that this is a purely rhetorical statement in the manner of establishing patronage, or a sense of authenticity. It is nevertheless unclear how well known the French romance may have been in England prior to its translation. The fact that the text does state that it 'was ful vnkowthe and lytel knowe' raises the question whether it was indeed unknown in England at that time, or whether such a comment was intended as ironic, as it was on the contrary quite familiar. Such familiarity may nevertheless have been limited to certain audiences or geographical locations. It is of significance here that this passage is only recorded in British Library Add. 35388. It is missing in University College C.188, which, like Add. 35388, recounts how Partonope spends his time in leisure and delight until the year has passed without the intermittent passage (2,323–52) that relates how the translator was instructed by his sovereign to turn the French story into English.

[41] It is of note here that the B group refers to Marmoria's father as 'Emanuel Griklandß kongur' (B 1) (Emanuel, king of Greece), indicating some corruption along the way or different textual

The Old French text reveals her name and status once the seduction has taken place as she declares that 'tote Basence est mes empires' (1,341) (all of Byzantium is my empire) and later that her name is Melior (1,769).[42] The corresponding section is missing in the longer English translation, but she is referred to as Melior throughout the remainder of the text and the extent of her rule is assumed to be Byzantium, indicating that the missing section is likely to have contained a similar revelation to the French text.

Penny Simons and Penny Eley suggest in two recent articles on the French *Partonopeu de Blois* that the romance may originally have been written as a conscious means of furthering a certain political agenda of the house of Blois and that later revisions show a deliberate subversion of that political subtext to further the cause of the Plantaganet dynasty.[43] Regardless of the potential existence of such a deliberate political agenda, the localising details (house of Blois, the French king, Constantinople etc.) place the text in a historical and ideological context both familiar and evocative for its French (and English) audience. Such references of necessity contain within them direct or indirect allusions to the contemporary political and social concerns of the respective reading communities. Both their French and English readers would thus have brought their own unique experiences and perception to the elucidation of the text. If one assumes a common French origin for both English versions, it is conceivable that the short version was intended for a lower class or a mixed public, perhaps not so familiar with the conceptual framework of the story and less interested in the political subtext than in the tale of the two lovers.[44] The focus would thus have been directed at the narrative

influences in the two groups. All the other extant manuscripts refer to her father as Saragus 'keisari fyrir Mykla gardi' (A 1) (emperor of Constantinople) and the B version subsequently refers to the city of her rule as 'Mikla gardi' (Constantinople) (B 1–2).

[42] The reference here to 'Basence' is unclear, but given the geographical location of her empire (Constantinople) I translate it here as 'Byzantium'. The term 'Byzantium' was not coined until the sixteenth century when the previous name 'basileia ton Rhomaion' was replaced by the Latin neuter word 'Byzantium', created from the name of an ancient Greek town Byzantion. The city of Constantinople was founded in close proximity to the old Greek town (Helen C. Evans, ed., *Byzantium: Faith and Power (1261–1557)*, New Haven and London: Yale University Press, 2004, 5). It is possible that the word as used in the French text draws on 'basileus', the ancient Greek term for 'sovereign', which was used by the Byzantine monarchs for the emperor in Constantinople, indicating again the geographical area that later become known as Byzantium (see for instance Warren T. Treadgold, *A History of the Byzantine State and Society*, Stanford: Stanford University Press, 1997, and Michael Angold, *The Byzantine Aristocracy: IX–XII Centuries*, Oxford: BAR International Series, 1984).

[43] Their theory is based on a close reading of manuscript copies, one of which they claim contains an earlier text which shows signs of a deliberate political objective behind the textual production. The other manuscript copies therefore reveal later efforts to minimise the criticism of the English and to subvert the intrinsic political agenda. Obviously such a text would have appealed to English readers in the fifteenth century ('The Prologue to *Partonopeus de Blois*' and 'A Subtext and its Subversion').

[44] It is also possible that the fragment represents an earlier version of the story, perhaps more closely related to the Cupid and Psyche myth. The extant French and longer English versions would thus represent the later historical contextualisation of the tale. The narrative details contained in the other corresponding versions (such as the Norse text), however, contradict such an interpretation. Since they belong to the same variant the only explanation for the

matter, the story of the two young lovers, rather than on the external details. The redirection of the political component of the text shows similarities to the cultural modifications wrought upon the Norse text, thereby revealing their common effort of reorienting the narrative sphere to a context familiar to the presumed new public. The modifications also disclose, however, some surprising correlations between the Norse text and the French and the longer English version against that of the fragment, despite the fact that it contains a rendition of the story equivalent to the Norse one. The difference between the Norse text and English fragment could imply multiple stages of rewriting and reshaping of the romance, where the existing versions represent the various stages through the inclusion of more or less narrative detail and the adaptation of the thematic orientation of the text to either specific authorial agendas or to the generalised cultural concerns of their reading communities.[45]

In the hunting incident there is an additional disagreement between the Icelandic text and the English fragment, where the Icelandic version agrees with the Old French and the longer English version. In both the French text and the long English version the hunting scene precedes the revelation of Melior's involvement in Partonopeu's disappearance, which thus leaves the reader as much in the dark as the protagonist as to what is about to transpire. This differs from the Norse text and the fragment, where the hunting episode takes place after we have witnessed Melior's observations of the knight and her selection of him as her future husband. In the French text, Partonopeu is hunting a wild boar ('sengler' 604) when he finds himself lost in the woods. The English translator faithfully renders it as 'wylde boore' (long 541). In the short version the incident is related as follows:

> Thee kyng on huntynge he wolde ryde
> W*ith* horn and howndys for to play.
> Pertinope wentte by his side.
> Thorghw enchauntement of that may
> They Reysede an hart w*ith* hornis wyde. (98–102)

The magical powers deployed by Melior in conjuring the animal which will lead Partonope astray, as yet undisclosed in the French text, are here made clear ('thorghw enchauntement'), thereby reducing the sense of mystery and

---

inclusion of such localising information would have been through the cross-contamination between the earlier version and later revisions at the level of the various national translations, which is highly unlikely.

[45] If the second version originated in France and spread from there to other countries, it would have to have included some of the narrative details recorded in the Norse version (unless one assumes the translator had access to both French versions). A comparative reading with the Spanish and Catalan versions would establish the extent of such textual correlation. The fragment would then represent a radical revision of this text. If, conversely, one assumes the text came to England in the first form and was reshaped there the fragment must again present a later stage in the revisions than the text that was used for the Norse translation. Again, much more research must be done on the various versions to establish such textual connections.

suspense. The wild boar of the French text has, moreover, metamorphosed into a stag.

In the Norse text the two redactions disagree on the type of the animal. In the A version Partalopi sees 'hlavpa fyrir hvndvnvm einn mikinn *villi gǫllt' (A 10) (running before the dogs a large wild boar) (135), thus agreeing with the French original. In the B version, on the other hand, Partalopi sees 'hiǫrt eirn mikinn laupa at sier' (B 10) (a large stag running at him) (135), recalling the text of the English fragment. Neither version proclaims that Marmoria is orchestrating the pursuit, as they both depict the scene in a similar manner to the French and the longer English versions. The only difference is that the hunting episode is directly preceded by Marmoria's resolve to 'leyniliga med þessv mali fara ok fa hann þo' (A 9) (secretly deal with this matter and get him nevertheless) (134), suggesting that the reader is to expect some sort of wily scheme that will involve the unknowing Partalopi.[46] The reader is thus complicit in the plot, thereby shifting his orientation within the text from the unsuspecting Partalopi to Marmoria. The suspense is thus not eliminated, but its narrative focus is simply shifted from 'what' is happening to Partonope in the French and English text to 'how' Marmoria will carry out her plan and whether it will succeed in the Norse text. It is thus quite possible that the Icelandic version and the English fragment are both examples of a more or less developed story stemming from an original French text, which began with an account of Melior. Then again it is conceivable that the English fragment is a much simplified and reworked version of an original text (whether French or English) that resembled more closely the narrative structure of the Norse text and the longer Middle English version (albeit with a different order of events).[47] Perhaps such a text was indeed intended for an audience differing in social status, or in gender composition, from that of the longer version, which would explain the disparity in narrative emphasis and representation.[48]

The fragment is in fact written in a manner reminiscent of other vernacular English romances where the original material is abridged and simplified,

---

[46] The B version fundamentally agrees here with the A and is only slightly more specific: 'hugde leyneliga at fara med þessu radi, ok ottadist fyrir at fa mann med vielum or Fracklandi' (9) (intended to proceed secretly with this plan and was afraid to get a man from France by means of artifices) (134). It is possible that the text is somewhat corrupt here. It is unlikely that 'ottadist' (feared) would have stood alone in this syntactical position and it does not agree with what has been stated before. It is probable that it should instead have said 'ottadist eigi', meaning 'feared not', which would be more in accordance with the tone of the passage. The B text shows some signs of such textual corruption or unclear passages in other instances.

[47] There are instances where the fragment agrees more closely with the longer English version than the Old Norse one. Partonope is, for instance, the cousin of the king of France in both English versions (as well as the French), whereas he has become the son of the king of France in the Icelandic version (the B version states that he ruled over 'Saxlande' (Saxony), but it is subsequently referred to as France in the text) (see p. 4 in the Norse text, line 59 in the fragment, lines 492–9 in the long English version, and line 535 in the Old French text).

[48] Unfortunately a more comprehensive comparison is impossible owing to the fragmented state of the text, which prevents a detailed reading of both versions concentrating on textual deviations shared by those texts against other versions.

stripped of its emotional and philosophical layers to procure a fast-paced account focused on the move from one narrative unit to the next rather than on the visual or sensual elaboration of the scenes themselves. While it is unclear how long the whole text must have been, it manages to describe the background of Melior, the search for a marital candidate, followed by the hunting scene and arrival in the fairy city, along with the seduction and subsequent revelation of Melior's identity (which ends abruptly before the shift to the tournament) in 276 lines. The equivalent material extends over more than nineteen hundred lines in the longer version, indicating that the text is extensively curtailed. Similarly, the delocalisation of the action and the characters removes the text from its social context, making it both more generalised and more applicable to a reading community formed of multiple diverse layers of society. It shifts the narrative emphasis from the Byzantine-France connection (and any tension between Eastern and Western Christianity) to the motif of the human and the fairy lover, common in the Breton lays.[49]

There is an additional minor change observable in the fragment, which, however, significantly alters the narrative rubric of the text when compared with the French story. The short version makes no mention of Partonope's age, as in the French source and the longer version. He is consistently referred to as 'chyilde', underscoring his youth, yet indicating that he is of marriageable age.[50] When Melior is introduced it is stated that she herself is young, suggesting that they are both of a tender age: 'He [the king] hadde thanne two dowghttris yinge' (7). This minor change signals a move away from the thematic fabric of the French source, where it is explicitly stated that Partonopeu is thirteen years old, and hence too young to marry Melior, who, on the other hand, seems to be somewhat older, as her advisors are in a great hurry to marry her off: 'Et si n'avoit que sol treze ans' (543) (and he was only thirteen years old). The 'que sol' further emphasises the young age of Partonopeu, intimating that his youth is of significance within the narrative framework.

This focus on his age is absent in the fragment. Yet there is a noticeable emphasis on his youth in the repeated references to him as 'young knight'. It is only after the seduction scene that the English fragment refers to Partonope not as 'chyilde', but as a man: 'Thyself art stalworth stowt man and gay', indicating that a shift has occurred with the sexual initiation (271). The

---

[49] See for instance *Lanval, Graelent, Désiré, Sir Launfal* and *Guingamor*. For information on connections of the Partonope story to folk tales, the Breton *lais*, the *matière de Bretagne*, and to the classical legend of Cupid and Psyche, see Helaine Newstead, 'The Traditional Background of *Partonopeus de Blois*', *Proceedings of the Modern Language Association of America* 61 (1946), 916–46; Lilian M. McCobb, 'The Traditional Bakground of *Partonopeu de Blois*. An Additional Note', *Neophilologus* 60 (1976), 608–10; and Colleen P. Donagher, 'Socializing the Sorceress: The Fairy Mistress in *Lanval, Le Bel Inconnu* and *Partonopeu de Blois*', *Essays in Medieval Studies* 4 (1987), 69–90.

[50] *The Middle English Dictionary* (ed. Hans Kurath *et al.*, Ann Arbor: The University of Michigan Press, 1969) gives multiple potential meanings for the word 'child' in Middle English. While the term could denote a boy or a girl (usually to the age of puberty) it frequently referred to a young man, often a youth of a noble birth (a young knight). All of the references have, however, in common the association of youth and innocence or inexperience associated with young age.

seduction scene itself is surprisingly gentle, intimating the mutual consent of both parties, which is quite different from the apparent rape scene in the French text:

> In Armes hee klipte that wo*m*man free.
> Softe as selk hee gan hiere fynde.
> And hee was bothe soft and swete
> In Armes bothe to fele and fooled.
> Of loue longynge hee wolde nowt lete,
> But wrovghtte his will w*ith* the byerde boolde.
> Whanne he hadde his [will] so wrovght,
> Thanne spake to hym that lady gente:
> 'Pertinope, myscvmforte thee nowght.'
> And w*ith* loue in Armes sche hym hente. (235–44)

The adjectives 'soft' and 'sweet' give the scene a sense of peace and sensuality that is devoid of any impression of brutality. There is no reference to Melior refusing or resisting his advances and her loving embrace after the event has occurred indicates it has overall been a successful experience on all parts.

Female Agency and Masculine Authority

The seduction scene is, as a matter of fact, of such fundamental importance for understanding the various transmission patterns of the romance that it is worth analysing in detail the diverse variations of the narrative portrayal of this scene within the different versions. The presentational alterations are directly linked to a larger and more complex thematic and ideological shift in the reconfiguration of the romance within each specific reading community. As we have seen in the English fragment the scene is portrayed as a mutually satisfying sexual experience of two young people that is brought about by Melior herself, but initiated by Partonope. The result is a textual shift in address from 'chyilde' to 'man'. Whether this was sustained throughout cannot be determined as the remainder of the text is missing, but there is no reason to think it would not have been so. In the very short account from the tournament that follows this scene, Partonope is no longer referred to as 'chyilde' (that is, as a *young* knight), but rather as 'knyght' (278, 297) and 'lord' (293), signalling that he has moved from the status of inexperienced youth to a grown man, a knight worthy of the hand of Melior.[51]

In the French *Partonopeu de Blois*, the seduction scene is also a turning point in the story. Since the account begins with the description of Partonopeu's Trojan ancestry and makes no mention of Melior, both Partonopeu and the audience are unaware of her existence and hence of the identity of the mysterious body that enters Partonopeu's bed in the dark. It is not until the seduction has taken place that her identity is revealed and thereby the entire machination that brought him to her in the first place. Preceding the

---

[51] The only reference to 'child' is in the speech of the duke, where he addresses his followers, 'now come my children that wole abyde', and is thus not directed at Partonope (299–300).

seduction the text focuses on the youth and immaturity of Partonopeu. He is systematically referred to as 'l'enfant' (child), as in the English fragment. As he rides out on a hunt with his uncle, the king of France, he is separated from his companions while hunting the boar and subsequently loses his way in the woods. The desperate search by the king's men that ensues intimates his inexperience and thus foregrounds his youth. He wanders through the forest, intermittently crying and calling out for help. The effect of the anticipation and suspense is heightened by the use of focalisation. The narrative is depicted through Partonopeu, who is himself unaware of what is going on and is, moreover, terrified. As he comes to the sea he finds a ship that then carries him to a magical city. He proceeds through the city until he comes to a palace, where he is served food by invisible hands and ultimately led to a bedchamber. There he lies down and is soon after joined by the mysterious personage, who, as we later find out, is Melior, the queen of Constantinople.

As the encounter takes place Partonopeu has lain down in bed and the chamber is plunged into dark, thus obscuring the usual sense of visualisation and intensifying both the aural and physical effects of the event:

> La cambre devint molt oscure
> ...
> Or crient il molt que vegne l'ore
> Que vif maufé li corent sore.
> Atant une fee vient al lit,
> Pas por pas, petit a petit,
> ...
> Mais ço est une damoisele.   (1,119–33)

> [The chamber becomes very dark
> ...
> Now he cries out loudly when the time comes
> that the devil incarnate is running towards him
> At that instant a fay comes to the bed,
> Step by step, little by little,
> ...
> But it is a lady.]

The dramatic effect is increased by relating the encounter through the perception of Partonopeu. Partonopeu *hears* the steps in the dark and instantly assumes it to be an evil spirit and then a fairy, until we discover it is simply a maiden. The discovery by the maiden herself of this unknown person in her bed is similarly depicted in physical terms as 'son pié le tousle sent' (1,144) (her foot touches him). Her reaction indicates that the maiden is startled:

> Et quant l'a sentu, si tressaut,
> Escrïa soi et nient trop haut:
> 'Comment! fait ele, qui es tu?
> Qui t'a en mon lit enbattu?
> Ice que est, Virgene Marie?'   (1,145–9)

> [And when she feels him, she shudders
> she cries out not too loudly:
> 'What!' she says, 'who are you?
> Who has thrown you in my bed?
> Who are you, Virgin Mary?']

The discovery is followed by an extended dialogue between the two, where Partonopeu begs for mercy and she demands that he leave her bed at once. Despite the orders for Partonopeu to leave the bed, the text gives some indications that the maiden has softened towards the intruder as it states that she feels 'a molt grant pitié' (1,249) (a great pity) towards him, which is followed by her turning towards the wall, at which point he subjugates her:

> Vers li se trait et met sa main
> Sor le costé soëf et plain;
> ...
> Vers lui se torne et dist: 'Laissiés!
> Grans folie est que vos caciés.'
> ...
> Et il le prent par les costés;
> Cele ses jambes ferme et lace,
> Et cil l'estraint, vers soi l'embrace.
> ...
> Les flors del pucelage a prises.
> Florse i dona et flors i prist.   (1,271–1,305)

> [He turned towards her and put his hand
> On her waist gently and smoothly
> ...
> She turns to him and says: 'Let me be!
> You have been smitten by madness.'
> ...
> And he takes her by the waist
> He grabs and entraps her legs
> And he clasps her and turning her towards him he
>   embraces her
> ...
> He has taken her flowers of maidenhood
> He gives flowers and he takes them.]

Melior's initial dismissals are in line with the standard mode of representing the sexual conquest of a modest maiden, yet the text gives indications before the sexual act takes place that she is indeed growing more amiable towards him. While the text makes it unclear whether or not it was specifically her intention that the seduction take place, it is nevertheless clear that she does not regret it having taken place afterwards as she addresses him as her 'amis' (friend or lover) and asks him to listen to her as she explains who she is and how he came to her (1,334). The seduction is thus instantly followed by her revelation that she is empress of Byzantium and that she brought him to her. She declares that she desired him as her husband, but that in view of his young age she cannot marry him yet, and they will have to wait for two and a half years until he is at the appropriate age to be dubbed knight and hence become her lawful husband. His youthfulness is again stressed as the reason behind the subterfuge: 'un enfant de petit aé' (1,366) (a child of a tender age). This is of significance within the context of textual transmission as both the longer English version and the Icelandic change the age (the fragment does not specify the age) and thereby shift the underlying motive of the entire scheme. The longer version changes it to eighteen years, indicating either that the translator had some moral qualms about subjecting his young protagonist to the sexual initiation and has thus changed his age, or, alternatively, that it is simply the result of a scribal mistake, since the text otherwise follows the source relatively closely and does maintain the references to Partonope's youth.[52]

Sarah Kay speculates whether the age of thirteen would have been too young for sexual initiation for the audience, as Partonopeu is still a *puer* (the period of *pueritia* was generally considered to be from age seven to fourteen for boys) and has therefore not yet reached adulthood and the necessary age for marital consent and sexual activity.[53] While marriages between children under the age of fourteen took place among the aristocracy, the translator may have changed the age to remove the connotations in the French text of an apparent 'indecent' seduction. In the Norse text both Partalopi and Marmoria are fifteen years old, indicating that with the age difference, which is the underlying reason behind the entire narrative motivation in the French text, being removed it is no longer a question of an experienced woman seducing a young adolescent, but rather of two equally experienced (or rather inexperienced) individuals.[54]

Partonopeu's age is thus a significant motif that plays a fundamental role in the narrative structure and dramatic movement of the story. Kay in fact attributes Melior's use of magic in the French text to an effort to 'conceal a relationship perceived as transgressive in the world of the romance'.[55] This becomes apparent in the expulsion of Partonopeu from Melior's kingdom once he breaks his promise and exposes himself and their relationship to the other inhabitants of the palace. As the candidate chosen by her emissaries as her future husband is still of a young age she must secure his love, yet such a relationship cannot be conducted in public and hence it has to take place within the privacy of her magically created realm of invisibility. While the French text thus plays on the ethical and moral codes of medieval society with respect to appropriate age for sexual initiation and marriage, the Icelandic text eliminates any such social coding involving age and replaces it with the notion of power and authority.

---

[52] With eighteen years, Partonope would still have been described as young and the references to him as 'chylde' (which also has the meaning of young knight) is thus not at odds with his age in the English text.
[53] *Courtly Contradictions. The Emergence of the Literary Object in the Twelfth Century* (Stanford: Stanford University Press, 2001), 281 and footnote 19, p. 349.
[54] The B version omits Marmoria's age (see pp. 2 and 4).
[55] *Courtly Contradictions*, 281.

This scene becomes highly problematic in the longer English version. Given the relative fidelity to the source by the English translator, any deviations from the original are thus of considerable importance in establishing authorial intent, or the possible motivations behind the textual modifications. The English text follows the French source closely, relating the story much in the same manner and with multiple verbal parallels. Apart from the opening lines of the English text, which differ from the French source as the redactor has added what amounts to a standard address to the reader, the translator recounts the Trojan genealogy of Partonope relatively faithfully.[56] As in the French text, Partonope goes hunting with his uncle, the French king, and becomes lost in the forest while pursuing a boar. The king mounts a search for his nephew and meanwhile Partonope wanders alone in the forest, frightened and weary, until he arrives at the seashore and sees the ship which will carry him to the magic realm of Melior's kingdom.

There is, however, a slight difference in narratorial distance between the two protagonists. The audience is positioned with the narrator in the French text, observing the young Partonopeu as he finds himself in this foreign place, thus increasing the narrative distancing between reader and protagonist while simultaneously increasing the sympathy for the weary child. The shift in focalisation from the external narratorial viewpoint to that of Partonopeu in the bedroom scene is therefore all the more effective. The English text lessens this effect as Partonope is given more direct speech while removing the intermediating agency of the narrator himself.[57] Once Partonope finds himself in the bedchamber the text follows the French source closely until the room has been plunged in darkness and Partonope hears 'a þynge fulle softely what euer hyt were' (1,182). Here there is no mentioning of an evil spirit or a fairy, rather the redactor states that it was 'a yonge mayde' (1,193) and then goes on to declare: 'the story in frensche, þer shalle he se / She was a laydy of grette degre, / That homely to hyr owne bedde come' (1,194–6). This minor narratorial addition radically changes the positioning of the reader within the narrative framework. Rather than being subject to the gradual elucidation of the visitor's identity along with the protagonist, the narrator here interposes to declare not only her identity, but also to point out his engagement with his source text. The audience is thus posed on the side of the narrator, who possesses information that the protagonist himself does not possess and which will, moreover, be revealed in the French text in due course, as the narrator indicates.

The following interpolation by the English redactor, which occurs prior to

---

[56] The English translator makes some minor changes to his source throughout the text that cannot all be listed here. There is some general reduction in narratorial intrusion and deliberations on love along with some minor additions. Apart from these it is apparent that the redactor worked directly from a manuscript copy of the French text.

[57] The English redactor also makes some minor additions that assert what is simply hinted at or left unsaid in the French text. Once Partonope sees the ship arrive, for example, he declares: 'Thys ys a Shyppe of ffayre' (743), alluding to what is later to come. There is, conversely, no mentioning of 'fairy' in the French text in connection with the boat, which remains simply a mysterious means of transportation to the magical realm across the sea (see lines 729–63).

the actual seduction, shows a deliberate and conscious interaction with the source material by the redactor:

> A-shamed she ys for wommanhede,
> Thynkenge þat she haþe in here bedde
> A lusty man, and she I-wys
> Wettynge welle a mayde she ys,
> Here maydenhode so yonge forto lese.   (Long 1,214–18)

He ascribes an inner feeling to Melior as she lies in bed, which goes directly against the mode of focalisation in the French source, where she is perceived through Partonopeu, and this sense is transmitted solely through her touch and her voice. The attribution of shame to Melior indicates a lack of active involvement by her in the arrival of Partonope in her maiden bed. The fact that the redactor interposes his own meditations at this point indicates that he may possibly have had some moral misgivings about what is to come and sought to minimise the moral culpability of both of his protagonists by explaining and rationalising how these two young people could have found themselves in such an unseemly situation. These deliberations similarly hint at the narrator's own preoccupation with female sexuality and with the part played by women in sexual encounters. It is, however, made clear that it is in fact Melior herself who has brought herself into this situation, whether she is at this point pleased with it or not, and the narrator is clear about his own opinion of this female folly:

> Supposyng welle she may not chese,
> As she þat had in soche plychte
> Here-selfe broghte; for alle here delyte
> And all here plesaunce was hym to haue
> To here husbande, and so to saue
> Here worshyppe; for fully þys was her þo3te.
>   (Long 1,219–24)

After the appropriate deliberations on Melior's lack of prudence in bringing herself into such a situation, the narrator returns to his source:

> Ther-fore fully I me purpose
> After myn auctor to make an ende.
> Thy[s] fayre lady þat was so hende,
> Streyghte forþe here legge, *and* happed to ffele,
> Trewly þe ffrenshe boke seyeth þe hele.   (Long 1,295–9)

The double reference to the source shifts the authorial responsibility onto the French text at this delicate moment. The narrator then makes a second significant departure from his source by relating her identity before the actual sexual consummation has taken place, declaring her to be 'quene *and* lady of þys londe' (1,329). This revelation of her identity prior to the sexual act alters the established relationship between the two. In the French text, both Partonopeu and the audience are unaware of the identity of the mystery lady that has come to him. Moreover, the multiple references to 'maufé' (demon) and 'fée' (fairy), both in the seduction scene itself and later by his mother when she hears of the relationship, underscore the sense of the supernatural and Melior's fairy-like attributes. Partonopeu himself refers to the unknown creature as 'maufé' twice (1,124, 1,131) and the narrator subsequently states that it is 'une fee' (a fairy) that has come to the bed (1,125). His mother similarly alludes to her son's lover as a demon when telling the king about Partonopeu's affair and states that as he was lost in the forest 'uns dïables a soi le traist; / en sanblant de feme se mist' (3,936, 3,946–7) (he was approached by a demon, who assumed the shape of a woman). In the English text, it is only Partonope's mother who later refers to 'deuyllys Enchauntemente' (long 5,056), and there is no mention of the supernatural in the bed scene itself.

There thus appears to be a reduction in the sense of magic about Melior in the English text that becomes even more apparent in the Norse text, where much of the fairy-like qualities have disappeared and Melior assumes more human characteristics. While the English text retains much of the folklore and fairy connections there seems to be an effort at rationalising the events that is consistent with the pattern of modifications observable in many of the other Middle English romance translations.[58] This shift not only implicates the reader in the scheme, but significantly alters the impression of the sexual conquest. In Kay's construing of a transgressive love affair between an older woman and a minor in the French text, it is vital that the revelation of her identity and motives take place afterwards.[59] There it serves to justify the act by recounting the basic causes for both the 'abduction' (Melior fell in love with Partonopeu) and the necessary wait (he is still too young for them to marry). This emphasis on love in the French text is significantly reduced in the English, thus curtailing the impact of love as the underlying motive. Similarly, the modification of Partonope's age removes the *raison d'être* for the entire scheme, that is that they must wait until Partonope reaches the age (and experience) to form a suitable marital candidate for the queen of Constantinople. The disclosure before the act thus changes the audience's perception of both the act itself and the characters engaged in it. It similarly moves it conceptually closer to the shorter fragmented version, where the reader is complicit from the beginning. The shift, in focalisation as well as in narrative order, removes the sense of mystery and deprives the audience of the stance of objectivity made possible through the mode of focalisation in the French text. Instead, the audience is made complicit in the scene, thereby engaging their pre-existing moral values in judgements of gendered culpability and accountability.

---

[58] This tendency to rationalise becomes even more evident in the Norse text, where the translator makes every effort to validate her supernatural skills by explaining that 'hon kvnni svo vel stiǫrnvbok at hon matti því til leidar koma sem sv list ma efla' (A 2) (she knew the book of astrology so well that she could bring about that which that art can accomplish) (130). The Norse redactor moreover makes clear that when she goes to France to see Partalopi for herself she did so 'med lærdoms prettvm ok velvm stiǫrnv bokar' (A 6–7) (by means of tricks of learning and devices of the astrology book) (133), thereby clarifying the mystery of her magical travel.

[59] *Courtly Contradictions*, 281.

The sexual consummation itself is described much in the same manner as in the French text.[60] After the alternations between her ordering him from her bed and his pleading for her mercy, she ultimately turns from him, as in the French text. He subsequently puts his arms around her, at which point she again orders him to let her be. This is then followed by the sexual conquest:

> And w*yth* þ*at* worde a-none ganne he
> In hys armes her fast to hy*m* brase.
> And fulle softely þen she sayde: 'Allas!'
> And her legges sho gan to knytte,
> And w*yth* hys knees he gan hem on-shote.
> And þ*er*-w*yth* all she sayde: 'Syr, mercy!'
> He wolde not lefe ne be þ*er*-by;
> For of her wordes toke he no hede;
> But þys a-way her maydenhede
> Haþe he þen rafte, *and* geffe her hys.
>   (Long 1,562–71)[61]

It is not until after the fact that the English Melior seems much more distressed by the event than her French counterpart. In the French text Melior announces that she is, in the appropriate maidenly fashion, affronted by Partonopeu's behaviour – which leads directly to the explanation of her identity (already established in the English text). It is not so much the act itself that is the source of complaint, but the behaviour traits of men and women in such a situation and his status with respect to her. The English version on the other hand depicts a much less satisfied Melior as she begins to weep and apparently mourn this unfortunate event:

> 'Ye shulde not haue had þat now ye haue.
> But welle I wotte, so Gode me safe,
> Myne a-mendes yes all I-made.'
> And w*yth* þ*at* worde she wox all sadde,
> And tenderly she gan to wepe.
> 'My sorowe,' sho sayde, 'ys not to seke.'
>   (Long 1,585–90).

While the English text thus follows the French in narrative progress prior to the seduction, inasmuch as it depicts how Melior sends for Partonope and encounters him in her bed, the reaction to the sexual act itself is rather different from the French Melior, revealing the dissimilar narrative concerns at stake.

As has been stated before, only one of the English manuscripts, Add. 35288, contains this part of the text. All the other manuscripts are defective at the beginning, and it is not until after the seduction scene that the University

---

[60] See lines 1,521–71 in the French text.
[61] The English redactor in the usual manner of directly expressing what is merely alluded to in his source replaces the symbolic rose with the more pointed 'maydenhede' as Partonope deprives Melior of her virginity (1,570–1).

College manuscript begins (the Rawl. Poet. manuscript commences with the battle with the Saracens, line 2964, while the two fragments contain text from even later in the story). Significantly, however, Add. 35288 has a curious lacuna right at this point. The text breaks off as Partonope is comforting the weeping Melior (1,598) and resumes as she is presumably telling him about the emissaries she had sent to find her a husband and how they had found him. Bödtker states in his edition of the text that there is a leaf missing in the middle.[62] When put side by side with the French text, however, there is in fact very little text missing. When compared with the last line before the lacuna and the first line after the lacuna that directly matches the French text there are only about 45 lines missing from the French text, hardly enough to fill an entire leaf.[63] Given that the English redactor has already explained who Melior is, there would seem to be even less need for additional text.[64] One might therefore assume that the missing leaf contained part of the equivalent lines in the French text along with some additional material that would have filled up the remainder of the leaf.

There is, however, an additional fact about the manuscript that makes the lacuna all the more intriguing. The text leading up to the lacuna, including the seduction scene, is written on vellum, whereas the remainder of the manuscript, with a new quire beginning after the lacuna, is written on paper. The collation of vellum and paper in one manuscript, while not unheard of in English medieval manuscripts, is unusual, and its incongruity is amplified by the fact of the lacuna. The hand of both parts appears to be the same, excluding the possibility of a later scribe having added text to an existing copy. The curious collation does invite the possibility, nevertheless, that the two parts of the manuscript may originally have been separate texts (one written on vellum, the other on paper), perhaps in a commercial scriptorium, which were put together for a patron.[65] They obviously contained the same story and the absence of the missing leaf may thus be due to the fact that it contained text that either overlapped with, or was of a different nature from, the resuming

---

[62] *The Middle-English Versions of Partonope of Blois*, 43.

[63] The relevant lines are 1,580 and 1,603 in the English text, which are the direct verbal translation of lines 1,312 and 1,357 in the French text. There are notably twenty-three additional lines in the English text between the lines mentioned which do not directly match the French text, although they contain similar material, that is, the complaint of Melior, which if taken into account reduces the number of missing lines even further.

[64] Melior has already declared to Partonope that she is 'queen *and* lady of þys londe' (1,329), thereby further reducing the necessity of such elaborations on her identity, except perhaps with respect to the extent of her rule, which, however, requires only a single line in the French text: 'tote Basence est mes empires' (1,341) (all of Byzantium is my empire).

[65] Gisela Guddat-Figge comments that the manuscript is 'unobtrusive but professional-looking' and states that it was 'probably produced in a bookshop', thus substantiating the theory that the manuscript was indeed produced for commercial purposes. This is further supported by the fact that there are three scribes responsible for the text (two northern ones and a southern one) and that the third scribe seems to have used different paper, as the watermark changes when he takes over (*Catalogue of Manuscripts Containing Middle English Romances*, 164–5). The notion of a bookshop with scribes copying the text of *Partonope of Blois* makes the theory applicable that there might originally have been two separate manuscript copies that for whatever reason were gathered in one volume and preserved in that condition.

text of the paper copy. The other part could also simply have been damaged, or missing, which would explain why the separate manuscript copies were placed together to begin with. The catchword on folio 19 verso (last vellum folio) does not match the lines on folio 20 recto (first paper folio), confirming that a leaf is indeed missing from the vellum quire.[66]

The lacuna and the interesting compilation of vellum and paper are significant here, as there is an observable narrative shift that occurs at this point. This shift is furthermore fundamentally connected to the different character representation evident in the various versions of the Partonope story. The Melior that appears after the lacuna is a self-assured, sexually demanding woman, quite different from the seemingly affronted and much-subdued Melior of the previous scene. This change in perspective is significant in connection with the Norse version, which features a figure reminiscent of this autonomous, self-possessed Melior who exerts her will. The narrative shift in the story itself thus forms a part of the *mouvance* of the romance within English literary history. While the fragment and the longer version bear witness to the active engagement with the Partonope story within possibly diverse English reading communities, the perplexing disparity between the vellum and the paper part in Add. 35288 and the fact that none of the other manuscripts contain this first half of the story might suggest further rewritings of the romance to engage the differing concerns of particular reading communities.

While this shift occurs in the French text as well, there is a difference both in effect and in degree. The focus in the French text is on the love that has captivated Melior, and she is thus portrayed, as much as Partonopeu himself, as the victim of Eros.[67] Her magical illusions are created specifically for the sake of containing and sustaining that love until it is publicly acceptable. In the English text the emphasis is less on the philosophical dilemma of love, underlined by the many narratorial intrusions in the French text on the topic of love, but rather on the authority and the command of power of Melior herself. It is in fact she who initiates and desires sexual contact at this point:

>   Offte sho was In porpose hy*m* to wake
>   To haue more plesauns of hy*m* þat ys her make.
>   Wyth hy*m* to play was all her most delyte.
>   Yette alle her luste sho woll putte In respyte.
>   She þo3te grette trauayly all þat ny3te had he;
>   Hy*m* to wake hyt had ben grette pyte.
>   (Long 1,923–8)[68]

---

[66] The vellum part of the manuscript is made up of two quires of five bifolia. The last leaf of the second quire is thus missing. The paper quires are intact (see Guddat-Figge, *Catalogue of Manuscripts Containing Middle English Romances*, 164).

[67] The multiple narratorial intrusions on the topic of love and how the lover (in this case the narrator himself) is the captive of his emotions for the beloved support the notion of love being the underlying motivation rather than sexual gratification. Sexual pleasure is directly linked with the concept of love and thus exists because of it.

[68] The corresponding passage in the French text is somewhat more subdued; the minor addition of 'lust' in the English translation shifts the focus of the scene from a natural expression of love to the physical gratification of bodily desires (1,577–80).

Here it is Partonope who is sleeping, out of sheer exhaustion it seems, and Melior who is observing him, with pleasure and desire, imagining the delights she might have with him.[69] The traditional masculine gaze that objectifies the female body is here appropriated by the female herself and directed at the unknowing sleeping body of Partonope. She is no longer the object of his desires, as in the prior seduction scene, where he is presented as the masculine aggressor overcoming his feminine object. Partonope is sleeping, making him both passive and vulnerable. She is the one awake, watching him and envisioning the physical pleasures she might enjoy with him. Melior must in fact contain her 'luste' to allow her poor lover to rest.[70]

This depiction reverses the traditional portrayal of desire in courtly literature. The representation of the French narrator as a lover, who is himself (in opposition to Partonopeu) restrained by the physical inaccessibility of the object of his love, draws attention to the underlying cultural context of courtly love. Joan M. Ferrante comments on the role played by women in the courtly literature of the twelfth century: 'They function . . . primarily as the inspiration of the male poet, lover, or hero, and they are usually presented as projections of the male ideal or the male fantasy.'[71] In the English text this mode of representation is sustained in the first half, but in effect reversed in the second, where she is no longer a projection of his fantasy, as they have already consummated their love. Moreover, the scene inverts the agency of desire and visualisation, as he is asleep and she is the one projecting her own subjective physical longings upon his 'absent' body.

The somewhat surprising correlation between the Norse *Marmoria* and some aspects of the English *Melior* raises questions of textual transmission and cultural appeal. While the longer English version is obviously a translation of the French text, the subtle reorganisation of some narrative units and the shift in character portrayal indicates the adaptation of the French material to its new reading community. The depiction of the seduction scene directly relates to a larger and more complex question of the engagement with the framework of meaning of the source text by the redactor. This becomes particularly evident in the diverse narrative representations of the scene of the sexual consummation. There is a distinct move away from the courtly context of the French text in the translations to incorporate the ideological values of

[69] While the text faithfully recites passages in the French text that deal with the sexual pleasure of the couple, it is apparent in the way in which the translator shapes these passages that the signifying framework to which he is referring is of a different nature from that of the French text. While the love-making of the French Melior is to a certain extent the natural result of the previously inspired love she had felt for his image, in the English text both the narrator and his characters seem to have some ambivalent reactions to the seduction itself. This leads to some perplexing multiplicity in the portrayal of Melior, which is of significance when the text is considered in the context of textual transmission of the romance and the impact of cultural reception.
[70] For a comparison of the moral portrayals of Melior in the French and English text see Brenda Hosington 'Voices of Protest and Submission: Portraits of Women in *Partonopeu de Blois* and its Middle English Translation', *Reading Medieval Studies* 17 (1991), 51–75.
[71] 'Male Fantasy and Female Reality in Courtly Literature', *Women's Studies* 11 (1984), 67–97, at 67.

their new reading communities. This is most notable in the Norse text, where it is no longer a question of two children coming together innocently (as in the English fragment), or the illicit love affair between a woman and an adolescent (as in the French text), or the sexual conquest of a woman (depicted in the longer English version), but rather the mutual gratification of equal individuals. The cultural adaptation that has occurred in the translation process thus becomes apparent in the character portrayal, and in the representation of gender roles, social obligations and behaviour. The extant texts are in fact the different productions of the story in its various contexts.

Gender Roles and Power

The existence of both versions in English raises some interesting questions as to paths of transmission and modes of textual reconstruction within specific reading communities. The distinct differences, thematic and representational, between the English fragment and the Norse text indicate that they served a different purpose, and the texts therefore show signs of the material having been modified to accommodate new functions, despite their belonging to the same textual family. The somewhat minor structural change made by the English redactor of the longer version in shifting the revelation of Melior's identity to before the seduction itself shows a distinct deviation from the French source, that is similarly reflected in the Norse version. This modification is in turn intertwined with the perplexing shift in Melior's personality. The reworking of the ideologically based content of the text shows the adaptation of the text to its new English reading community, reflected most strongly in the representation of gender roles and notions of power.

Roberta L. Krueger points out that 'notions of idealized "masculine" and "feminine" comportments were so forcefully articulated in medieval romance and didactic literature that their outlines survived well beyond the Victorian age'.[72] Yet she also notes that the romances often 'opened up discursive space where gender roles were scrutinized and where underlying social and sexual tensions were explored'.[73] The romance as a genre thus in a sense prescribed gendered behavioural codes within courtly society, while it simultaneously provided the means of questioning such gender constructions.[74]

---

[72] 'Question of Gender in Old French Courtly Romance', in *The Cambridge Companion to Medieval Romance*, ed. Roberta L. Krueger (Cambridge: Cambridge University Press, 2000), 132–49, at 132.
[73] Ibid. 132.
[74] Much work has been done recently on gender roles in both the French *Partonopeu de Blois* and its English translation. For critical work on the former see Matilda Tomaryn Bruckner, 'The Interplay of Gender and Genres in *Partonopeu de Blois*', in her *Shaping Romance. Interpretation, Truth, and Closure in Twelfth-Century French Fictions* (Philadelphia: University of Pennsylvania Press, 1993), 109–56; Eley and Simons, '*Partonopeus de Blois* and Chrétien de Troyes'; and Penny Simons and Penny Eley, 'Male Beauty and Sexual Orientation in *Partonopeus de Blois*', *Romance Studies* 17 (1999), 41–56. For a discussion of gender in the Middle English translation see Gretchen Mieszkowski, 'Urake and the Gender Roles of *Partonope of Blois*', *Mediaevalia* 25 (2004), 181–96; Hosington, 'Voices of Protest and

The depiction of the destabilisation of gender-constructed social barriers provided an opportunity to reflect on the status of women.[75] The autonomy and self-government denied historical women in the Middle Ages becomes a major theme in the Partonope story, and one that is approached from different angles in all the various versions discussed here.

The subtle modifications apparent in the longer English version regarding Partonope's age and the ambiguous seduction scene has left the English redactor with a dilemma that is absent from his French source, that is how to justify his female protagonist's appropriation of power and pleasure, traditionally reserved for men. While Melior is admittedly royal, and thus automatically in possession of power, the insistence by her advisor that she be married indicates that a female rule is not an acceptable long-term option and that a husband must be found to replace her as the dominant force in the kingdom. Similarly, her fairy-like features seem to indicate that she exists outside the traditional social boundaries of ethical and moral behaviour. Yet the reaction of her court once the spell is broken and Partonopeu becomes visible to the inhabitants of the castle shows that, as Sarah Kay has pointed out, the relationship is indeed perceived as socially transgressive. By removing the need for the postponement of the nuptials (due to Partonope's youth) the balance of power in the relationships is shifted. It is no longer a question of an adolescent that must mature before he can take on his rightful position as commander as in the French text. At eighteen years of age, Partonope should rightfully be able to assume that authority.

The problem of gender and authority is thus much more conspicuous in the English text. It is also directly linked with the public and private realm. In her bedchamber, Melior is not subject to the social rules that exist outside of this private domain. Once Partonope is brought into her chamber, he is also removed from the gendered behavioural patterns and hierarchies. It is of significance within the textual realm that his mother is appalled when she hears of his love-affair, as it contravenes in her eyes all established social rules of male and female interactions:

> He made wyth hyr covenaunte
> To be hyr loue *and* hyr seruante.
> He louethe * hyr beste of any creature.
> Yette of hur persone, shappe, ne fygure,
> Wyth hys eyen he neuer [had] syghte trewly.
> Þys ys, me þynketh, a mervelowse ffoly.   (Long 5,080–5)

Submission'; and Amy N. Vines, 'A Woman's "Crafte": Melior as Lover, Teacher, and Patron in the Middle English Partonope of Blois', *Modern Philology* 105 (2007), 245–70.

[75] Noblewomen formed an important part of the audience of courtly literature in Anglo-Norman and northern French courts from the twelfth century onwards. While there are no extensive records of women writers (although to what extent they did compose poetry is perhaps unknown), aristocratic women figure prominently as readers and patrons of lyric and narrative poetry (see Krueger, 'Question of Gender in Old French Courtly Romance', 133–5). The preservation of texts written by elite women shows that they were in fact literate and took part in the tradition of the courtly romance.

She makes it clear that Partonope has been tricked into a 'covenaunte' that goes against social customs, as he has not even seen his beloved. The conventional procedure of both courtly love and medieval marital agreements has thus been breached. Her solution is to provide him with a socially acceptable alternative, the king's niece, and thereby re-establish both his senses and the proper order of gendered relations within the world of the romance.

The narrative plays on this movement between the public and private realm and the conflicting notion of identities that each space allows and accepts. The text emphasises the ambivalence of the correlation between space, the authority inherent in that space and the concept of privacy.[76] Melior appropriates the power that is intrinsic to her royal chamber as the symbol of the authority of the throne. She uses that power, however, to negotiate a private space that is denied her by the public office of her position. The royal chamber, which functions as the source of her power, ironically becomes her private space of desire and love, the two concepts historically denied a woman in her position.[77]

It is significant that when Partonope enters the realm of her private desires he is invisible to the people in the city and he himself cannot see anyone. The magical domain is thus directly connected with a private space that is removed from social obligations and constraints. In this realm, Melior is in full control and Partonope must bow to her authority and more importantly to her desires. Most significantly he is unable to see her, which removes the appropriating and objectifying power of the male gaze. A. C. Spearing considers sight to be in its essence masculine, as it is 'usually conceptualized as penetrative and dominating'.[78] While sight in the medieval period was considered to be a physiological capacity, directly related to the capacity to fall in love (which occurred as the image of the loved one penetrated through the eyes) and hence attributable to both men and women, courtly literature tends to reserve such visual penetrations for their male characters.[79] The lady is thus, at least at the beginning, a passive agent and one that is subject to the gaze of her male lover.[80]

---

[76] For information on the changing notion of 'chamber' itself in the late twelfth century and its connection to the conception of private and public see *A History of Private Life*, ed. Georges Duby, trans. Arthur Goldhammer, vol. 2, *Revelations of the Medieval World* (Cambridge: The Belknap Press of Harvard University Press, 1988), particularly 60–8, 323–32, 408–23.

[77] While the courtly romances elevate the concept of love and desire, the reality of aristocratic women was something entirely different. Their marital prospects were based on political liaisons and agreements and had little to do with personal choice or emotions. In fact, feminine desire was a particular threat to the throne as it could endanger the bloodline. Royal daughters and wives were thus less in possession of their own bodies than women of the lower social classes, as their position enforced upon them a public function that further limited their selfhood, despite the apparent impressions of power and privilege.

[78] '*Partonope of Blois*', in his *The Medieval Poet as Voyeur* (Cambridge: Cambridge University Press, 1993), 140–54, at 145.

[79] In *Yvain*, for instance, it is the sight of Laudine that causes Yvain to fall in love with her. He is, in fact, literally struck by the vision of her (by the arrows of Eros), while she, on the other hand, falls in love with the idea of him before she has ever even laid eyes on him.

[80] Michael Camille comments on the predominance of the gender delineations where

This process is reversed in the Partonope story, where it is in fact Melior who falls in love with Partonopeu's image. The text additionally plays on the interrelation of the visual and the aural in the passage, as Partonopeu is unable to *see* her and only *hears* her (while she has already seen him, as we find out later). The apparent irregularity of this is signalled in the English text by his mother's words that 'Yette of hur pe*r*sone, shappe, ne fygure, / Wy*th* h*y*s eyen he neu*er* [had] syghte trewly. / Þys ys, me þynketh, a m*er*velowse ffoly' (5,083–5), which implies the significance of vision (and more importantly 'hys' vision) for such a process to take place. Spearing in fact notes that the 'English redactor of *Partonope of Blois* intensifies the sensory effects already present in the French' (145), suggesting the intentional emphasis of the implications of sight (or lack of it) in the passage and the shift in meaning of the seduction scene itself from the French to the English text.

Partonope is thus deprived of the control inherent in the nature of masculine visualisation and observation of the female body. He must re-establish his masculine identity through the re-appropriation of control and it can only be done by shattering the illusion of a private realm created by Melior. Claire M. Jackson associates the female body with the city in *Partonope of Blois*, stating that 'from the beginning Melior is inextricably linked with her setting'.[81] The figurative space created by Melior can thus be seen as a reflection of her interior – a realm of desire that is protected from societal control precisely because it is invisible to the members of that society, that is her own people. With the collapse of the spell the city is metamorphosed and becomes simply an ordinary city, bound by the common social codes of communal life, just as Melior becomes a mortal woman restricted by those very same codes. Despite her royal status she is accountable for her behaviour to her people, and, in fact, less in possession of her selfhood and the privacy implicit in that selfhood because of her public role.

Melior's own words, spoken after Partonope has broken his promise, illustrate the collapse of the division between her public reputation and her private world in which she is free to make use of her conventionally masculine skills and powers: 'My shame þe*n* shall I se *opynly*, / That haþe be hyd full *preuely* / þorowe my connynge *and* my scyence' (long 5,988–90, my italics). She distinguishes between what will be perceived publicly, that is 'opynly', and what she can do as long as it is hidden and 'preuely', indicating that the two

---

women tend to be the objects of the male gaze both in medieval literature and art, but notes additionally that there is an apparent shift in the late fourteenth century, when the male body comes to be eroticised for the first time. Yet while the female body is presented as naked and open to this masculine gaze, the male body is 'all surface . . . surrounded by and protected by armor and heraldry that announces its strength and impenetrability' (*The Medieval Art of Love. Objects and Subjects of Desire*, New York: Harry N. Abrams, 1998, 34–40, at 35). The naked, vulnerable body of Partonope in the previous scene is thus feminised as the object of Melior's erotic gaze, despite the apparent instability of the power inherent in visualisation and subject–object relations.

[81] Jackson argues that Melior and her city are 'interdependent and inseparable' and that the romance explores Melior's relationship with Partonope through the portrayal of space, hence the connection between Melior's body and her city ('The City as Two-Way Mirror in the Middle English *Partonope of Blois*', *Mediaevalia* 25 (2004), 197–208, at 198–9).

realms represent on the one hand the social constraints of public opinion and on the other the freedom of personal will and lack of gendered constraints. The emphasis on '*my* connynge and *my* scyence' reveals the conscious separation of her private space, where she is free to exercise her will and knowledge, and the public space, where it will only bring her shame.[82]

Partonope must thus erase the distinction to force her to assume her female role. To do so he must shatter her illusion, but he is unable to do it while under her command. The paradox of his apparent subservience to her power and the necessity of reinstating gendered hierarchy draws attention to the inherent contradiction between women's position within the fictional realm of the romance and the reality of courtly life. On the one hand, they are the venerated objects of the knight's love and fully in possession of power over him, yet within the actual social structures their authority over themselves is severely limited and dependent on the dictates of their husbands or fathers. It is of significance that it is Partonope's mother and the bishop who bring about the collapse of the magical realm and thus force Melior to adapt her public role as an inner one as well. The Church here is, of course, aligned with the patriarchal order and serves a fundamental role in preserving and instituting gender structures and hierarchy.[83] His mother signifies the appropriate female role and position in society and hence serves as the instrument to guide Partonope in the effort to regain his masculine position.[84] Significantly

---

[82] Sarah Kay proposes that the empty city is in fact 'the realm of the dead' as the name, Chef d'Oire, could also mean 'journey's end'. This, she claims, is supported by the play on the words *oirre* (journey), *Loire* (4,123–4), and *l'Oirre*, which indicate the connections between the two worlds. The apparent invisibility of the inhabitants of Blois to Chef d'Oire and vice versa thus signals the movement between the two realms, where figures either appear or disappear as they cross the water (*Courtly Contradictions* 275–9, at 276). Kay's convincing reading of the inhabitants of the city as 'dead', however, does not take into account the fact that Partonopeu has been transplanted into a foreign city, amidst people presumably speaking a foreign tongue. He is therefore not surrounded by the 'dead', but rather an unfamiliar and incomprehensible 'other'. He might as well, in fact, be invisible to the inhabitants in view of his inability to communicate or otherwise engage with this community of 'others' in which he finds himself. The word *oire* could, however, also be a play on *oir* (to hear), especially given the emphasis on the aural over the visual in the magical city. This interpretation is supported by the foregrounding of sensory effects and hearing in the descriptions of Partonopeu's experiences in Chef d'Oire. The English text faithfully translates the name as 'Chyffe De Oyre' (2,158) ('Chief doire' in the University College MS), but the act of linguistic transfer removes the symbolic connotations attached to the name in the French text. Similarly the shift in attention from Melior's supernatural elements in the French text to her function within the social fabric in the English indicates a redirection of the narrative focus from the marvellous to the social implications of the relationship. This is even more pronounced in the Norse text, where the mystical has been completely subsumed by the exploration of authority and dominion and gendered balance.

[83] Despite the role of the Church in the twelfth century in instituting a more mutual marriage through advocating the necessity of female consent, its tenets are nevertheless fundamentally traditional in the sense that the Church requires the conformity to certain social structures (such as marriage, hierarchy, etc.) for the perpetuation of its doctrine within those social structures.

[84] It is of note here that in the Icelandic text it is no longer the mother who acts as the corrective agent, but rather Partalopi's father, the king of France. Moreover, the bishop is

the spell is broken by sight. By re-appropriating his privilege of the male gaze he is able to shatter the illusion that separated the private from the public, re-establish her as a female body (quite literally) and enforce the social coding of gendered behaviour:

> Hys launterne he pute vp wyth hys lyghte.
> Alle naked þer had he þe syghte
> Off þe ffeyrest shape creature
> That euer was formed þorowe nature.
> When þys lady dyd þys a-spye,
> On hym she caste a pytuos eye,
> and sowned wyth a dedely chere. (Long 5,862–8)

By the simple act of shining a lantern on her body and thus exposing her to his gaze she is robbed of the control she has hitherto had both over him and over her own body.

While the act of exposing the unknown lover by means of a lantern reflects the underlying mythological story of Cupid and Psyche it assumes here a different function and new connotations. Psyche disobeys her unknown lover for fear that he will devour her, and her action is brought about by her own innocence and her sisters' jealousy.[85] Partonopeu, on the other hand, is giving in to the dictates of his mother and the bishop. He is assuming control that, as his mother's words indicate, is rightfully his. His is not an act of innocence, but rather a correction of a presumed imbalance of authority in the relationship, where he, as her lover, has a right and duty to *see* his beloved. Psyche, on the other hand, acts out of fear for her life and that of her unborn child and the intention is not to re-establish the balance of power, but to kill a monster before it has a chance to kill her.[86] The text thus not only reverses the gender structures of the lovers, but it additionally shifts the focus from the play on immortal power and female innocence of the mythical story to the questioning of gendered patterns

---

depicted as Partalopi's maternal uncle, thereby making it a familial affair, rather than a social concern symbolised by the ecclesiastic figure of the bishop in the English text.

[85] Psyche's sisters warn her that she is sharing her bed with 'an immense serpent, writhing its manifold coils, its bloody jaws dripping deadly poison, its maw gaping deep' (Apuleius, *Cupid and Psyche*, 69). The text foregrounds the fact that Psyche is naive and states that 'poor Psyche, simple and immature creature that she was, was seized by fear at these grim words' and in fear of her life brings the lamp and a sharp blade to sever the serpent's throat only to find out as she shines the light on her sleeping lover, that her husband is no monster, but the deity Cupid (71–5).

[86] It is significant here that while Partonopeu is in France when the discussion with his mother and the bishop takes place, Psyche is in the mysterious realm of her husband and apparently unable to leave. While she is thus in his power, both literally and figuratively, Partonopeu is absent from the magical domain of his beloved and in no danger for his life. He in fact returns to Melior out of love (and perhaps to keep his promise in the English text). While the impulse behind the lantern scene in the Cupid story is one of feminine naïveté and fear, it becomes more complex in *Partonopeu*. The travel between the magical city and his motherland draws attention to the movement between the familiar and the unfamiliar; the established social structures of the kingdom of France and the threatening reversion of those structures by the 'other' that is absent in the myth.

of behaviour and the notion of feminine sovereignty.

As soon as Partonope has betrayed Melior's command and hence forced her to assume her feminine role she does so in an appropriately conventional manner and swoons. As she laments her fate her speech slowly becomes imbued with the socially coded conventions and the consequences of her breach of those conventions:

> Fo[r] to se me oponly;
> And nowe shull they knowe a-pertely
> þat I haue kepte yowe for my loue.
> Allas! wyche shame *and* wyche reproue
> Ye shalle þen be to me,
> And yette I telle yowe trewly þat ye
> Haue do worse to me þen all thys:
> Ye haue rafte me my wordely blys,
> My maydenhode, my honowre, *and* my name,
> My Ioye, my boldenes, *and* all my game.
> (Long 6,038–47)

She oscillates in her lament between the regret for the loss of her authority and the shame she will be subjected to as a result of the exposure. This move between social opinion and her own thoughts in her speech indicates that the two realms have begun to merge. The loss of the bliss of their secret relationship is juxtaposed with 'my maydenhode, my honowre, and my name', which is then again followed by her love, her boldness (as in freedom of behaviour) and her game (presumably the entire scheme). She voices the judgement of society, while simultaneously mourning the loss of her previous privilege and freedom. She is thus robbed not only of her public position, but also of the interior space, the magic realm created to satisfy her private desires, where the crossing of gender-coded rules of behaviour could take place.

The text subsequently plays on the subtle references to 'man' and 'womanhede' in order to explore the notion of masculine and feminine behaviour until appropriate gender constructions can be re-established at the end, where Partonope assumes his masculine authoritative position as husband and hence ruler of what had previously been Melior's kingdom. As becomes apparent in the Norse text, the positions of an emperor and his empress are not equal. While Melior is in power as the empress prior to her wedding, she is so only until she is married off, at which point she must delegate the authority to her husband as her rightful superior. Once she relinquishes her status as sole empress, she is subject to Partonope, sharing her kingdom with an emperor. While she retains her position of power as empress (and Byzantium admittedly had its share of strong empresses), that power is nevertheless secondary to that of her husband by virtue of the gender codes depicted and reinforced in the text itself.

The move from private to public and social coding in the long English version is noticeably absent in *Partalopa saga*. The use of narrative focalisation and structuring in the Icelandic version moves the emphasis away from this notion of private and public realms that delineates the gender barriers and the societal codes of conduct of the English text. By focusing on Melior as the protagonist from the beginning, her autonomy is foregrounded irrespective of such demarcations of public and private behaviour. The narrative thus becomes less about establishing and correcting the gendered roles of the protagonists and more about finding the equilibrium of evenly matched individuals who in a union form a stronger unit than they would have done separately. Partalopi must in fact prove himself to be not only a man, but a man worthy of conquering Marmoria and hence assuming her hand in marriage.

While the only significant difference between the two versions of the Partonope story is in the way in which the romance begins, this seemingly insignificant narrative reorganisation has a profound effect upon the representational impression and character construction, which completely changes the way in which the audience is made to engage with the text. The narrative reconfiguration therefore has a deep impact upon each version's potential to convey meaning. It similarly influences the ideological framework of character portrayal. As the cultural structures that dictated the pattern of meaning of the French text are either non-existent or non-applicable to their new reading communities, the translators must reconstruct the narrative material in a manner that is both relevant and comprehensible to its new audience. The shift in textual perception by the translator and his presumed public thus guides the translation process and reconstruction of the text and thereby incorporates the redactor's conceptualisation of his source text as well as of his intended public. While the short English version is based, for instance, on the same narrative structure as the Norse text, it is in fact conceptually closer to the French original, as it retains the sense of Partonope's youth and innocence and the fairy-like qualities of Melior. The longer English version is, on the other hand, obviously a translation of a French source, but shows some deliberate reworking and modifications that shift the foundation of the text's meaning. Some of those textual moves are in fact captured and expanded in the Norse text.

The Norse text exhibits the profound impact of cultural transmission, as it contains and presents all the narrative elements present in the French text, but in a manner that has transformed the story into something quite different. Any political subtext and allusions to social expectations of sexual behaviour have vanished in the journey from the original twelfth-century French context to fourteenth-century Icelandic society. What we have instead is an exploration of female independence, a battle of the sexes in a sense, that is brought to a satisfying conclusion in the final marriage of Marmoria and Partalopi.[87]

---

[87] Most of the French manuscripts describe a single wedding (that of Partonope and Melior), which is then followed by a continuation of the narrative (which is not apparent in any of the translations and hence will not be addressed here). MS Arsenal 2986 in Bibliothèque de l'Arsenal in Paris (MS A) describes a triple wedding including, besides the hero and the heroine, the king of France, who marries Melior's sister Urrake, and Partonopeu's companion Gaudin, who marries Persewis (for a discussion of the variant endings of the French text see Simons and Eley, 'A Subtext and its Subversion'). The longer English version has adopted the single wedding, whereas the Icelandic one ends with a double marriage where Marmoria's sister, Urækia, marries Barbarus, Partalopi's companion. The triple wedding of the A

The difference in representation between the Old Norse and the other versions is that whereas the English and French text show the process of female subjugation through the establishment of male authority and patriarchal hierarchy, the Norse text appears to celebrate the union of two equally powerful individuals. Marmoria can succumb in marriage to Partalopi only because he has proven himself to be *as worthy* of his position as she is of hers. He does not replace her, but rather complements her existing power and authority.

The English text reveals, on the other hand, contemporary social anxieties about female consent and gendered power dynamics that are played out in the longer version. The existence of the two versions within England in the fifteenth century and the conflicting narrative strains contained within the manuscript copies of the longer version similarly suggest the sometimes contradictory influences of local textual communities versus those of the larger linguistic and cultural community within which authors and their audiences co-exist. The multitude of cultural interpretations therefore reveals the multiple layers of signification inherent in the romance of Partonopeu. Each textual community thus recaptures, repeats and rewrites the story to reflect the uniquely culturally determined concerns of its author and his readers, which ultimately reveals the profound impact of cultural context in the textual transmission of narrative material.

---

manuscript of the French text indicates a socially acceptable conclusion within Francophone context, where the king of France is given his due through the marriage to Melior's sister. Owing to the abridged nature of the Icelandic version and the lack of a comparable political context connected to the figure of the French king, the relationship is shifted to the more prominent figures of Urækia and Barbarus. It is unclear what resolution the English fragment had to the story as the ending has not been preserved.

Appendix

Summaries of the Versions of *Partonopeu de Blois*

Old French version
(Based on the outline in Gildea's edition)

Long English version

1. Introduction

(Lines 1–134)
The author will write the story for the benefit and entertainment of his reader.

(Lines 1–71)
The author states the reader will find many marvels in his story.

2. Genealogy

(135–498)
Describes how Marcomiris, the youngest son of Priam, escapes to France at the end of the Trojan war. His descendants become the royal line of France. Clovis, the king of France, has a favourite nephew by the name of Partonopeus de Blois.

(72–522)
Tells of Priam, Marcomiris, and the battle of Troy. Marcomiris goes to France and his descendants become kings of France. Clovis, the king of France, has a favourite nephew by the name of Partonope of Blois.

1. Introduction of Melior

2. Introduction of Partonope

3. Hunting scene

(499–1062)
During a hunt in the Ardennes with his uncle, Partonopeu pursues a boar and is lost in the forest. He wanders through the night until he arrives at the sea where he sees a boat guided by unseen hands that carries him to a magical city, Chief d'Oire. He finds no living being and proceeds to a castle, where he is served food by invisible servants. He is led to a bedchamber by torches.

(523–1128)
Partonope goes hunting with his uncle in the Ardennes. He pursues a boar and is lost in the forest. He wanders through the forest that night and the following day until he arrives at the sea, where a boat guided by unseen hands carries him to a magical city. He sees no one and proceeds to a castle, where he is served food by invisible servants. He is led to a bedchamber by torches.

Versions of 'Partonopeu de Blois'

Short English version	Old Norse version
	(The outline is based on chapter divisions in the Icelandic manuscripts, but owing to inconsistencies between the manuscripts some deviations will occur in an effort to accommodate the outline to the other texts.)
(Lines 1–52) A noble king dies, leaving his two daughters, Melior and Urake. Melior, who is both wise and skilled in magic, inherits the kingdom.	(Pages 1–4) Saragus, emperor of Constantinople, dies, leaving as heir his daughter, Marmoria, who is both wise and skilled in necromancy.
(53–96) Messengers are sent to find her a husband. Pertinope de Bloys, the nephew of the king of France, exceeds all others. Melior goes to see him herself and decides to carry him off.	(4–9) King Hlodvir, ruler of France, has a son by the name of Partalopi, who surpasses other men. Marmoria hears of this and proceeds to see for herself.
(97–208) The king and Pertinope go out hunting. Melior raises a hart by means of her magic crafts. Pertinope follows it till he comes to the sea. Melior sends a ship for him. There is no one aboard. He is carried to a magical city, where he proceeds to a castle. He is served food by invisible servants. He is then led to a bedchamber by torches.	(10–21) The king and Partalopi go hunting and during a pursuit of a boar (A)/stag (B) Partalopi is separated from the king. The boar/stag disappears. Partalopi comes to a cliff at a beach where he sits down. He sees a ship guided by unseen hands that carries him to a city. He proceeds to a castle where he is served food by invisible servants. He is then led to a bedchamber by torches.

4. *Seduction scene*

(1063–1334)

Partonopeu retires to bed. The chamber becomes dark. He is joined by a mysterious person in bed that turns out to be a woman. She orders him out of her bed and he begs for her mercy. She pities him and allows him to remain. He then subdues her and robs her of her virginity. Melior complains about men and tells him he must honour her as she is now his lover.

5. *Revelation*

(1335–1580)

Melior reveals her name, declaring that she is empress of Constantinople and that she has chosen him as her future husband, but that in view of his youth they must wait. She explains how she heard of him and visited his court unseen and caused him to be brought to her city. He is to remain with her for two and a half years until they can be married. Meanwhile he can stay with her at night and entertain himself in her kingdom during the day, unseen by the inhabitants. The only condition is that he can not see her until the time comes, when she will dub him knight and present him to her counsellors as her chosen husband.

6. *Partonopeu dwells with Melior*

(1581–1886)

Partonopeu wakes in the morning to find Melior gone. She has left him beautiful clothes. He entertains himself during the day and at night they remain together.

7. *Partonopeu returns to France*

(1887–2078)

After a year in Chief d'Oire, Partonopeu requests permission to visit France. Melior notifies him of the death of his father and of Clovis, his uncle, and grants him leave. She presents him with much wealth. He returns to France to find it under siege by 'Saracens of the North'. He recaptures castles in Blois and offers his assistance to Lohier, the young king of France.

(1129–1598)

Partonope goes to bed and the chamber becomes dark. He is joined by a mysterious person in bed that turns out to be the queen of the city. She orders him out of her bed and he begs for her mercy. She angrily declares that she is the queen of the country. She turns from him and he then subdues her and robs her of her virginity. Melior is dismayed and sorrowful to find herself in this situation.

(1599–1932)

Lacuna (shift in Add. 35288 from vellum to paper, University College 188 commences). Melior recounts how her envoys told her of Partonope and how she went to France herself to see him. She made him follow the boar and brought him to her city. Partonope warns her against jealousy. He wants to see her, but is not allowed until a year and a half has passed, at which time they will be married. He will remain with her at night and during the day he can entertain himself in her kingdom, unseen by the inhabitants, but he must not try to see her. They can have the pleasure they want from each other.

(1933–2351)

Partonope wakes in the morning to find Melior gone. She has left him beautiful clothes. He entertains himself during the day and at night they remain together.

(2352–2655)

After a year has passed, Partonope requests leave to visit France. Melior grants him leave and tells him that his father and Clovis, his uncle, are dead and that enemies have invaded France. She reminds him of his promise. He returns to Blois with much gold from her. Partonope recaptures his mother's castles and offers his assistance to the king of France.

(209–44)
Pertinope goes to bed and is joined by a lady. She orders him to leave and he begs her to have mercy on him. He embraces her and they consummate their love. She embraces him with love.

(21–33)
Partalopi retires and the chamber becomes dark. He is joined by a maiden. He puts his arms around her and she declares that she is the queen of the city and of many lands. He refuses to leave her bed and claims he was brought there through her schemes and that he will rather die defending himself than flee before her knights. She admires his courage and they spend the night in pleasure.

(245–76)
Melior reveals that she brought him to her by means of magic. He is not to see her until twelve months have passed. If he does as she says he will have riches and pleasures.

(33–7)
Partalopi wakes in the morning to find Marmoria gone. She has left him beautiful clothes. He entertains himself during the day and at night they remain together.

(37–43)
Marmoria tells him that Markauld (A)/ Mannhaulld (B), king of Bretons, has besieged his father's kingdom and that he should return to assist him. She tells him to challenge the king to a dual for the kingdom to prove his prowess to her. She equips him with much wealth. Partalopi returns to Paris. King Hlodvir asks his advice and Partalopi suggests a single combat.

8. Partonopeu battles with Sornegur (Markauld)
(2079–3844)

The leader of the enemies is called Sornegur. He challenges Lohier to single combat for the kingdom. Partonopeu persuades his cousin to allow him to fight Sornegur for him. The combat is long and difficult, but eventually Partonopeu is inspired by thoughts of Melior and gains advantage. Marés, Sornegur's favourite, breaches the agreement and invades the field to save his lord. A general battle ensues. Sornegur surrenders and peace is made. The 'Saracens' execute Marés for his treachery and surrender Partonopeu, who had been held captive by the traitor. The enemies return home with pledges of friendship.

(2656–4939)

The heathen kings Agisor and Sornegour have attacked the country and outnumber the French. Partonope fights the Saracen armies. The heathen kings hold council. Sornegour proposes a single battle for the kingdom. Partonope offers himself. The combat is long and difficult. Partonope is inspired by thoughts of Melior and gains advantage. Marres, Sornegour's steward, breaches the agreement and invades the field to save his lord. General battle ensues and Partonope is captured. Sornegour surrenders and peace is made. Marres is executed for his treachery and Partonope is surrendered. The enemies return home with pledges of friendship.

9. His mother's secret plan/ (father's plan)
(3845–4202)

Partonopeu tells his mother about the love affair with Melior. She believes he has been enchanted by a fairy. She plots to make him fall in love with the king's niece by means of a potion. Partonopeu surrenders to the maiden, but when she mentions his old love he regains his senses and escapes from Paris to Blois. He locks himself in a room, but then realises he has not broken his oath and returns to Chief d'Oire and begs for forgiveness. Melior grants it and reminds him again of his oath not to try to see her.

(4340–5499)

Partonope confesses his love affair to this mother. She believes he has been tricked by some evil enchantments. She plots to make him fall in love with the king's niece by means of a potent drink. He agrees to marry the maiden and the king carries out the nuptials. When she mentions his old love, Partonope regains his senses and returns to Blois. He locks himself in a room weeping and decides to ask her forgiveness. He returns to Melior, who forgives him, but warns him to beware of treason.

10. Partonopeu's betrayal
(4203–5172)

After half a year has passed Partonopeu becomes homesick again. Melior grants him leave reluctantly and reminds him of his promise. Partonopeu returns home and his mother turns to the archbishop of Paris to help her. Partonopeu receives a miraculous lantern and returns to Chief d'Oire. He violates the oath and shines the lantern on Melior and discovers that she is the most beautiful woman he has seen. Melior tells him that he has destroyed her powers of magic and grieves over her lost powers, her reputation and her lover. They are now exposed to the court. The ladies all admire his beauty, particularly Urraque, the queen's sister. She escorts Partonopeu out of the castle and sends him back to France after having tried to appease Melior's anger.

(5500–6416)

After a fortnight, Partonope thinks of his home again and requests leave to return. Melior reminds him of his mother's ploys and his promise to her. Partonope returns home and his mother enlists the help of the bishop of Paris. She then gives Partonope a lantern to be able to see the lady at the advice of the bishop. Partonope then returns to Melior. At night he takes out the lantern and discovers that she is the most beautiful woman he has ever seen. Melior swoons. She laments the loss of her magical powers, as well as the disgrace and his betrayal. They are now exposed to the court. The ladies chastise Melior for her behaviour, but admire his beauty. Urake, Melior's sister, begs her to forgive him, but to no avail. Urake accompanies him out of the castle and sends him back to France.

(43–53)
King Hlodvir asks his knights who would be willing to battle Markauld. Partalopi offers to ride against him. The king is hesitant, but in the end accepts. Partalopi and Markauld do battle and Partalopi allows Markauld to exchange his broken spear for a new one three times. Partalopi then unhorses him and when his men see this they invade the field to help their lord. A great bird appears and grabs Partalopi and returns him to the king. The treacherous knights are slain and King Hlodvir and King Markauld make peace and Markauld returns to Brittany.

(53–7)
The king asks him where he has been and Partalopi tells him about Marmoria. The king believes it to be a delusion. He sends for two girls. Partalopi is drunk and looses his senses and begins to play with them. He proposes to one and the other leaves. He then intends to sleep with her, but is overcome with thoughts of Marmoria. He leaves the city and returns to Constantinople. Marmoria tells him that she took him from the knights and the girl, but that eventually his father will have the better of them.

(57–70)
Partalopi remains another twelve months with Marmoria. He then says he would like to return to see about affairs in his homelands. She says he will be tempted, but that if he follows her advice then he will be the most powerful man in his family. He returns to France. His father urges him to turn from the delusion. He seeks the advice of the wisest men in France. The bishop, Partalopi's maternal uncle, gives him a stone that prevents spells from being cast upon whoever is holding it. He then returns to Marmoria. She suspects some deception, but he denies it and she falls asleep. He takes the stone and exposes Marmoria's beauty. Her knights rush in and capture him. Urækia, Marmoria's sister, asks that he be handed to her, claiming she will have him killed. She takes him to the sea and sends him back.

11. *Partonopeu is expelled from Constantinople*

(5173–5834)
Partonopeu is heartbroken and wishes to die. He locks himself in a room, refusing food and drink. He then decides to go into the Ardennes in the hope of being devoured by wild animals. His squire, Guillemot, who is the son of Sornegur, aids him and is baptised by Partonopeu, receiving the name Ansel. Partonopeu then rides off without him into the forest to await his death. His horse is wounded by a lion and flees towards the sea.

(6417–7145)
Partonope is heartbroken and wishes to die. He locks himself in a chamber and refuses to talk to anyone. He eats and drinks little and lives in misery. He decides to go to the Ardennes in the hope of being devoured by wild animals. He asks a boy to help him. His name is Gilamour, the nephew of Sornegour. He baptises the boy, who receives the name Anselote. Partonope then rides off without him. Anselote follows him, but loses his tracks at night. Partonope awaits his death. His horse is wounded by a lion and flees towards the sea.

12. *Urraque and Partonopeu*

(5835–6788)
The neighing of the horse is heard by people on a ship nearby that is owned by Urraque. The pilot, Maruc, claims to be able to charm wild animals and they go ashore and into the forest, where they discover Partonopeu, who is almost unrecognisable. Urraque falsely claims that Melior sent her to find him and promises to conceal him until she can bring him to Melior. Urraque and her lady-in-waiting, Persewis, nurse Partonopeu back to health. Meanwhile Urraque returns to the court of her sister and finds out that a tournament has been planned and the winner is to receive her hand in marriage. Melior laments the loss of her lover and tells her sister that her councillor, Ernol, has made the plans. Urraque does not reveal that she has found Partonopeu, but rather claims that he has lost his mind as a result of Melior's actions.

(7146–8283)
The neighing of the horse is heard by people on a ship anchored nearby that is owned by a lady. A sailor by the name of Maroke suggests that the horse and owner have been lost in the forest. He claims to be able to charm animals. They go on land. The lady finds Partonope who is unrecognisable. She states that her name is Urake and when he swoons she recognises him as well. She falsely claims that Melior has sent her and invites him to her castle. He is tended by Urake and a maiden by the name of Persewisse. Urake returns to the court of her sister and finds her mourning her lover. Urake states that she has heard that he had lost his mind because of Melior's actions. Melior tells her that it has been decided that a tournament be held and that the winner is to receive her hand in marriage.

13. *Urraque's plan*

(6789–7634)
Urraque returns to Salence and interrupts the growing love of Persewis for Partonopeu. She tells him of her discoveries and conceives a plan that will bring the two together again. She brings him fine armour. Partonopeu refuses to let her gird him, as he had promised Melior that she would dub him as knight. Urraque returns to Chief d'Oire and has her sister tell her which knights will attend the tournament. She presents Partonopeu, who has his helmet closed, and Melior dubs him without recognising him. She is, however, overcome with emotion and must postpone the dubbings. Urraque, Persewis and Partonopeu return to Salance to wait for the tournament to begin.

(8284–9173)
Urake returns to Salence and tells Partonope about the tournament. She brings him fine armour and a horse. Partonope refuses to let her gird him as he had promised Melior the honour of dubbing him. Urake returns to Chief de Oire. She torments her sister and asks about the details of the tournament. Melior girds Partonope without recognising him. They are both distressed. They return to Salence with Persewisse, who is falling in love with Partonope.

(70–82)
Partalopi returns to Paris and locks himself in his hall. He refuses to speak to anyone. He remains there for seven days without food and drink. Then a man comes to the city and asks to speak to Partalopi. He states that his name is Hlodvir (A)/Lodver (B) and that he is the son of Markauld, the king of Brittany. He has been sent to Partalopi to learn the arts of knighthood. He breaks open the door and forces Partalopi to eat and drink. They ride away together and Partalopi baptises him, giving him the name Barbarus. He then steals away in the night and goes back to the cliff overlooking the sea.

(82–92)
Urækia returns to Constantinople and states that Partalopi has been killed. Marmoria grieves. A council is summoned as she seems no longer in a state to rule. It is decided that a tournament will be held and she will thus be able to choose the best knight as her husband. Urækia then returns to the cliff and sees a horse running from a lion. She finds Partalopi in the forest and brings him with her to her castle on an island. Urækia then goes back to her sister and scolds her for her inconstancy.

(92–5)
Urækia returns to the island and tells Partalopi about the proposed tournament. She gives him advice. He is to say he is Hugi (B), the son of the duke of Normandy. They separate for the time being.
[(A) One day he goes riding about and the people in the castle notice a knight; they ask who he might be and he says he is Hugi, the son of the earl of Normandy. Urækia welcomes him and he remains with her.]
[(B) Urækia torments her sister much for having caused the death of her beloved.]

14. Partonopeu's adventures

(7635–7904)
One day Partonopeu goes out in a boat. He is driven off shore by a storm and lands on an island that belongs to a villainous lord, Armant, who imprisons him. Urraque searches for him in vain and goes to Chief d'Oire with a heavy heart. Armant departs for the tournament as well. Partonopeu wins over his wife, who agrees to release him on the condition that he return. She gives him equipment. Partonopeu departs for the tournament and on his way encounters a Spanish knight, Gaudin. They decide to enter the tournament as companions.

(9174–9525)
One day Partonope goes out on a boat and is driven off shore by a violent storm. He lands on the isle of Tenodoen, ruled by the fierce lord, Armaunt, who captures Partonope. Urake and Persewis search for him in vain and go to the court with heavy hearts. Armaunt also leaves to partake in the tournament. His wife pities Partonope and releases him on the condition that he return after the tournament. She provides him with equipment. He departs for the tournament and meets with a Spanish knight, whose name is Gaudyn le Bloys. They ride together to the tournament.

15. The three-day tournament

(7905–9694)
Partonopeu and Gaudin enter the lists. They receive admiration. Partonopeu and the sultan of Persia joust. Partonopeu is unhorsed, but recovers and pursues the Saracens. Gaudin comes to his rescue. They joust the king of Syria and his forces before nightfall and Partonopeu rescues his friend. Partonope is sad at the end of the day and Gaudin attempts to cheer him up. The second day, Partonopeu fights the sultan again. This time it is the sultan who is unhorsed. Partonopeu finds himself near the tower and seeks to present Melior with his gonfanon. Melior draws both banner and lance into the tower. She does not comprehend the act, but Urraque does and she explains the incident to her sister. Meanwhile, Lohier is rescued by Partonopeu from the followers of the emperor of Germany. Partonopeu again saves Gaudin. An intense battle follows between the Germans and the French. On the third day Partonopeu unhorses the villain, Armant. Armant allies himself with the kings of Mec and Syria and is killed by Partonopeu. He battles with Margaris, forcing him into the tower. In the end the judges descend and order him out. Partonopeu retires, thinking that he has lost the tournament.

(9526–11218)
Partonope and Gaudin enter the lists. They receive admiration. Partonope jousts the sultan of Persia. Their spears break and Partonope pierces his shield and loses his own. He gets a new spear and attacks Armaunt. He is attacked by the Sultan again after unhorsing one of his friends. He pursues the sultan and Gaudin comes to his rescue. The king of Syria unhorses Gaudin and is unhorsed by Partonope in turn. Despite the success of the day, Partonope is sad and Gaudin attempts to cheer him up. The second day, Partonope fights the sultan again and overthrows him. He passes by Melior and offers her the flag. She takes it, but does not hear his words. Urake has recognised Partonope and confesses to her sister. Meanwhile, the king of France is fighting the emperor of Germany. Partonope goes to his rescue. An intense battle follows between the Germans and the French. Partonope rescues Gaudin from the sultan. On the third day Partonope unhorses Armaunt. He unhorses the king of Mede, nephew of the king of Syria, and kills Armaunt. He encounters the sultan and they fight fiercely. The end of the combat is signalled. Partonope retires, thinking that he has lost the tournament.

Versions of 'Partonopeu de Blois'

(95–111)
One day Partalopi goes out on a boat and is driven out to sea. He lands on an island and comes to a castle where there is a fierce-looking man (A) / giant (B) by the name of Gram (A) / Grimar (B), who captures him. He is freed by his wife, who tells him that her husband has departed to take part in the tournament. She gives him armour and he promises to return. On his way he meets a knight, who turns out to be his squire Barbarus, who had travelled far searching for him. They now ride after Gram. Partalopi kills him and Barbarus kills his squire. They return to his wife and tell her about her husband's death. She has been held captive for twenty years and rejoices that she is finally free. They release all the other prisoners. The next morning they depart for the tournament.

(111–15)
Partalopi and Barbarus ride to the tournament. There are two knights who surpass all others. They encounter Partalopi and Barbarus and are overcome by them.
[(A) Partalopi asks them their names. They are brothers by the names of Heinrikur and Vilhialmur, sons of the duke of Braband, and they tell him that they had come to the tournament to seek Partalopi and to offer him their services. They are pleased to discover they have found him.]

Gaudyn encourages Pertinope to fight well and promises to help him. They hear mass and then ride to the field. The king of France lines up his knights.
(End of fragment)

Marmoria witnesses the battle. Partalopi is praised by all, but Marmoria is desolate as she believes he is dead.

161

16. *Conclusion*

(9695–10,656)
Partonopeu returns to the island with Gaudin. He is released by Armant's wife after she hears of her husband's death. They return to Chief d'Oire. The judges deliberate. Gaudin sees Urraque and falls in love. The judges debate the knights selected; Lohier, Partonopeu, Gaudin, the sultan Margaris of Persia, Sadés, king of Syria, and Aupatris, king of Nubia. The final vote is between Margaris and Partonopeu. Corsolt advises that the decision be based on their physical appearance and Partonopeu wins the prize. The sultan departs angry and Melior and Partonopeu celebrate their marriage. The author takes leave of his audience. He promises to tell, at his lady's command, the history of Anselot, the love affair of Anselot, the love affair of Gaudin, and the war with the sultan.

(11,219–12,195)
Partonope returns to Tenodoen. Armaunt's wife releases him upon hearing of her husband's death. They return to the city. Gaudin falls in love with Urake. The judges deliberate between the king of France, Gaudin, Partonope, the Sultan Margarise, Sades, the king of Syria, and Anpatrys, the king of Nubia. The judges debate between the Sultan and Partonope. Corsolt advises that the decision be made based upon their appearance. Partonope is chosen. The sultan departs, bent on vengeance. Melior and Partonope are united in marriage. The author takes leave of his audience.

(116–26)
[(A) Partalopi rides to the castle that Gram owned. Urækia rides out to him and he welcomes her. Barbarus serves them and she is very taken by him. The next day they ride back. Urækia reveals to Marmoria that the knight who won the tournament is Partalopi. Marmoria calls all the chieftains. The king of France declares that Partalopi must be dead since he had not seen him. Partalopi enters and they embrace. Partalopi tells her of all the things that have happened. The chieftains choose him as their emperor. Partalopi requests that Barbarus marry Urækia. Urækia declares that she wishes to marry him and no other man. They are wedded, along with Partalopi and Marmoria. Partalopi releases his father, the king of France, from any obligations to the emperor of Constantinople. Partalopi and Marmoria rule Constantinople and all of Greece and many other countries.]
[(B) Partalopi rides to Urækia. He is served by Barbarus, and Urækia is much taken by him. Partalopi is led into the hall and is chosen as emperor. Marmoria reluctantly agrees. Partalopi reveals himself and Urækia then tells of all that she has done. Marmoria is happy and so is King Hlodvir. Partalopi and Marmoria are joined in matrimony and Partalopi then unites Urækia and Barbarus in marriage as well. Partalopi and Marmoria reign in peace.]

Conclusion

THE USE OF THE WORD 'TRANSLATION' in the title of this book brings to the fore the ambiguity inherent in the word itself. It is this intrinsic tension in the understanding of what constitutes a translation that underlies the analysis of the works discussed. These works form a corpus of literature, both in Norse and in English, that are often disregarded precisely because they are translations, when, in effect, medieval literature as such can be viewed as fundamentally translational in nature. Authors in the Middle Ages borrowed, reshaped and combined narrative content, ideas and rhetorical forms from various different sources, both native and foreign, to create their own works, scarcely distinguishing between what was borrowed and what was new. It is the distinction between medieval and modern conceptions of 'translation' that creates a disjunction in our perception of literary creativity in the Middle Ages. To acknowledge the cultural value of pre-modern translations as evidence of the various reading communities' narrative predilections and of the fundamental mobility of texts is to recognise medieval perceptions of text as fluid and mobile. It similarly reveals the lack of such rigid distinctions between native and foreign within medieval reading communities, where many different linguistic registers and textual traditions often co-existed, as in the case of England.

The meaning of the Latin *translatio*, 'carrying across', captures the sense of movement not only of the text, but also of the entire cultural subtext contained within. Relevant here is the notion of *translatio studii et imperii*, of the geographical transfer of learning and power from East to West, that is later replicated in the move of the French material to the North. The metaphor also foregrounds the medieval perception of the relation between language and empire and the fact that such power could in fact be transferred by means of texts. The conceptualisation of cultural imperialism proposed in the first chapter shows how literary material could be used as social or political propaganda, while it simultaneously reveals the subversive potential inherent in linguistic and rhetorical reconfiguration. The imperial momentum depicted here is therefore negated by the very means of its promotion, that is, through the textual and linguistic appropriation of its power to convey meaning.

The notion of translation signals, moreover, not only the movement of textual material, but also its refashioning within the new system of meaning. The translation of a text requires the decoding of the source and the reassembly of this decoded meaning in the target language. It thus involves both an interpretation of the source text and the envisioning of the text within the linguistic and literary structures available to the translator. This cognitive process of decoding and recoding the source text of necessity involves and affects various aspects of the text, such as ideological components, rhetorical force, narrative elements, behavioural patterns and socially determined codes of conduct. For a text to be intelligible to its audience it must draw on systems of meaning that are comprehensible to that audience and related to their social and cultural conditions. The various approaches and topics in the previous chapters highlight the multiplicity of textual transmission. Each work discussed here in fact presented unique dimensions of translation, thereby inviting a differing critical approach. This inherent complexity of textual transfer reveals the part played by translations in the negotiations of cultural identity and establishment of cultural boundaries.

The question of the literary impact of linguistic hegemony is acted out in the Middle English versions of Marie de France's *Lais* discussed in Chapter 1. The modifications in textual representation range from minor deviations, such as rhetorical nuances in *Lay le Freine*, to the more substantial semiotic reconfiguration through ironic representation and subversion apparent in *Sir Launfal*. Each in turn foregrounds the differing modes of textual engagement with literary material as a means of either establishing boundaries or crossing those boundaries. The contradictory impulses present in *Strengleikar* similarly denote the complexity of cultural interaction and the influence of such interaction on the formation of cultural identity. While the first chapter explored the effects of cultural transmission on a national level, the second chapter examined such effects within the context of linguistic and behavioural conventions. The heroic ethos of the *chanson de geste* tradition echoes the pre-existing Germanic traditions of warrior mentality, codes of honour and masculine ideals in medieval Scandinavia, thereby revealing cultural correlations that become apparent in the familiarity of literary representation and narrative progress. The systematic reduction of elements representing foreign and unfamiliar codes of conduct and moral values indicates an effort at integration that intensifies as the translation progresses. It similarly reveals the translator's awareness that the interpretation of language is not only a linguistic but also a cultural act.

The third chapter moved from the social and ideological codes embedded in linguistic and literary representation to narrative and structural aspects of textual transmission. The recasting of Chrétien's *Yvain* in Old Norse and Middle English foregrounds the different narrative preoccupations of the authors that in turn reveal the unique culturally determined readings of the source text by each (or every) author. The concern with knightly behaviour and codes of honour in both homosocial and heterosexual relationships in *Ywain and Gawain* reveals a shift in orientation from the individual to social structures. The multiple layers of influence apparent in *Ívens saga*, in turn, expose the instability of medieval textuality and the active engagement of authors, scribes and their audiences with literary material. Ultimately, this mobility of texts, both geographically and figuratively, was interrogated in the fourth chapter by deliberating on manuscript transmission, textual variants and, finally, the socially and culturally coded conceptualisations of gender and power in the various versions of *Partonopeu de Blois*. Thus the final chapter, like Chapters 2 and 3, explored textual transmission in terms of the narrative content and its power to convey meaning, but it also brought the discussion back to the notion of trans-historical and international literary dialogue between and among cultures proposed in the first chapter.

The movement of texts from northern France into England and Scandinavia parallels a different historical movement, that is, the migration of peoples across Europe. It reverses the previous migratory influx of Vikings into England and northern France in the flow of narrative material and ideas back into England following the Conquest and into Norway and Iceland through political and mercantile relationships in the following centuries. This pattern of migration and settlement that is reflected in the movement of texts and in the resulting complex cultural relations calls attention to the potential relevance of post-colonial theories for medieval studies. The editors of a recent work on post-colonial approaches to medievalism connect the concept of translation to the notion of cultural encounters, stating that translation in fact serves as a 'metaphor for cultures in contact, confrontation, and competition' and hence as 'metaphor for post-colonial writing itself'.[1] Yet cultures are not static, but are continually being reshaped and reformed through that very process of contact and engagement. Part of cultural formation is in fact cultural transformation. Translations are not only the meeting place of cultures; they also reveal the complex relations of semiotic, conceptual, social and poetic conventions in the movement of texts between linguistic, geographical and temporal realms. The cross-cultural reading of texts and their translations thus provides a model for the study of textual transmission that takes into account the complexity and volatility of cultural interaction in the Middle Ages.

The time period of the works discussed also coincides with a different, albeit just as significant, historical event: the establishment and institution of the vernacular in Europe. The formation of the French romance in the twelfth century signals the beginning of 'romance' as a literary language as well as a literary form. The Middle English and Old Norse translations of the French romances, the *chansons de geste* and the *Lais* similarly belong to some of the earliest literary writing in the vernacular. They reveal not only the engagement with foreign material, but also the appraisal of the capacities of a spoken tongue to represent literary ideas. The translations hence expose literary experimentations with the various modes of expressing ideas in conjunction with established and pre-existing modes of verbalisation and narrative procedures. The translations thus form part of the establishment of the native tongue as a literary language, while they simultaneously seek to extend the linguistic and formal capacities of the native tongue to accommodate different literary models and poetic structures.

The temporal gap between the source texts and their translations, and between the translations and their manuscript copies raises questions of cultural relevance of the texts in connection with their historical audiences. As stated above, the French romances and Marie de France's *Lais* stem from a

---

[1] Ananya Jahanara Kabir and Deanne Williams, eds., *Postcolonial Approaches to the European Middle Ages. Translating Cultures* (Cambridge: Cambridge University Press, 2005), 6.

Conclusion

momentum of a civilising force of courtly society and changes in the social structures of twelfth-century France. The Norse translations at the court of the Norwegian king, Hákon Hákonarson, however, introduce questions of authorial intent and political intricacies with respect to literary production that come back to the notion of imperialistic tendencies. The political shifts taking place in fourteenth-century England re-engage questions of cultural identity. The re-enactment and reformulation of the pre-existing French material in the native tongue similarly calls attention to the disintegrating relation with the French crown and, by extension, with Anglo-Norman as a dominating literary language. As in Iceland in the fourteenth century, the translations of romances and other French material took place alongside original native creations. Both linguistic communities in fact exhibit a flourishing production of native romances beside the translations, intimating an active experimentation with form, literary voice and modes of cultural articulation that demonstrates the significance of translations as means of probing questions of cultural demarcations and identity.

The romance of *Partonopeu de Blois* is of particular relevance here. The refashioning of this twelfth-century French romance in two different versions in fourteenth-century England, and possibly in Iceland at the same time, shows the active engagement of authors with literary material that reveals different and very unique narrative concerns. The existence of both versions and in such different forms in England raises questions of the reading communities that instigated and preserved those texts. It similarly foregrounds the complexity of English literary tradition where texts might have been circulating at the same time in different localities (or even within the same localities, but within different reading communities), unbeknownst to each other. Christopher Cannon calls attention to this co-existence of texts that are nevertheless disconnected from and unrelated to each other in a recent work that seeks to foreground precisely this multiplicity of early English literary production.[2] With the manuscript copies stemming from the same century (except notably Add. 35288, which is later than the others), the question remains whether the two versions co-existed in separate geographic regions, or whether they form two different strains of the story, one earlier and the other a later variation, or, then again, whether they were intentionally composed for different audiences. Was the longer version possibly commissioned for a particular audience accustomed to or familiar with Chaucerian modes of articulation and representation revealed in the literary echoes of and conceptual similarities to Chaucer's works? While such deliberations remain beyond the scope of this work, they foreground the relevance of those texts in the conceptualisations

---

[2] *The Grounds of English Literature* (Oxford: Oxford University Press, 2004). Cannon's argument centres on the value (in Marxist terms) of the text as cultural production unrelated to its place among and relation to other texts. I would argue that such value is in no way lessened through inter-textual connections and that cross-cultural reading of texts in fact locates such inherent cultural values through differences and parallelisms of source and target texts. David Lawton elaborated on this inherent mobility of the romance itself, both as matter and form, in an as yet unpublished lecture, 'For God and Werewolf: A Reading History of *Guillaume de Palerne*', given at the University of Oxford on 17 October 2005.

of medieval writing and reading practices. What is clear, however, is that the various versions reveal the profound influences of the cultural and literary traditions of their receptive communities, as is evident in the reshaping of the narrative material to reveal the unique cultural concerns and moral inclinations of their authors or their presumed public.

Ultimately, I have tried to argue for the repositioning of Middle English and Old Norse translations within literary history; to consider them as evidence not of the lack of literary sophistication on the part of their authors, but of the variety, multiplicity and richness of vernacular literary writing. When the works are examined in connection with, yet as independent from, their source texts, their significance is revealed in the affirmation of the cultural conceptualisations and literary predilections of their reading communities. Each chapter in turn approaches the question of cultural transfer from a different angle; that of national linguistic re-enactment and cultural dissidence, through behavioural and narratological transformations, to questions of transmission patterns and socially determined codes of conduct. The diversity in approach recalls the inherent complexity of cultural encounter evident in the texts discussed above. In the end, the model of cultural transformations proposed here seeks to engage the reality of medieval textual *mouvance*, not only within manuscript transmission, but across national and linguistic boundaries, foregrounding the continual movement of cultural ideas and literary forms and material across Europe in the Middle Ages.

Bibliography

Manuscripts

Bibliothèque Nationale, Paris
Arsenal 2986
Arsenal 6565

Bodleian Library, Oxford
Eng. Poet. C. 3
Rawl. Poet. 14
Lat. Misc. B. 17
University College 188

British Library, London
Add. 35.288
Add. 38.663
Cotton Caligula A.ii
Cotton Galba E.ix
Cotton Vitellius D.iii
Egerton 2862
Harley 978 (Microfilm 1090)

Cambridge University Library, Cambridge
Gg.iv.26.2
Gg.iv.27.1
Gg.iv.27.2

Landsbókasafn Íslands – Háskólabókasafn, Reykjavík
ÍB 51 fol.
ÍB 423 4to
ÍBR 5 fol.
ÍBR 39 8vo
JS 8 fol.
JS 27 fol.
LBS 272 fol.
LBS 840 4to
LBS 1654 4to
LBS 2146 4to

Stofnun Árna Magnússonar, Reykjavík
AM 489 4to

Primary Works

Apuleius, *Cupid and Psyche*, ed. E. J. Kenney. Cambridge: Cambridge University Press, 2001.
Bevers saga, ed. Christopher Sanders. With the text of the Anglo-Norman *Boeve de Haumtone*. Reykjavík: Stofnun Árna Magnússonar á Íslandi, 2001.
Brennu-Njáls saga, ed. Einar Ólafur Sveinsson. Reykjavík: Hið íslenzka fornritafélag, 1954.
La Chanson de Roland, ed. and trans. Gerard J. Brault. Oxford text and English translation. University Park: The Pennsylvania State University Press, 1984.
Chestre, Thomas, *Sir Launfal*, ed. A. J. Bliss. Nelson's Medieval and Renaissance Library. London: Thomas Nelson and Sons, 1960.
Chrétien de Troyes, *The Complete Romances of Chrétien de Troyes*, trans. David Staines. Bloomington: Indiana University Press, 1990.
—— *Erec and Enide*, ed. and trans. Carleton W. Carroll. New York: Garland Publishing, 1987.
—— *The Knight with the Lion, or Yvain (Le Chevalier au Lion)*, ed. and trans. William W. Kibler. Garland Library of Medieval Literature 48. New York: Garland Publishing, 1985.
—— *Yvain (Der Löwenritter)*, ed. W. Foerster. Halle: Verlag von Max Niemeyer, 1902.
—— *Yvain ou Le Chevalier au Lion*, ed. Jan Nelson, Carleton W. Carroll. New York: Appleton-Century-Crofts, 1968.
Clari saga, in *Riddarasögur*, ed. Bjarni Vilhjálmsson, vol. 5. Reykjavík: Íslendingasagnaútgáfan, 1951, 1–61.
Elis saga, Strengleikar and Other Texts. Uppsala University Library Delagardieska Samlingen Nos. 4–7 Folio and AM 666 b Quarto, ed. Mattias Tveitane. Corpus codicum norvegicorum medii aevi, quarto serie, vol. 4. Oslo: The Society for Publications of Old Norwegian Manuscripts, 1972.
Elis saga ok Rósamundu, ed. Eugen Kölbing. Heilbronn: Verlag von Gebr. Henninger, 1881.
The English Charlemagne Romances Part II, ed. Sidney J. H. Herrtage from the Landsdowne MS 388. Early English Text Society, Extra Series 35. London: The Early English Text Society, 1880.
The English Charlemagne Romances Part VI, ed. Sidney J. H. Herrtage. *The Taill of Rauf Coilȝear from Lekpreviks edition of 1572 with the fragments of Roland and Vernagu and Otuel from the Auchinleck Manuscript*. Early English Text Society, Extra Series 39. London: The Early English Text Society, 1882.
Erex saga, ed. Gustaf Cereschiöld. Samfund til udgivelse af gammel nordisk literature 3. Copenhagen: STUAGNL, 1880.
Erex saga and Ívens saga: The Old Norse Versions of Chrétien de Troyes's 'Erec' and 'Yvain', trans. Foster W. Blaisdell and Marianne E. Kalinke. Lincoln: University of Nebraska Press, 1977.
Facsimile Udgave af Flores oc Blantzeflor, ed. Gotfred af Ghemens (1509 edn). Copenhagen: Hermann-Petersens forlag, 1910.
Firumbras and Otuel and Roland, ed. Mary Isabelle O'Sullivan from MS Brit. Mus. Addit. 37492. Early English Text Society, Original Series 198. London: Oxford University Press, 1935.
Flores och Blanzeflor, ed. Emil Olson. Samlingar utgivna av svenska fornskrift-sällskapet 157. Lund: Berlingska Boktryckeriet, 1921.
Flóres saga og Blankiflúr, in *Riddarasögur*, ed. Bjarni Vilhjálmsson, vol. 4. Reykjavík: Íslendingasagnaútgáfan, 1951, 137–94.

Flóres saga ok Blankiflúr, ed. Eugen Kölbing. Altnordische Saga-bibliothek 5. Halle A. S: Max Niemeyer, 1896.
A Fragment of 'Partonope of Blois', from a Manuscript at Vale Royal in the Possession of Lord Delamere, ed. R. C. N. London: Nichols and Sons, 1873.
'Graelent' and 'Guingamor': Two Breton Lays, ed. and trans. Russel Weingartner. Garland Library of Medieval Literature 37. New York: Garland Publishing 1985.
Guillaume de Palerne. An English Translation of the Twelfth Century French Verse Romance, ed. and trans. Leslie A. Sconduto. Jefferson: McFarland & Co., 2004.
Herr Ivan, ed. Erik Noreen. Samlingar utg. av svensk fornskrift-sällskap 50. Uppsala: Almquist & Wiksells boktryckeri, 1931.
Ívens saga, ed. Eugen Kölbing. Altnordische Saga-bibliothek 7. Halle A. S.: Max Niemeyer, 1898.
Ívens saga, ed. Foster W. Blaisdell. Editiones Arnamagnæanæ, Series B, 18. Copenhagen: C. A. Reitzels Boghandel, 1979.
Karlamagnús saga. The Saga of Charlemagne and his Heroes, trans. Constance B. Hieatt, vol. 3. Toronto: Pontifical Institute of Medieval Studies, 1980.
Karlamagnus saga ok kappa hans, ed. C. R. Unger. Christiania: H. J. Jensen, 1860.
King Horn. A Middle-English Romance, ed. Joseph Hall. Oxford: Clarendon Press, 1901.
King Horn, Floris and Blauncheflur, The Assumption of our Lady, ed. George H. McKnight. Early English Text Society, Original Series 14. First edited in 1866 by J. Rawson Lumby, re-edited 1901, 2nd reprint. London: Oxford University Press, 1990.
The King's Mirror (Speculum Regale – Konungs skuggsjá), trans. Laurence Marcellus Larson. Scandinavian Monographs 3. New York: The American-Scandinavian Foundation, 1917.
Laȝamon, *Brut*, ed. G. L. Brook and R. F. Leslie. Early English Text Society, Original Series 250 and 277. London: Oxford University Press, 1963–78.
Langland, William, *The Vision of Piers Plowman*, ed. A. V. C. Schmidt. London: The Everyman Library, 1995.
Late Medieval Icelandic Romances, ed. Agnete Loth. 5 vols. Editiones Arnamagnæanæ, Series B, 20–4. Copenhagen: The Arnamagnæan Institute, 1962–5.
Marie de France, *Les Lais de Marie de France*, ed. Jean Rychner. Les classiques français du moyen age 93. Paris: Éditions Champion, 1966.
—— *The Lais of Marie de France*, trans. Robert Hanning and Joan Ferrante. New York: E. P. Dutton, 1978.
The Middle English Breton Lays, ed. Anne Laskaya and Eve Salisbury. TEAMS Middle English Text Series. Kalamazoo: Medieval Institute Publications, 1995.
The Middle-English Versions of Partonope of Blois, ed. A. Trampe Bödtker. Early English Text Society, Extra Series 109. Millwood: Kraus Reprint, 1981 [1912].
Njal's saga, trans. Robert Cook. London: Penguin Books, 2001.
Die nordische und die englische Version der Tristan-Sage, ed. Eugen Kölbing. Heilbronn: Verlag von Gebr. Henninger, 1878.
Parcevals saga, in *Riddarasögur*, ed. Bjarni Vilhjálmsson, vol. 4. Reykjavík: Íslendingasagnaútgáfan, 1951, 195–285.
Partalopa saga, ed. Lise Præstgaard Andersen. Editiones Arnamagnæanæ, Series B, 28. Copenhagen: C. A. Reitzels Forlag, 1983.
Partalopa saga, ed. Oscar Klockhoff. Uppsala: Akademiska Bokhandeln, 1877.
Partonope of Blois, ed. David Lawton and Sif Rikhardsdottir. TEAMS Middle English Text Series. Kalamazoo: The Medieval Institute Publications, forthcoming.
Partonopeus de Blois, ed. A. C. M. Robert and G.-A. Crapelet, 2 vols. Paris: G.-A. Crapelet, 1834.

Partonopeu de Blois. A French Romance of the Twelfth Century, ed. Joseph Gildae, 2 vols. Villanova: Villanova University Press, 1967–70.

Persenober og Konstantianobis. Danske Folkebøger fra 16. og 17. Århundrede, ed. J. P. Jakobsen, Jørgen Olrik and R. Paulli, vol. 6. Copenhagen: Gyldendal, 1915–36.

The Pseudo-Turpin, ed. H. M. Smyser from Bibliothèque Nationale, fonds latin, MS 17656. Cambridge, Mass.: The Medieval Academy of America, 1937.

Renart, Jean, *L'escoufle: roman d'aventure*, ed. H. Michelant and D. Meyer. Publications de le Société des anciens textes français. Paris: Firmin Didot et cie, 1894.

—— *The Romance of the Rose or Guillaume de Dole*, trans. Patricia Terry and Nancy Vine Durling. Philadelphia: University of Pennsylvania Press, 1993.

Riddarasögur. Parcevals saga, Valvers þáttr, Ívents saga, Mírmans saga, ed. Eugen Kölbing. Strassburg: Karl J. Trübner, 1872.

Le Roman de Partonopeu de Blois, ed. and trans. Olivier Collet and Pierre-Marie Joris. Paris: Librairie générale française, 2005.

Le Roman de Thèbes, ed. Guy Raynaud de Lage. 2 vols. Les classiques français du moyen âge 94. Paris: H. Champion, 1966–8.

The Romance of Sir Beues of Hamtoun, ed. Eugen Kölbing. Early English Text Society, Extra Series 46, 48 and 65. Millwood: Kraus Reprint Co., 1978 [1885, 1886 and 1894].

Saga af Tristram ok Ísodd, ed. Peter Jorgensen, trans. Joyce Hill, in *Norse Romance*, ed. Marianne E. Kalinke, vol. 1, *The Tristan Legend*. Arthurian Archives 3. Cambridge: D. S. Brewer, 1999, 241–92.

Saga af Tristram ok Ísönd samt Möttuls saga, ed. Gísli Brynjúlfsson. Copenhagen: Det Kongelige nordiske oldskrift-selskab, 1878.

Saxo Grammaticus, *The History of the Danes*, ed. Hilda Ellis Davidson, trans. Peter Fisher. Cambridge: D. S. Brewer, 1979.

The Sege off Melayne, The Romance of Duke Rowland and Sir Otuell of Spayne, The Song of Roland, ed. Sidney J. Herrtage. Early English Text Society, Extra Series 35. New York: Kraus Reprint, 1981.

Sigurðar saga þögla, in *Riddarasögur*, ed. Bjarni Vilhjálmsson, vol. 3. Reykjavik: Íslendingasagnaútgáfan, 1953, 95–267.

Sir Gawain and the Green Knight, Pearl, Cleanness, Patience, ed. J. J. Anderson. London: Everyman's Library, 1998.

Sir Perceval of Galles and Ywain and Gawain, ed. Mary Flowers Braswell. TEAMS Middle English Text Series. Kalamazoo: The Medieval Institute Publications, 1995.

The Song of Roland, trans. D. D. R. Owen. Woodbridge: The Boydell Press, 1990.

Speculum Regale. Ein altnorwegischer Dialog nach Cod. Arnamagn. 243 Fol. B und den ältesten Fragmenten, ed. Oscar Brenner. Munich: Christian Kaiser, 1881.

Statius, P. Papinius, *Thebaid*, trans. A. D. Melville. Oxford: Clarendon Press, 1992.

Strengleikar. An Old Norse Translation of Twenty-one Old French Lais, ed. Robert Cook and Mattias Tveitane from the manuscript Uppsala De la Gardie 4–7 – AM 666 b, 4to. Oslo: Norsk historisk kjeldeskrift-institutt, 1979.

Strengleikar eða Lioðabok. En Samling af Romantiske Fortællinger efter Bretoniske Folkesange (Lais), ed. R. Keyser and C. R. Unger. Christiania: Carl C. Werner & Comp.s Bogtrykkeri, 1850.

Sturla Þórðarson, *Hákonar saga Hákonarsonar*, in *Konungasögur*, ed. Guðni Jónsson, vol. 3. Reykjavik: Íslendingasagnaútgáfan, 1957, 1–464.

Thomas of Britain, *Tristran*, ed. Stewart Gregory. Garland Library of Medieval Literature 78. New York: Garland Publishing, 1991.

Tiodielis saga, ed. Tove Hovn Ohlsson. Reykjavík: Stofnun Árna Magnússonar í íslenskum fræðum, 2009.

Tristrams saga ok Ísöndar, ed. and trans. Peter Jorgensen, in *Norse Romance*, ed. Marianne E. Kalinke, vol. 1, *The Tristan Legend*. Arthurian Archives 3. Cambridge: D. S. Brewer, 1999, 23–226.
Ywain and Gawain, ed. Albert B. Friedman and Norman T. Harrington. Early English Text Society, Original Series 254. London: Oxford University Press, 1964.
Ywain and Gawain, ed. Gustav Schleich. Oppeln: E. Franck's Buchhandlung, 1887.

Reference Works

Alexander Jóhannesson, *Isländisches etymologisches Wörterbuch*. Bern: Francke Verlag, 1956.
Ásgeir Blöndal Magnússon, *Íslensk orðsifjabók*. Reykjavík: Orðabók Háskólans, Stofnun Árna Magnússonar í íslenskum fræðum, 1989.
Emden, A. B., *A Biographical Register of the University of Oxford to A.D. 1500*. Oxford: Oxford University Press, 1957–9.
Fritzner, Johan, *Ordbog over det gamle norske Sprog*, 3 vols., 2nd edn. Kristiania: Den norske Forlagsforening, 1886–96.
Greimas, Algirdas Julien, and Teresa Mary Keane, *Dictionnaire du moyen français*. Paris: Larousse, 2001.
Hindley, Alan, Frederick W. Langley and Brian J. Levy, *Old French–English Dictionary*. Cambridge: Cambridge University Press, 2000.
Hunt, Richard William, and Falconer Madan, *A Summary Catalogue of Western Manuscripts in the Bodleian Library at Oxford*. Oxford: Clarendon Press, 1953.
Knudsen, Trygve, and Alf Sommerfelt, eds., *Norsk riksmålsordbok*, vol. 3. Oslo: Det Norske Akademi for Sprog og Litteratur, og Kunnskapsforlaget, 1991.
Knirk, James E., Helle Degnbol, Bent C. Jacobsen, Eva Rode, Christopher Sanders and Þorbjörg Helgadóttir, *Ordbog over det norrøne prosasprog*. Copenhagen: Den arnamagnæanske kommission, 1989 –.
Kurath, Hans, *et al.*, eds., *The Middle English Dictionary*. Ann Arbor: The University of Michigan Press, 1954 –.
McIntosh, Angus, M. L. Samuels and Michael Benskin, eds. (with assistance from Margaret Laing and Keith Williamson), *A Linguistic Atlas of Late Medieval English*. Aberdeen: Aberdeen University Press, 1986.
Wells, John E., ed., *A Manual of Writings in Middle English 1050–1400*. New Haven: Yale University Press, 1916.

Secondary Works

Adler, Alfred, 'Sovereignty in Chrétien's *Yvain*', *Proceedings of the Modern Language Association of America* 62 (1947), 281–305.
Aebischer, Paul, *Les différents états de la Karlamagnús saga*. Berlin: Akademie Verlag, 1956.
Andersen, Lise Præstgaard, '*Partalopa saga*, homologue scandinave d'*Eros et Psyché*', *Revue des langues romanes* 102 (1998), 57–64.
Angold, Michael, *The Byzantine Aristocracy: IX–XII Centuries*. Oxford: BAR International Series, 1984.
Apter, Emily, *The Translation Zone: A New Comparative Literature*. Princeton: Princeton University Press, 2006.
Ármann Jakobsson, *Staður í nýjum heimi: konungasagan Morkinskinna*. Reykjavík: Háskólaútgáfan, 2002.

Ármann Jakobsson, 'Uppreisn æskunnar: unglingasagan um Flóres og Blankiflúr', *Skírnir* 176 (2002), 89–112.

Árni Böðvarsson, *Handritalestur og gotneskt letur*. Reykjavík: Iðunn, 1974.

Ashcroft, Bill, Introduction, *The Post-Colonial Studies Reader*, ed. Bill Ashcroft, Gareth Griffiths and Helen Tiffin. London: Routledge, 1995, 1–4.

——, Gareth Griffiths and Helen Tiffin, eds., *The Post-Colonial Studies Reader*. London: Routledge, 1995.

Auerbach, Erich, 'The Knight Sets Forth', *Mimesis. The Representation of Reality in Western Literature*, trans. Willard R. Trask. Princeton: Princeton University Press, 2003, 123–42.

Baldwin, John W., *Aristocratic Life in Medieval France. The Romances of Jean Renart and Gerbert de Montreuil 1190–1230*. Baltimore: The Johns Hopkins University Press, 2000.

Barnes, Geraldine, 'The Riddarasögur: A Medieval Exercise in Translation', *Saga-Book of the Viking Society* 19 (1977), 403–41.

—— 'Romance in Iceland', in *Old Icelandic Literature and Society*, ed. Margaret Clunies Ross. Cambridge: Cambridge University Press, 2000, 266–86.

—— 'Some Observations on Flóres saga ok Blankiflúr', *Scandinavian Studies* 49.1 (1977), 48–66.

Bartlett, Robert, *The Hanged Man. A Story of Miracle, Memory, and Colonialism in the Middle Ages*. Princeton: Princeton University Press, 2004.

—— *The Making of Europe. Conquest, Colonization and Cultural Change 950–1350*. Princeton: Princeton University Press, 1994.

Bassnet, Susan, *Translation Studies*. Rev. edn. London: Routledge, 1994.

—— and André Lefevere, *Constructing Cultures*. Clevedon: Multilingual Matters, 1998.

Bateman, J. Chimène, 'Problems of Recognition: The Fallible Narrator and the Female Addressee in *Partonopeu de Blois*', *Mediaevalia* 25 (2004), 163–81. Special Issue: *Partonopeus in Europe. An Old French Romance and its Adaptations*, ed. Catherine Hanley, Mario Longtin and Penny Eley. New York: The Center for Medieval and Renaissance Studies, 2004.

Beadle, Richard, 'Middle English Texts and their Transmission, 1350–1500: Some Geographical Criteria', in *Speaking in our Tongues. Proceedings of a Colloquium on Medieval Dialectology and Related Disciplines*, ed. Margaret Laing and Keith Williamson. Cambridge: D. S. Brewer, 1994, 69–92.

—— 'Prolegomena to a Literary Geography of Later Medieval Norfolk', in *Regionalism in Late Medieval Manuscripts and Texts*, ed. Felicity Riddy. York Manuscript Conferences: Proceedings Series. Cambridge: D. S. Brewer, 1991, 89–108.

Beckmann, Gustav Adolf, 'Schwierigkeiten und Triumph einer Überhöhung: zur Erzählkunst im Rolandslied', *Romantisches Jahrbuch* 59 (2008), 128–56.

Beer, Jeanette, ed., *Medieval Translators and their Craft*. Kalamazoo: Medieval Institute Publications, 1989.

—— 'The State of the Question', *New Medieval Literatures* 9 (2007), 181–4.

Benjamin, Walter, 'The Task of the Translator', trans. Harry Zohn, in *Theories of Translation. An Anthology of Essays from Dryden to Derrida*, ed. Rainer Schulte and John Biguenet. Chicago: The University of Chicago Press, 1992, 71–82.

Bennett, J. A. W., and G. V. Smithers, eds., *Early Middle English Verse and Prose*. Oxford: Oxford University Press, 1966.

Bennett, Michael, 'France in England: Anglo-French Culture in the Reign of Edward III', in *Language and Culture. The French of England c.1100–c.1500*, ed. Jocelyn Wogan-Browne et al. York: York Medieval Press, 2009, 320–33.

Bennett, Philip E, 'Origins of the French Epic: The *Song of Roland* and Other French

Epics', in *Approaches to Teaching the 'Song of Roland'*, ed. William W. Kibler and Leslie Zarker Morgan. New York: The Modern Language Association of America, 2006, 57–65.
Berndt, Rolf, 'The Period of the Final Decline of French in Medieval England (Fourteenth and Early Fifteenth Centuries)', *Zeitschrift für Anglistik und Amerikanistik* 20 (1972), 341–69.
Bhabha, Homi K., *The Location of Culture*. London: Routledge, 1994.
Bloch, Howard, *The Anonymous Marie de France*. Chicago: University of Chicago Press, 2003.
Bödtker, A. Trampe, *Parténopeus de Blois. Étude comparative des versions islandaise et danoise*. Videnskabs-selskabets skrifter 2. Hist.-Filos. Kt. 1904. No. 3. Christiania: J. Dybwad, 1904.
Bollard, John K., '*Hende wordes*: The Theme of Courtesy in *Ywain and Gawain*', *Neophilologus* 78 (1994), 655–70.
Boyd, Matthieu, 'The Ring, the Sword, the Fancy Dress, and the Posthumous Child: Background to the Element of Heroic Biography in Marie de France's *Yonec*', *Romance Quarterly* 55 (2008), 205–30.
Brault, Gerard, 'Coping with the Death of Roland', in *Approaches to Teaching the 'Song of Roland'*, ed. William W. Kibler and Leslie Zarker Morgan. New York: The Modern Language Association of America, 2006, 207–12.
Brown, Thomas H., 'The Relationship between *Partonopeus de Blois* and the Cupid and Psyche Tradition', *Brigham Young University Studies* 5 (1964)6: 193–202.
Brownlee, Kevin, and Marina Scordilis Brownlee, *Romance. Generic Transformation from Chrétien de Troyes to Cervantes*. Hanover: University Press of New England, 1985.
Brownlee, Kevin, Tony Hunt, Ian Johnson, Alastair Minnis and Nigel F. Palmer, 'Vernacular Literary Consciousness *c*.1100–*c*.1500: French, German and English Evidence', *The Cambridge History of Literary Criticism: The Middle Ages*, ed. Alastair Minnis and Ian Johnson, vol 2. Cambridge: Cambridge University Press, 2005, 422–71.
Brownlee, Marina, 'Comparatists in Translation: A Premodern Example', *New Medieval Literatures* 9 (2007), 203–6.
——, Kevin Brownlee and Stephen G. Nichols, eds., *The New Medievalism*. Baltimore: The Johns Hopkins University Press, 1991.
Brownrigg, Linda L., ed., *Medieval Book Production. Assessing the Evidence*. Los Altos Hills: Anderson-Lovelace, 1990.
Bruckner, Matilda Tomaryn, '*Le Fresne*'s Model for Twinning in the *Lais* of Marie de France', *Modern Language Notes* 121 (2006), 946–60.
—— 'The Interplay of Gender and Genres in *Partonopeu de Blois*', in her *Shaping Romance. Interpretation, Truth, and Closure in Twelfth-Century French Fictions*. Philadelphia: University of Pennsylvania Press, 1993, 109–56.
—— 'Intertextuality', in *The Legacy of Chrétien de Troyes*, ed. Norris J. Lacy, Douglas Kelly and Keith Busby, vol. 1. Amsterdam: Rodopi, 1987, 223–65.
—— 'Romancing History and Rewriting the Game of Fiction: Jean Renart's *Rose* through the Looking Glass of *Partonopeu de Blois*', in *The World and its Rival. Essays on Literary Imagination in Honor of Per Nykrog*, ed. Kathryn Karczewska and Tom Conley. Amsterdam: Rodopi, 1999, 93–118.
—— 'The Shape of Romance in Medieval France', *The Cambridge Companion to Medieval Romance*, ed. Roberta L. Krueger. Cambridge: Cambridge University Press, 2000, 13–28.
—— and Glyn S. Burgess, 'Arthur in the Narrative Lay', in *The Arthur of the French*, ed. Glyn S. Burgess and Karen Pratt. Cardiff: University of Wales Press, 2005, 186–214.

Brunner, Karl, 'Middle English Metrical Romances and their Audience', *Studies in Medieval Literature. In Honor of Professor Albert Croll Baugh*, ed. MacEdward Leach. Philadelphia: University of Pennsylvania Press, 1961, 219–27.

——'Die Überlieferung der mittelenglischen Versromanzen', *Anglia* 76 (1958), 64–73.

Burgess, Glyn S., *Marie de France. An Analytical Bibliography. Supplement no. 3.* Woodbridge: Tamesis, 2007.

Busby, Keith, 'The Characters and the Setting', in *The Legacy of Chrétien de Troyes*, ed. Norris J. Lacy, Douglas Kelly and Keith Busby, vol. 1. Amsterdam: Rodopi, 1987, 57–90.

——'Chrétien de Troyes English'd', *Neophilologus* 71 (1987), 596–613.

Butterfield, Ardis, *The Familiar Enemy: Chaucer, Language and Nation in the Hundred Years War*. Oxford: Oxford University Press, 2009.

Bynum, Caroline Walker, 'Wonder', *The American Historical Review* 102 (1997), 1–26.

Byock, Jesse, *Feud in the Icelandic Saga*. Berkeley: University of California Press, 1982.

Caluwé-Dor, Juliette de, 'Yvain's Lion Again: A Comparative Analysis of its Personality and Function in the Welsh, French and English Versions', in *An Arthurian Tapestry. Essays in Memory of Lewis Thorpe*, ed. Kenneth Varty. Glasgow: University of Glasgow, 1981, 229–38.

Camille, Michael, *The Medieval Art of Love. Objects and Subjects of Desire*. New York: Harry N. Abrams, 1998.

Cannon, Christopher, *The Grounds of English Literature*. Oxford: Oxford University Press, 2004.

Carruthers, Mary J., *The Book of Memory. A Study of Memory in Medieval Culture*. Cambridge: Cambridge University Press, 1990.

Cartlidge, Neil, ed., *Boundaries in Medieval Romance*. Cambridge: D. S. Brewer, 2008.

Cerquiglini, Bernard, *Éloge de la variante: histoire critique de la philology*. Paris: Seuil, 1989.

——*In Praise of the Variant: A Critical History of Philology*, trans. Betsy Wing. Baltimore: Johns Hopkins University Press, 1999.

Cheyfitz, Eric, *The Poetics of Imperialism. Translation and Colonization from 'The Tempest' to 'Tarzan'*. Expanded edn. Philadelphia: University of Pennsylvania Press, 1997.

Clover, Carol J., *The Medieval Saga*. Ithaca: Cornell University Press, 1982.

Clunies Ross, Margaret, *A History of Old Norse Poetry and Poetics*. Cambridge: D. S. Brewer, 2005.

——'Medieval Iceland and the European Middle Ages', *International Scandinavian and Medieval Studies in Memory of Gerd Wolfgang Weber*, ed. Michael Dallapiazza, Olaf Hansen, Preben Meulengracht Sørensen and Yvonne S. Bonnetain. Trieste: Edizioni Parnaso, 2000, 111–20.

——'Medieval Icelandic Textual Culture', *Gripla* 20 (2009), 163–81.

——ed., *Old Icelandic Literature and Society*. Cambridge Studies in Medieval Literature 42. Cambridge: Cambridge University Press, 2000.

Cohen, Jeffrey Jerome, ed., *The Postcolonial Middle Ages*. New York: St Martin's Press, 2000.

Cohen-Mushlin, Aliza, 'The Twelfth-Century Scriptorium of Frankenthal', in *Medieval Book Production. Assessing the Evidence*, ed. Linda L. Brownrigg. Proceedings of the Second Conference of the Seminar in the History of the Book to 1500, Oxford, July 1988. Los Altos Hills: Anderson-Lovelace, 1990, 85–102.

Cooper, Helen, *The English Romance in Time. Transforming Motifs from Geoffrey of Monmouth to the Death of Shakespeare*. Oxford: Oxford University Press, 2004.

Copeland, Rita, 'Childhood, Pedagogy, and the Literal Sense', *New Medieval Literatures* 1 (1997), 125–56.
—— ed., *Criticism and Dissent in the Middle Ages*. Cambridge: Cambridge University Press, 1996.
—— *Rhetoric, Hermeneutics, and Translation in the Middle Ages. Academic Traditions and Vernacular Texts*. Cambridge Studies in Medieval Literature 11. Cambridge: Cambridge University Press, 1991.
——, David Lawton and Wendy Scase, eds., *New Medieval Literatures*, 12 vols. Oxford: Oxford University Press, 1997–2005 (vols. 1–7), Turnhout: Brepols, 2006–10 (vols. 8–12).
Crane, Susan, 'Anglo-Norman Cultures in England, 1066–1460', in *The Cambridge History of Medieval English Literature*, ed. David Wallace. Cambridge: Cambridge University Press, 1999, 35–60.
Culler, Jonathan, *Structuralist Poetics. Structuralism, Linguistics, and the Study of Literature*. Ithaca: Cornell University Press, 1993.
Davies, R. R., *The First English Empire. Power and Identities in the British Isles 1093–1343*. Oxford: Oxford University Press, 2000.
Dennison, Lynda, 'Oxford, Exeter College MS 47: The Importance of Stylistic and Codicological Analysis in its Dating and Localization', in *Medieval Book Production. Assessing the Evidence*, ed. Linda L. Brownrigg. Proceedings of the Second Conference of the Seminar in the History of the Book to 1500, Oxford, July 1988. Los Altos Hills: Anderson-Lovelace, 1990, 41–60.
Deschamps, Eustache, *L'art de dictier*, ed. and trans. Deborah M. Sinnreich-Levi. Medieval Texts and Studies 13. East Lansing: Colleagues Press, 1994.
DeVries, Kelly, *The Norwegian Invasion of England in 1066*. Woodbridge: Boydell Press, 2003.
Donagher, Colleen P., 'Socializing the Sorceress: The Fairy Mistress in *Lanval, Le Bel Inconnu* and *Partonopeu de Blois*', *Essays in Medieval Studies* 4 (1987), 69–90.
Donovan, Mortimer J., *The Breton Lay: A Guide to Varieties*. Notre Dame: University of Notre Dame Press, 1969.
Doyle, A. I., 'Book Production by the Monastic Orders in England (c.1375–1530): Assessing the Evidence', in *Medieval Book Production. Assessing the Evidence*, ed. Linda L. Brownrigg. Proceedings of the Second Conference of the Seminar in the History of the Book to 1500, Oxford, July 1988. Los Altos Hills: Anderson-Lovelace, 1990, 1–20.
Doyle, Michael, *Empires*. Ithaca: Cornell University Press, 1986.
Driscoll, Matthew James, 'Þögnin mikla. Hugleiðingar um riddarasögur og stöðu þeirra í íslenskum bókmenntum', *Skáldskaparmál* 1 (1990), 157–68.
Duby, Georges, ed., *A History of Private Life. Revelations of the Medieval World*, trans. Arthur Goldhammer, vol. 2. Cambridge: The Belknap Press of Harvard University Press, 1988.
Duggan, Joseph J., 'Beyond the Oxford Text: The Songs of Roland', *Approaches to Teaching the 'Song of Roland'*, ed. William W. Kibler and Leslie Zarker Morgan. New York: The Modern Language Association of America, 2006, 66–72.
—— *The Romances of Chrétien de Troyes*. New Haven: Yale University Press, 2001.
Edwards, Robert R., 'Invention and Closure in Chrétien's *Yvain*', in his *Ratio and Invention. A Study of Medieval Lyric and Narrative*. Nashville: Vanderbilt University Press, 1989, 102–14.
—— 'Invention and Poetic Emblems: *Partonopeu de Blois* and *Sir Gawain and the Green Knight*', in his *Ratio and Invention. A Study of Medieval Lyric and Narrative*. Nashville: Vanderbilt University Press, 1989, 115–30.

Edwards, Robert R., *Ratio and Invention. A Study of Medieval Lyric and Narrative*. Nashville: Vanderbilt University Press, 1989.
Eley, Penny, Catherine Henley, Marion Longtin and Penny Simons, '*Cristal et Clarie* and a Lost Manuscript of *Partonopeus de Blois*', Romania 121 (2003), 329–47.
Eley, Penny, and Penny Simons, '*Partonopeus de Blois* and Chrétien de Troyes: A Re-assessment', Romania 117 (1999), 316–41.
Ellis, Roger, and Ruth Evans, eds., *The Medieval Translator IV*. Binghampton: Medieval and Renaissance Texts and Studies, 1994.
Ellis, Roger, and René Tixier, eds., *The Medieval Translator V*. Turnhout: Brepols, 1996.
Enders, Jody, 'Medieval Death, Modern Morality, and the Fallacies of Intention', New Medieval Literatures 5 (2002), 87–114.
Ernst, Lorenz, *Floire und Blantscheflur. Studie zur vergleichenden Literaturewissenschaft*. Quellen und Forschungen zur Sprach- und Culturgeschichte der germanischen Völker 118. Strassburg: Karl J. Trübner, 1912.
Evans, Helen C., ed., *Byzantium: Faith and Power (1261–1557)*. New Haven: Yale University Press, 2004.
Evans, Murray J., *Rereading Middle English Romance. Manuscript Layout, Decoration, and the Rhetoric of Composite Structure*. Montreal: McGill-Queen's University Press, 1995.
Everett, Dorothy, 'A Characterization of the English Medieval Romance', *Essays on Middle English Literature*, ed. Patricia Kean. Oxford: Clarendon Press, 1955, 1–22.
Faris, David E., 'The Art of Adventure in the Middle English Romance: *Ywain and Gawain, Eger and Grime*', Studia Neophilologica 53 (1981), 91–100.
Fawcett, Robin P., M. A. K. Halliday, Sydney M. Lamb and Adam Makkai, eds., *The Semiotics of Culture and Language*, 2 vols. London: Frances Pinter, 1984.
Ferrante, Joan M., 'Courtly Literature', *Woman as Image in Medieval Literature. From the Twelfth Century to Dante*. New York: Columbia University Press, 1975.
—— 'Male Fantasy and Female Reality in Courtly Literature', Women's Studies 11 (1984), 67–97.
—— 'Public Postures and Private Maneuvers: Roles Medieval Women Play', *Women and Power in the Middle Ages*, ed. Mary Erler and Maryanne Kowaleski. Athens: The University of Georgia Press, 1983, 213–29.
Field, Rosalind, 'The Anglo-Norman Background to Alliterative Romance', in *Middle English Alliterative Poetry and its Literary Background*, ed. David Lawton. Cambridge: D. S. Brewer, 1982, 54–69.
—— 'Romance in England, 1066–1400', in *The Cambridge History of Medieval English Literature*, ed. David Wallace. Cambridge: Cambridge University Press, 1999, 152–76.
Finlayson, John, '*Ywain and Gawain* and the Meaning of Adventure', Anglia 87 (1969), 312–37.
Folz, Robert, *The Concept of Empire in Western Europe from the Fifth to the Fourteenth Century*, trans. Sheila Ann Ogilvie. New York: J. & J. Harper Editions, 1969.
Foote, Peter G., *The Pseudo-Turpin Chronicle in Iceland*. London: London Mediæval Studies, 1959.
Fourrier, Anthime, *Le courant réaliste dans le roman courtois en France au moyen-âge*. Paris: Nizet, 1960.
—— 'Encore la chronologie des oeuvres de Chrétien de Troyes', Bulletin bibliographique de la Sociéte internationale Arthurienne 2 (1950), 69–88.
Fradenburg, Louise O., '"Voice Memorial": Loss and Reparation in Chaucer's Poetry', Exemplaria 2 (1990), 169–202.

Bibliography

Frappier, Jean, *Chrétien de Troyes. The Man and his Work*, trans. Raymond J. Cormier. Athens: Othio University Press, 1982.
—— *Etude sur Yvain ou Le Chevalier au Lion de Chrétien de Troyes*. Paris: Sedes, 1969.
Freeman, Michelle A., *The Poetics of Translatio Studii and Conjointure. Chrétien de Troyes's Cligés*. Lexington: French Forum Publishers, 1979.
Fuchs, Barbara, 'Imperium Studies: Theorizing Early Modern Expansion', in *Postcolonial Moves: Medieval Through Modern*, ed. Patricial Clare Ingham and Michelle R. Warren. New York: Palgrave Macmillan, 2003, 71–90.
Furnish, Shearle, 'Thematic Structure and Symbolic Motif in the Middle English Breton Lays', *Traditio* 62 (2007), 83–116.
Furrow, Melissa, *Expectations of Romance. The Reception of a Genre in Medieval England*. Cambridge: D. S. Brewer, 2009.
Gaunt, Simon, 'Romance and Other Genres', in *The Cambridge Companion to Medieval Romance*, ed. Roberta L. Krueger. Cambridge: Cambridge University Press, 2000, 45–59.
—— and Sarah Kay, *The Cambridge Companion to Medieval French Literature*. Cambridge: Cambridge University Press, 2008.
Geertz, Clifford, *The Interpretation of Cultures*. New York: Basic Books, 2000.
Genette, Gérard, *Narrative Discourse. An Essay in Method*, trans. Jane E. Lewin. Ithaca: Cornell University Press, 1980.
—— *Narrative Discourse Revisited*, trans. Jane E. Lewin. Ithaca: Cornell University Press, 1988.
Gilbert, Jane, 'The *Chanson de Roland*', in *The Cambridge Companion to Medieval French Literature*, ed. Simon Gaunt and Sarah Kay. Cambridge: Cambridge University Press, 2008, 21–34.
Gilbert, Martin, *The Routledge Atlas of British History*. 3rd edn. London: Routledge, 2003.
Gísli Sigurðsson, *Gaelic Influence in Iceland. Historical and Literary Contacts*. Studia Islandica 46. Reykjavík: Bókaútgáfa menningarsjóðs, 1988.
—— and Vésteinn Ólason, eds., *The Manuscripts of Iceland*, trans. Bernard Scudder. Reykjavík: Árni Magnússon Institute in Iceland, 2004.
Glauser, Jürg, 'Romance (Translated *Riddarasögur*)', *A Companion to Old Norse-Icelandic Literature and Culture*, ed. Rory McTurk. Oxford, Blackwell: 2005, 372–87.
le Goff, Jacques, *The Medieval Imagination*, trans. Arthur Goldhammer. Chicago: The University of Chicago Press, 1988.
Gorlée, Dinda L., *On Translating Signs: Exploring Text and Semio-Translation*. Amsterdam: Rodopi, 2004.
Goyet, Florence, 'Narrative Structure and Political Construction: The Epic at Work', *Oral Tradition* 23 (2008), 15–27.
Greimas, A. J., 'Narrative Grammar: Units and Levels', *Modern Language Notes* 86 (1971), 793–806.
Grieve, Patricia E., *Floire and Blancheflor and the European Romance*. Cambridge Studies in Medieval Literature 32. Cambridge: Cambridge University Press, 1997.
Griffiths, Jeremy, and Derek Pearsall, eds., *Book Production and Publishing in Britain 1375–1475*. Cambridge: Cambridge University Press, 1989.
Guddat-Figge, Gisela, *Catalogue of Manuscripts Containing Middle English Romances*. Münchener Universitäts-Schriften 4. Munich: Wilhelm Fink Verlag, 1976.
Gurevich, A. J., *Categories of Medieval Culture*, trans. G. L. Campbell. London: Routledge & Kegan Paul, 1985.

Guy-Bray, Stephen, 'Male Trouble: *Sir Launfal* and the Trials of Masculinity', *English Studies in Canada* 34 (2008), 31–48.
Haidu, Peter, 'The Episode as Semiotic Module in Twelfth-Century Romance', *Poetics Today* 4 (1983), 655–81.
—— 'Romance: Realistic Genre or Historical Text?', in *The Craft of Fiction. Essays in Medieval Poetics*, ed. Leigh A. Arrathoon. Rochester: Solaris Press, 1984, 1–46.
—— *The Subject Medieval/Modern. Text and Governance in the Middle Ages*. Standford, California: Stanford University Press, 2004.
Hallberg, Peter, 'Norröna riddarsagor. Några språkdrag', *Arkiv för nordisk filologi* 86 (1971), 114–38.
Halliday, M. A. K., 'Language as Code and Language as Behaviour', in *The Semiotics of Culture and Language*, ed. Robin P. Fawcett, M. A. K. Halliday, Sydney M. Lamb and Adam Makkai, vol. 1. London: Frances Pinter, 1984, 3–36.
Halvorsen, E. F., *The Norse Version of the Chanson de Roland*. Bibliotheca Arnamagnæana 19. Copenhagen: Ejnar Munksgaard, 1959.
Hamilton, Gayle K., 'The Breaking of the Troth in *Ywain and Gawain*', *Mediaevalia* 2 (1976), 111–35.
Hanna, Ralph, 'Analytical Survey 4: Middle English Manuscripts and the Study of Literarature', *New Medieval Literatures* 4 (2001), 242–64.
—— *London Literature, 1300–1380*. Cambridge: Cambridge University Press, 2005.
Harré, Rom, ed., *The Social Construction of Emotions*. Oxford: Blackwell, 1986.
—— and W. Parrott, eds., *The Emotions, Social, Cultural and Biological Dimensions*. London: Sage Publications, 1996.
Harrington, Norman T., 'The Problem of the Lacunae in *Ywain and Gawain*', *Journal of English and Germanic Philology* 69 (1970), 659–65.
Harris, Julian, 'The Rôle of the Lion in Chrétien de Troyes' *Yvain*', *Proceedings of the Modern Language Association of America* 64 (1949), 1143–63.
Hasan, Ruqaiya, 'Ways of Saying: Ways of Meaning', *The Semiotics of Culture and Language*, ed. Robin P. Fawcett, M. A. K. Halliday, Sydney M. Lamb and Adam Makkai, vol. 1. London: Frances Pinter, 1984, 105–62.
Hazell, Dinah, 'The Blinding of Gwennere: Thomas Chestre as Social Critic', *Arthurian Literature* 20 (2003), 123–43.
Helle, Knut, 'Anglo-Norwegian Relations in the Reign of Håkon Håkonsson (1217–63)', *Medieval Scandinavia* 1 (1968), 101–14.
—— ed., *The Cambridge History of Scandinavia*, vol. 1, *Prehistory to 1520*. Cambridge: Cambridge University Press, 2003.
Heng, Geraldine, *Empire of Magic. Medieval Romance and the Politics of Cultural Fantasy*. New York: Columbia University Press, 2003.
Hindman, Sandra, *Sealed in Parchment. Rereading of Knighthood in the Illuminated Manuscripts of Chrétien de Troyes*. Chicago: University of Chicago Press, 1994.
Hollengreen, Laura H., ed., *Translatio or the Transmission of Culture in the Middle Ages and the Renaissance. Modes and Messages*. Arizona Studies in the Middle Ages and the Renaissance 13. Turnhout: Brepols, 2008.
Holmes, James S., *Translated! Papers on Literary Translation and Translation Studies*. Amsterdam: Rodopi, 1988.
Hopkins, Amanda, 'Female Vulnerability as Catalyst in the Middle English Breton Lays', in *The Matter of Identity in Medieval Romance*, ed. Phillipa Hardman. Cambridge: D. S. Brewer, 2002, 43–58.
Hosington, Brenda, 'Proverb Translation as Linguistic and Cultural Transfer in Some Middle English Versions of Old French Romances', *The Medieval Translator. Traduire au moyen âge*, ed. Roger Ellis and René Tixier, vol. 5. Turnhout: Brepols, 1996, 170–86.

Hosington, Brenda, 'Voices of Protest and Submission: Portraits of Women in *Partonopeu de Blois* and its Middle English Translation', *Reading Medieval Studies* 17 (1991), 51–75.
von Humboldt, Wilhelm, 'From Introduction to his Translation of *Agamemnon*', in *Theories of Translation. An Anthology of Essays from Dryden to Derrida*, ed. Rainer Schulte and John Biguenet. Chicago: The University of Chicago Press, 1992, 55–9.
Hunt, Tony, 'Beginnings, Middles, and Ends: Some Interpretative Problems in Chrétien's *Yvain* and its Medieval Adaptations', in *The Craft of Fiction. Essays in Medieval Poetics*, ed. Leigh A. Arrathoon. Rochester: Solaris Press, 1984, 83–117.
—— 'The Lion and Yvain', in *The Legend of Arthur in the Middle Ages*, ed. P. B. Grout, R. A. Lodge, C. E. Pickford and E. K. C. Varty. Cambridge: D. S. Brewer, 1983, 86–98.
—— 'The Medieval Adaptations of Chrétien's *Yvain*: A Bibliographical Essay', in *An Arthurian Tapestry. Essays in Memory of Lewis Thorpe*, ed. Kenneth Varty. Glasgow: University of Glasgow, 1981, 203–13.
—— 'Redating Chrestien de Troyes', *Bulletin bibliographique de la Sociéte internationale Arthurienne* 30 (1978), 209–37.
Ihle, Sandra, 'The English *Partonope of Blois* as Exemplum', in *Courtly Literature. Culture and Context. Selected Papers from the 5th Triennial Congress of the International Courtly Literature Society, Dalfsen, The Netherlands, 9–16 August, 1986*, ed. Keith Busby and Erik Kooper. Amsterdam: John Benjamins, 1990, 301–11.
Ingham, Patricia Clare, '"In Contrayez Straunge": Colonial Relations, British Identity, and *Sir Gawain and the Green Knight*', *New Medieval Literatures* 4 (2001), 61–94.
—— *Sovereign Fantasies. Arthurian Romance and the Making of Britain*. Philadelphia: University of Pennsylvania Press, 2001.
—— and Michelle R. Warren, eds., *Postcolonial Moves: Medieval through Modern*. New York: Palgrave Macmillan, 2003.
Ingham, Richard, 'The Persistence of Anglo-Norman 1230–1362: A Linguistic Perspective', in *Language and Culture in Medieval Britain. The French of England c.1100–c.1500*, ed. Jocelyn Wogan-Browne *et al.* York: York Medieval Press, 2009, 44–54.
Jackson, Claire M., 'The City as Two-Way Mirror in the Middle English *Partonope of Blois*', *Mediaevalia* 25 (2004), 197–208. Special Issue: *Partonopeus in Europe. An Old French Romance and its Adaptations*, ed. Catherine Hanley, Mario Longtin and Penny Eley. New York: The Center for Medieval and Renaissance Studies, 2004.
Jaeger, C. Stephen, *The Origins of Courtliness. Civilizing Trends and the Formation of Courtly Ideals 939–1210*. Philadelphia: University of Pennsylvania Press, 1985.
—— 'Pessimism in the Twelfth-Century "Renaissance"', *Speculum* 78.4 (2003), 1,151–83.
Jakobson, Roman, 'On Linguistic Aspects of Translation', in *Theories of Translation. An Anthology of Essays from Dryden to Derrida*, ed. Rainer Schulte and John Biguenet. Chicago: The University of Chicago Press, 1992, 144–51.
Jauss, Hans Robert, *Toward an Aesthetic of Reception*, trans. Timothy Bahti. Theory and History of Literature, vol. 2. Minneapolis: University of Minnesota Press, 1982.
Jenkins, Jacqueline, and Olivier Bertrand, eds., *The Medieval Translator / Traduire au moyen âge 10*. Turnhout: Brepols, 2008.
Johnston, Grahame, 'The Breton Lays in Middle English', in *Iceland and the Mediaeval World. Studies in Honour of Ian Maxwell*, ed. Gabriel Turville-Petre and John Stanley Martin. Victoria: The Organizing Committee for Publishing a Volume in Honour of Professor Maxwell, 1974, 151–62.

Jones, Catherine M., 'Roland versus Oliver', in *Approaches to Teaching the 'Song of Roland'*, ed. William W. Kibler and Leslie Zarker Morgan. New York: The Modern Language Association of America, 2006, 201–6.

Jones, Chris, *Eclipse of Empire? Perceptions of the Western Empire and its Rulers in Late-Medieval France*. Turnhout: Brepols, 2007.

Jones, Peter Murray, 'British Library MS Sloane 76: A Translator's Holograph', in *Medieval Book Production. Assessing the Evidence*, ed. Linda L. Brownrigg. Proceedings of the Second Conference of The Seminar in the History of the Book to 1500, Oxford, July 1988. Los Altos Hills: Anderson-Lovelace, 1990, 21–40.

Jurasinski, Stefan, 'Treason and the Charge of Sodomy in the *Lai de Lanval*', *Romance Quarterly* 54 (2007), 290–302.

Kabir, Ananya Jahanara, and Deanne Williams, eds., *Postcolonial Approaches to the European Middle Ages. Translating Cultures*. Cambridge: Cambridge University Press, 2005.

Kalinke, Marianne E., *Bridal-Quest Romance in Medieval Iceland*. Islandica 46. Ithaca: Cornell University Press, 1990.

—— '*Gvímars saga*', *Opuscula* 7. Bibliotheca Arnamagnæana 34, Copenhagen: C. A. Reitzels boghandel, 1979, 106–39.

—— *King Arthur North-by-Northwest. The 'matière de Bretagne' in Old Norse-Icelandic Romances*. Bibliotheca Arnamagnæana 37. Copenhagen: C. A. Reitzels boghandel, 1981.

—— 'The Misogamous Maiden Kings of Icelandic Romances', *Scripta Islandica* 37 (1986), 47–71.

Kalinke, Marianne E., and P. M. Mitchell, eds., *Bibliography of Old Norse-Icelandic Romances*. Islandica 44. Ithaca: Cornell University Press, 1985.

Kay, Sarah, 'Analytical Survey 3: The New Philology', *New Medieval Literatures* 3 (1999), 295–326.

—— *Courtly Contradictions. The Emergence of the Literary Object in the Twelfth Century*. Stanford: Stanford University Press, 2001.

—— 'Courts, Clerks, and Courtly Love', in *The Cambridge Companion to Medieval Romance*, ed. Roberta L. Krueger. Cambridge: Cambridge University Press, 2000, 81–96.

—— 'Translating Theory', *New Medieval Literatures* 9 (2007), 199–202.

Kelly, Douglas, 'The Art of Description', in *The Legacy of Chrétien de Troyes*, ed. Norris J. Lacy, Douglas Kelly and Keith Busby, vol. 1. Amsterdam: Rodopi, 1987, 191–221.

—— 'Chrétien de Troyes: The Narrator and his Art', in *The Romances of Chrétien de Troyes, A Symposium*, ed. Douglas Kelly. Lexington: French Forum, Publishers, 1985, 13–47.

—— 'Romance and the Vanity of Chretien de Troyes', in *Romance. Generic Transformation from Chrétien de Troyes to Cervantes*, ed. Kevin Brownlee and Marina Scordilis Brownlee. Hanover: University Press of New England, 1985, 74–90.

—— ed., *The Romances of Chrétien de Troyes. A Symposium*. Lexington: French Forum, Publishers, 1985.

Kennedy, Ruth, and Simon Meecham-Jones, eds., *Authority and Subjugation in Writing in Medieval Wales*. New York: Palgrave Macmillan, 2008.

Ker, W. P., *English Literature Medieval*. London: Williams & Norgate, 1928.

—— *Epic and Romance. Essays on Medieval Literature*. New York: Dover Publications, 1957.

Kerby-Fulton, Kathryn, '*Piers Plowman*', in *The Cambridge History of Medieval English Literature*, ed. David Wallace. Cambridge: Cambridge University Press, 1999, 513–38.

Kibbee, Douglas A., 'Emigrant Languages and Acculturation: The Case of Anglo-French', in *The Origins and Development of Emigrant Languages. Proceedings from the Second Rask Colloquium, Odense University, November 1994*, ed. Hans F. Nielsen and Lene Schøsler. Odense: Odense University Press, 1996, 1–20.

—— *For to Speke Frenche Trewely. The French Language in England, 1000–1600: Its Status, Description and Instruction*. Amsterdam: John Benjamins Publishing Company, 1991.

Kinoshita, Sharon, *Medieval Boundaries. Rethinking Difference in Old French Literature*. Philadelphia: University of Pennsylvania Press, 2006.

Kittay, Jeffrey, and Wlad Godzich, *The Emergence of Prose. An Essay in Prosaics*. Minneapolis: University of Minnesota Press, 1987.

Kjær, Joanna, '*Karlamagnús saga*: la saga de Charlemagne', *Revue des langues romanes* 102 (1998), 7–24.

—— 'La réception scandinave de la littérature courtoise et l'exemple de la *Chanson de Roland* / *Af Rúnzivals bardaga*: Une épopée féodale transformée en roman courtois?', *Romania* 114 (1996), 50–69.

Klockhoff, Oskar, *Små bidrag til nordiska literaturehistorien under medeltiden*. Upsala: Esaias Edquists Boktryckeri, 1880.

Knight, Stephen, 'The Social Function of the Middle English Romances', in *Medieval Literature. Criticism, Ideology & History*, ed. David Aers. New York: St Martin's Press, 1986, 99–122.

Kölbing, Eugen, 'Über die verschiedenen Gestaltungen der Partonopeus-Sage', *Germanistische Studien* (Supplement zur Germania), ed. Karl Bartsch, vol. 2. Vienna: Druck und Verlag von Carl Gerold's Sohn, 1875.

Kramarz-Bein, Susanne, 'Geschichtsdenken in Skandinavien in der Tradition der *Chansons de geste* am Beispiel der *Karlamagnús saga*', in *Arbeiten zur Skandinavistik. XII Arbeitstagung der Deutschsprachigen Skandinavistik 16.–23. September 1995 in Greifswald*, ed. Walter Baumgartner und Hans Fix. Vienna: Fassbaender, 1996, 152–65.

—— 'Karl der Große in der skandinavischen Literatur des Mittelalters unter besonderer Berücksichtigung der altwestnordischen *Karlamagnús saga ok kappa hans* und ihres Erzählverfahrens', *Jahrbuch der Oswald von Wolkenstein-Gesellschaft* 16 (2006), 74–89.

—— 'Zur erzählstruktur der *Karlamagnús saga*', in *Arbeiten zur Skandinavistik (14. Arbeitstagung der Deutschsprachigen Skandinavistik 1–5.9 1999 in München)*, ed. Annegret Heitman. Frankfurt am Main: Peter Lang, 2001, 369–78.

Krueger, Roberta L., 'The Author's Voice: Narrators, Audiences, and the Problem of Interpretation', in *The Legacy of Chrétien de Troyes*, ed. Norris J. Lacy, Douglas Kelly and Keith Busby, vol. 1. Amsterdam: Rodopi, 1987, 115–40.

—— ed., *The Cambridge Companion to Medieval Romance*. Cambridge: Cambridge University Press, 2000.

—— 'Marie de France', in *The Cambridge Companion to Medieval Women's Writing*, ed. Carolyn Dinshaw and David Wallace. Cambridge: Cambridge University Press, 2003, 172–83.

—— 'Question of Gender in Old French Courtly Romance', in *The Cambridge Companion to Medieval Romance*, ed. Roberta L. Krueger. Cambridge: Cambridge University Press, 2000, 132–49.

—— 'The Shape of Romance in Medieval France', *The Cambridge Companion to Medieval Romance*, ed. Roberta L. Krueger. Cambridge: Cambridge University Press, 2000, 13–28.

—— 'Textuality and Performance in *Partonopeu de Blois*', *Assays* 3 (1985), 57–72.

Lacy, Norris J., *The Craft of Chrétien de Troyes: An Essay on Narrative Art*. Leiden: E. J. Brill, 1980.

Lacy, Norris J., 'Observations on Authority', *Arthuriana* 19 (2009), 72–9.
——, Douglas Kelly and Keith Busby, eds., *The Legacy of Chrétien de Troyes*, 2 vols. Amsterdam: Rodopi, 1987.
—— and Joan Tasker Grimbert, eds., *A Companion to Chrétien de Troyes*. Cambridge: D. S. Brewer, 2005.
Laing, Margaret, 'Anchor Texts and Literary Manuscripts in Early Middle English', in *Regionalism in Late Medieval Manuscripts and Texts*, ed. Felicity Riddy. York Manuscript Conferences: Proceedings Series. Cambridge: D. S. Brewer, 1991, 27–52.
Larrington, Carolyne, 'Queens and Bodies: The Norwegian Translated *lais* and Hákon IV's Kinswomen', *Journal of English and Germanic Philology* 108 (2009), 506–27.
—— 'The Translated *Lais*', in *King Arthur of the North*, ed. Marianne Kalinke. Cardiff: University of Wales Press, 2009, 77–97.
Laskaya, Anne, 'Thomas Chestre's Revision of Manhood in *Sir Launfal*', in *Retelling Tales: Essays in Honour of Russell Peck*, ed. Thomas Hahn and Alan Lupack. Cambridge: D. S. Brewer, 1997, 191–212.
Lawton, David, 'Analytical Survey 1: Literary History and Cultural Study', *New Medieval Literatures* 1 (1997), 237–69.
—— 'For God and Werewolf: A Reading History of *Guillaume de Palerne* 1190–1390'. Lecture, University of Oxford, 17 Oct. 2005.
—— ed., *William of Palerne*. TEAMS Middle English Text Series. Kalamazoo: The Medieval Institute Publications, forthcoming.
Leach, Henry Goddard, *Angevin Britain and Scandinavia*. Harvard Studies in Comparative Literature 6. Cambridge, Mass.: Harvard University Press, 1921.
Lee, Ashley, 'The Hind Episode in Marie de France's *Guigemar* and Medieval Vernacular Poetics', *Neophilologus* 93 (2009), 191–200.
Lefevere, André, and Susan Bassnett, *Constructing Cultures*. Clevedon: Multilingual Matters, 1998.
——— eds., *Translation, History, and Culture*. London: Pinter Publishers, 1990.
Legge, M. Dominica, *Anglo-Norman Literature and its Background*. Oxford: Clarendon Press, 1963.
Leicester, H. Marshall, Jr, 'The Voice of the Hind. The Emergence of Feminine Discontent in the *Lais* of Marie de France', in *Reading Medieval Culture. Essays in Honor of Robert W. Hanning*, ed. Robert M. Stein and Sandra Pierson Prior. Notre Dame, Indiana: University of Notre Dame Press, 2005, 132–69.
Liestøl, Knut, *The Origin of the Icelandic Family Sagas*, trans. A. G. Jayne. Oslo: H. Aschehoug & Co. (W. Nygaard), 1930.
Lönnroth, Lars, 'Charlemagne, Hrólf kraki, Óláf Tryggvason, Parallels in the Heroic Tradition', in *Les relations littéraires franco-scandinaves au moyen âge. Actes du colloque de Liège (avril 1972)*. Bibliothèque de la faculté de philosophie et lettres de l'Université de Liège Fasc. 208. Paris: Société d'édition 'Les belles lettres', 1975, 29–52.
—— *European Sources of Icelandic Saga-Writing*. Stockholm: Boktryckeri Aktiebolaget Thule, 1965.
Loomis, Roger Sherman, ed., *Arthurian Literature in the Middle Ages*. Oxford: Clarendon Press, 1959.
Lusignan, Serge, 'French Language in Contact with English: Social Context and Linguistic Change (mid-13th–14th centuries)', in *Language and Culture. The French of England c.1100–c.1500*, ed. Jocelyn Wogan-Browne *et al*. York: York Medieval Press, 2009, 19–30.
Malm, Mats, 'The Notion of Effeminate Language in Old Norse Literature', in *Learning and Understanding in the Old Norse World. Essays in Honour of Margaret Clunies Ross*, ed. Judy Quinn, Kate Heslop and Tarrin Wills. Turnhout: Brepols, 2007, 305–20.

Bibliography

Marvin, Julia, 'The Vitality of Anglo-Norman in Late Medieval England: The Case of the Prose *Brut* Chronicle', in *Language and Culture. The French of England c.1100–c.1500*, ed. Jocelyn Wogan-Browne *et al.* York: York Medieval Press, 2009, 303–19.
McCobb, Lilian M., 'The English *Partonope of Blois*, its French Source, and Chaucer's *Knight's Tale*', *The Chaucer Review* 11 (1977), 369–72.
—— 'The Traditional Background of *Partonopeu de Blois*. An Additional Note', *Neophilologus* 60 (1976), 608–10.
McCracken, Peggy, 'Translation and Animals in Marie de France's *Lais*', *Australian Journal of French Studies* 46 (2009): 206–18.
McCreesh, Bernardine, 'Translation and Adaptation in *Lay le Freine*', *Forum for Modern Language Studies* 35 (1999), 386–95.
Mehl, Dieter, *The Middle English Romances of the Thirteenth and Fourteenth Centuries*. London: Routledge & Kegan Paul, 1968.
Middleton, Anne, 'The Audience and Public of *Piers Plowman*', in *Middle English Alliterative Poetry and its Literary Background*, ed. David Lawton. Cambridge: D. S. Brewer, 1982, 101–23.
Mieszkowski, Gretchen, 'Urake and the Gender Roles of *Partonope of Blois*', *Mediaevalia* 25 (2004), 181–96. Special Issue: *Partonopeus in Europe. An Old French Romance and its Adaptations*, ed. Catherine Hanley, Mario Longtin and Penny Eley. New York: The Center for Medieval and Renaissance Studies, 2004.
Mills, Madwyn, *et al.*, 'Chivalric Romance', *The Arthur of the English. The Arthurian Legend in Medieval English Life and Literature*, ed. W. R. J. Barron. Arthurian Literature in the Middle Ages 2. Cardiff: University of Wales Press, 2001, 113–84.
Minnis, A. J., 'Medieval Imagination and Memory', in *The Cambridge History of Literary Criticism: The Middle Ages*, ed. Alastair Minnis and Ian Johnson, vol 2. Cambridge: Cambridge University Press, 2005, 239–74.
—— *Medieval Theory of Authorship. Scholastic Literary Attitudes in the later Middle Ages*. 2nd edn. Philadelphia: University of Pennsylvania Press, 1988.
Minnis, Alastair, and Ian Johnson, eds., *The Cambridge History of Literary Criticism: The Middle Ages*, vol. 2. Cambridge: Cambridge University Press, 2005.
Mommsen, Wolfgang J., *Theories of Imperialism*, trans. P. S. Falla. New York: Random House, 1980.
Nelting, David, 'Literalität und Spiritualität im altfranzösischen Rolandslied', *Romanische Forschungen* 119 (2007), 203–15.
Newstead, Helaine, 'Narrative Techniques in Chrétien's *Yvain*', *Romance Philology* 30 (1977), 431–41.
—— 'The Traditional Background of *Partonopeus de Blois*', *Proceedings of the Modern Language Association of America* 61 (1946), 916–46.
Ney, Agnete, Ármann Jakobsson and Annette Larsen, eds., *Fornaldarsagaerne: Myter og virkelighed*. Copenhagen: Museum Tusculanums Forlag, 2008.
Nicholls, Jonathan, *The Matter of Courtesy. Medieval Courtesy Books and the Gawain-Poet*. Cambridge: D. S. Brewer, 1985.
Nichols, Stephen G., 'The New Medievalism: Tradition and Discontinuity in Medieval Culture', in *The New Medievalism*, ed. Marina S. Brownlee, Kevin Brownlee and Stephen G. Nichols. Baltimore: The Johns Hopkins University Press, 1991, 1–26.
Noble, Peter S., '*Partonopeu de Blois* and Chrétien de Troyes', in *Studies in Honor of Hans-Erich Keller*, ed. Rupert T. Pickens. Kalamazoo: Medieval Institute Publications, 1993, 195–211.
Nordal, Guðrún, *Tools of Literacy: The Role of Skaldic Verse in Icelandic Textual Culture of the Twelfth and Thirteenth Centuries*. Toronto: University of Toronto Press, 2001.

Nordal, Guðrún, and Vésteinn Ólason, eds., *Íslensk bókmenntasaga*, vol. 1. Reykjavík: Mál og menning, 1992.
Ormrod, W. Mark, 'The Language of Complaint: Multilingualism and Petitioning in Later Medieval England', in *Language and Culture. The French of England c.1100–c.1500*, ed. Jocelyn Wogan-Browne et al. York: York Medieval Press, 2009, 31–43.
—— 'The Use of English: Language, Law, and Political Culture in Fourteenth-Century England', *Speculum* 78 (2003), 750–87.
Owen, D. D. R., *Eleanor of Aquitaine. Queen and Legend*. Oxford: Blackwell, 1993.
Parkes, M. B., *Scribes, Scripts and Readers. Studies in the Communication, Presentation and Dissemination of Medieval Texts*. London: The Hambledon Press, 1991.
Pearman, Tory Vandeventer, 'Refiguring Disability: Deviance, Blinding, and the Supernatural in Thomas Chestre's *Sir Launfal*', *Journal of Literary and Cultural Disability Studies* 3 (2009), 131–46.
Pearsall, Derek, *Old English and Middle English Poetry*. The Routledge History of English Poetry 1. London: Routledge & Kegan Paul, 1977.
Petrilli, Susan, ed., *Translation Translation*. Amsterdam: Rodopi, 2003.
Power, Rosemary, '*Le Lai de Lanval* and *Helga þáttr Þórissonar*', *Opuscula* 8. Bibliotheca Arnamagnæana 38. Copenhagen: The Arnamagnæan Commission, 1985, 158–61.
Psaki, Regina F., 'Women's Counsel in the Riddarasögur: The Case of *Parcevals saga*', in *Cold Counsel: Women in Old Norse Literature and Mythology*, ed. Sarah M. Anderson and Karen Swenson. New York: Routledge: 2002, 201–24.
Rabassa, Gregory, 'Words Cannot Express . . . The Translation of Cultures', in *Translation Horizons. Beyond the Boundaries of Translation Spectrum*, ed. Marilyn Gaddis Rose. Binghampton: State University of New York, 1996, 183–94.
Raffel, Burton, 'Translating Medieval European Poetry', in *The Craft of Translation*, ed. John Biguenet and Rainer Schulte. Chicago: the University of Chicago Press, 1989, 28–53.
Les relations littéraires franco-scandinaves au moyen âge. Actes du colloque de Liège (avril 1972). Bibliothèque de la faculté de philosophie et lettres de l'Université de Liège Fasc. 208. Paris: Société d'édition 'Les belles lettres', 1975.
Reynolds, Suzanne, *Medieval Reading. Grammar, Rhetoric and the Classical Text*. Cambridge Studies in Medieval Literature 27. Cambridge: Cambridge University Press, 1996.
Röder, Gabriele, 'Die *Chansons de geste* in der altnordischen *Karlamagnús saga*: Übersetzungen oder Adaptationen?', in *The Medieval Translator / Traduire au moyen âge*, ed. Roger Ellis, René Tixier and Bernd Weitemeier, vol. 6. Turnhout: Brepols, 1998, 134–58.
Rose, Marilyn Gaddis, ed., *Translation Horizons. Beyond the Boundaries of Translation Spectrum*. Binghampton: State University of New York, 1996.
Rosenwein, Barbara H., ed., *Anger's Past. The Social Uses of an Emotion in the Middle Ages*. Ithaca: Cornell University Press, 1998.
—— *Emotional Communities in the Early Middle Ages*. Ithaca: Cornell University Press, 2007.
Rothwell, W., 'Arrivals and Departures: The Adoption of French Terminology into Middle English', *English Studies* 79 (1998), 144–65.
—— 'Chaucer and Stratford ate Bowe', *Bulletin of the John Rylands University Library of Manchester* 74 (1992), 3–28.
—— 'English and French in England after 1362', *English Studies* 82 (2001), 539–59.
—— 'The Missing Link in English Etymology: Anglo-French', *Medium Aevum* 60 (1991), 173–96.

Rothwell, W., 'The Role of French in Thirteenth-Century England', *Bulletin of the John Rylands University Library of Manchester* 58 (1976), 445–66.
—— 'The Teaching of French in Medieval England', *Proceedings of the Modern Language Association of America* 63 (1968), 36–46.
—— 'The Trilingual England of Geoffrey Chaucer', *Studies in the Age of Chaucer* 16 (1994), 45–68.
Rowe, Elizabeth Ashman, 'Þorsteins þáttr uxafóts, Helga þáttr Þórissonar, and the Conversion Þættir', *Scandinavian Studies* 76 (2004), 459–74.
Said, Edward W., *Culture and Imperialism*. New York: Alfred A. Knopf, 1993.
Salter, Elizabeth, *English and International: Studies in the Literature, Art and Patronage of Medieval England*, ed. Derek Pearsall and Nicolette Zeeman. Cambridge: Cambridge University Press, 1988.
Salzman, L. F., *Henry II*. New York: Russel & Russel, 1967.
Sanders, Christopher, 'Hinn alkunni bókabévus', in *Sagnaþing helgað Jónasi Kristjánssyni sjötugum 10. apríl 1994*, ed. Gísli Sigurðsson, Guðrún Kvaran and Sigurgeir Steingrímsson, vol. 2. Reykjavik: Hið íslenska bókmenntafélag, 1994, 691–7.
Sandler, Lucy Freeman, '*Omne bonum*: Compilatio and Ordinatio in an English Illustrated Encyclopedia of the Fourteenth Century', in *Medieval Book Production. Assessing the Evidence*, ed. Linda L. Brownrigg. Proceedings of the Second Conference of the Seminar in the History of the Book to 1500, Oxford, July 1988. Los Altos Hills: Anderson-Lovelace, 1990, 183–200.
Saunders, Corinne, ed., *Cultural Encounters in the Romance of Medieval England*. Studies in Medieval Romance. Cambridge: D. S. Brewer, 2005.
Schach, Paul, 'The 'Saga af Tristram ok Ísodd': Summary or Satire?', *Modern Language Quarterly* 21 (1960), 336–52.
—— 'Some Observations on the Influence of *Tristrams saga ok Isöndar* on Old Icelandic Literature', in *Old Norse Literature and Mythology. A Symposium*, ed. Edgar C. Polomé. Austin: University of Texas Press, 1969, 81–130.
—— 'Some Observations on the Translations of Friar Robert', in *Les relations littéraires franco-scandinaves au moyen age. Actes du colloque de Liège (avril 1972)*. Bibliothèque de la faculté de philosophie et lettres de l'Université de Liège Fasc. 208. Paris: Société d'édition 'Les belles lettres', 1975, 117–36.
Schier, Kurt, 'Iceland and the Rise of Literature in "Terra Nova"', *Grípla* 1 (1975), 168–81.
Schiff, Randy P., 'Borderland Subversions: Anti-imperial Energies in *The Awntyrs off Arthure* and *Golagros and Gawane*', *Speculum* 84 (2009), 613–32.
Schlauch, Margaret, *Romance in Iceland*. Princeton: Princeton University Press, 1934.
Schleich, Gustav, *Über das Verhältnis der mittelenglischen Romanze Ywain and Gawain zu ihrer altfranzösischen Quelle*. Berlin: R. Gaertners Verlagsbuchhandlung, 1889.
Schleiermacher, Friedrich, 'From On the different Methods of Translating', trans. Waltraud Bartscht, in *Theories of Translation. An Anthology of Essays from Dryden to Derrida*, ed. Rainer Schulte and John Biguenet. Chicago: The University of Chicago Press, 1992, 36–54.
Seaman, Myra, 'Tomas Chestre's *Sir Launfal* and the Englishing of Medieval Romance', *Medieval Perspectives* 15 (2000), 105–19.
Sif Ríkharðsdóttir, 'Meykóngahefðin í riddarasögum: hugmyndafræðileg átök um kynhlutverk og þjóðfélagsstöðu', *Skírnir* 184 (2010), 410–33.
Simons, Penny C., 'A Romance Revisited: Reopening the Question of the Manuscript Tradition of *Partonopeus de Blois*', *Romania* 115 (1997), 368–405.

Simons, Penny C., and Penny Eley, 'Male Beauty and Sexual Orientation in *Partonopeus de Blois*', *Romance Studies* 17 (1999), 41–56.
—— 'The Prologue to *Partonopeus de Blois*: Text, Context and Subtext', *French Studies* 49 (1995), 1–16.
—— 'A Subtext and its Subversion: The Variant Endings to *Partonopeus de Blois*', *Neophilologus* 82 (1998), 181–97.
Snell-Hornby, Mary, *Translation Studies. An Integrated Approach*. Amsterdam: John Benjamins Publishing Company, 1995.
Spearing, A. C., 'The Lanval Story', *The Medieval Poet as Voyeur*. Cambridge: Cambridge University Press, 1993, 97–120.
—— 'Marie de France and Her Middle English Adapters', *Studies in the Age of Chaucer* 12 (1990), 117–57.
—— '*Partonope of Blois*', *The Medieval Poet as Voyeur*. Cambridge: Cambridge University Press, 1993, 140–54.
Spensley, Ronald, 'The Courtly Lady in *Partonope of Blois*', *Neuphilologische Mitteilungen* 74 (1973), 288–91.
Spiegel, Gabrielle, 'Épater les médiévistes', *History and Theory* 39 (2000), 243–50.
Stahuljak, Zrinka, *Bloodless Genealogies of the French Middle Ages. Translatio, Kinship, and Metaphor*. Gainesville: University Press of Florida, 2005.
—— 'An Epistemology of Tension. Translation and Multiculturalism', in *The Translator. Studies in Intercultural Communication* 10 (2004), 33–57.
Stein, Robert M., 'Acts of Translation', *New Medieval Literatures* 9 (2007), 185–90.
Stock, Brian, *The Implications of Literacy. Written Language and Models of Interpretation in the Eleventh and Twelfth Centuries*. Princeton: Princeton University Press, 1983.
—— *Listening for the Text. On the Uses of the Past*. Baltimore: The Johns Hopkins University Press, 1990.
Sunnen, Donald Robert, 'Medieval Translation as Certamen: The Germanic Versions of *Ivain, Le Chevalier au Lion*'. Dissertation, University of Illinois at Urbana-Champaign, 1990.
Sverrir Tómasson, 'Hvenær var Tristrams sögu snúið?', *Grípla* 2 (1977), 47–78.
——, Torfi H. Tulinius and Vésteinn Ólason, eds., *Íslensk bókmenntasaga*, vol. 2. Reykjavík: Mál og menning, 1993.
Thorrold, Craig, 'Mistranslation or Modification? Toponymical Transformation in *Partonope of Blois*', *Mediaevalia* 25 (2004), 1–25. Special Issue: *Partonopeus in Europe. An Old French Romance and its Adaptations*, ed. Catherine Hanley, Mario Longtin and Penny Eley. New York: The Center for Medieval and Renaissance Studies, 2004.
Tomlinson, John, *Cultural Imperialism*. Baltimore: The Johns Hopkins University Press, 1991.
Townsend, David, 'Scandals of Translation, Pragmatics of Desire', *New Medieval Literatures* 9 (2007), 207–11.
Treadgold, Warren T., *A History of the Byzantine State and Society*. Stanford: Stanford University Press, 1997.
Trounce, A. McI., 'The English Tail-Rhyme Romances', *Medium Ævum* 1 (1932), 87–108; *Medium Ævum* 2 (1933), 189–98; *Medium Ævum* 3 (1934), 30–50.
Tulinius, Torfi H., *The Matter of the North. The Rise of Literary Fiction in Thirteenth Century Iceland*, trans. Randi C. Eldevik. Odense: Odense University Press, 2002.
—— 'The Self as Other. Iceland and Christian Europe in the Middle Ages', *Grípla* 20 (2009), 199–215.
Turville-Petre, Thorlac, *England the Nation. Language, Literature, and National Identity, 1290–1340*. Oxford: Clarendon Press, 1996.

Turville-Petre, Thorlac, Introduction, *Alliterative Poetry of the Later Middle Ages. An Anthology*, ed. Thorlac Turville-Petre. Washington: The Catholic University of America Press, 1989, 1–8.
Uitti, Karl D., '*Le Chevalier au Lion* (*Yvain*)', in *The Romances of Chrétien de Troyes. A Symposium*, ed. Douglas Kelly. Lexington: French Forum, Publishers, 1985, 182–231.
—— with Michelle A. Freeman, *Chrétien de Troyes Revisited*. New York: Twayne Publishers, 1995.
Uri, S. P., 'Some Remarks on *Partonopeus de Blois*', *Neophilologus* 37 (1953), 83–98.
Vance, Eugene, *From Topic to Tale. Logic and Narrativity in the Middle Ages*. Theory and History of Literature 47. Minneapolis: University of Minnesota Press, 1987.
—— *Mervelous Signals. Poetics and Sign Theory in the Middle Ages*. Lincoln: University of Nebraska Press, 1986.
Veldhoen, Bart, 'Psychology and the Middle English Romances: Preliminaries to Readings of *Sir Gawain and the Green Knight, Sir Orfeo*, and *Sir Launfal*', in *Companion to Middle English Romances*, ed. Henk Aertsen and Alasdair A. MacDonald. Amsterdam: VU University Press, 1990, 101–28.
Venuti, Lawrence, 'Translation as a Social Practice: or, The Violence of Translation', in *Translation Horizons. Beyond the Boundaries of Translation Spectrum*, ed. Marilyn Gaddis Rose. Binghampton: State University of New York, 1996, 195–214.
Vinaver, Eugène, *The Rise of Romance*. Oxford: Oxford University Press, 1971.
Vines, Amy N., 'A Woman's "Crafte:" Melior as Lover, Teacher, and Patron in the Middle English *Partonope of Blois*', *Modern Philology* 105 (2007), 245–70.
Wallace, David, ed., *The Cambridge History of Medieval English Literature*. Cambridge: Cambridge University Press, 1999.
Walters, Lori, 'The Poet-Narrator's Address to his Lady as Structural Device in *Partonopeu de Blois*', *Medium Ævum* 61 (1992), 229–41.
Warren, Michelle R., *History on the Edge. Excalibur and the Borders of Britain 1100–1300*. Medieval Cultures 22. Minneapolis: University of Minnesota Press, 2000.
—— 'Translating in the Zone', *New Medieval Literatures* 9 (2007), 191–8.
—— 'Translation', in *Oxford Twenty-First Century Approaches to Literature: Middle English*, ed. Paul Strohm. Oxford: Oxford University Press, 2007, 51–67.
Watson, Nicholas, 'The Politics of Middle English Writing', *The Idea of the Vernacular. An Anthology of Middle English Literary Theory, 1280–1520*, ed. Jocelyn Wogan-Browne, Nicholas Watson, Andrew Taylor and Ruth Evans. University Park: The Pennsylvania State University Press, 1999, 331–52.
Whalen, Logan E., *Marie de France and the Poetics of Memory*. Washington, DC: The Catholic University of America Press, 2008.
Whiting, B. J., 'A Fifteenth Century Chaucerian: The Translator of *Partonope of Blois*', *Medieval Studies* 7 (1945), 40–54.
Windeatt, Barry, 'Chaucer and Fifteenth-Century Romance: *Partonope of Blois*', in *Chaucer Traditions. Studies in Honour of Derek Brewer*, ed. Ruth Morse and Barry Windeatt. Cambridge: Cambridge University Press, 1990, 1–20.
Wittig, Susan, *Stylistic and Narrative Structures in the Middle English Romances*. Austin: University of Texas Press, 1978.
Wogan-Browne, Jocelyn, 'Analytical Survey 5: "Reading is Good Prayer": Recent Research on Female Reading Communities', *New Medieval Literatures* 5 (2002), 229–97.
—— *et al.*, eds., *Language and Culture in Medieval Britain. The French of England c.1100–c.1500*. York: York Medieval Press, 2009.
——, Nicholas Watson, Andrew Taylor and Ruth Evans, eds., *The Idea of the Vernacular. An Anthology of Middle English Literary Theory, 1280–1520*. University Park: The Pennsylvania State University Press, 1999.

Wolf, H. J., 'Partonopeus und die Wikinger', in *Das Epos in der Romania. Festschrift für Dieter Kremers zum 65. Geburtstag*, ed. Susanne Knaller and Edith Mara. Tübingen: Gunter Narr Verlag, 1986, 431–46.

Wülker, R., 'Zu Partanope of Blois', *Anglia* 12 (1890), 607–20.

Zumthor, Paul, *Toward a Medieval Poetics*, trans. Philip Bennett. Minneapolis: University of Minnesota Press, 1992.

Index

adaptation 3, 5, 46, 94, 129
  cultural 21, 51–2, 53, 56, 72 n.45, 142–3
Adler, Alfred 88–9
Aebischer, Paul 72 n.44
agenda 38, 44 n.60, 83, 101, 103
  authorial 129
  cultural 17
  political 45, 128
Althing 19
amplification 61, 85, 88
  cultural 62
Andersen, Lise Præstgaard 117–18, 119
Anglo-Norman 4, 9, 19, 20, 33, 56: *see also* French
  as literary language 14, 167
  decline of 15–17, 36–7, 167
Anglo-Saxons 17
Apuleius 114 n.4, 116 n.9: *see also* Cupid and Psyche myth
  Metamorphoses 114 n.4
Ármann Jakobsson 59 n.19
Arthur, King: *see Sir Launfal* under Chestre, Thomas; *Yvain* under Chrétien de Troyes; *Lanval* under Marie de France
Ashcroft, Bill 35 [35 n.26]
audience 76, 112
  see also Sir Launfal under Chestre, Thomas; *Yvain* under Chrétien de Troyes; *under Lay le Freine*; *Lais* under Marie de France; *under Partalopa saga*; *under Partonope of Blois*; *under Partonopeu de Blois*; public; reader; reading community; *under Rúnzivals þáttr*; *under Strengleikar*; *under* translation; *under Ywain and Gawain*
  English 15–16, 48, 77, 93–5
  Francophone 61, 93–4, 144 n.75
  implied 59
  Nordic 21, 71–5, 91–3, 118, 124–5
  theory of 11–13, 94 n.52, 165–7

authority 2, 11, 147: *see also under Partalopa saga*; *Partonope of Blois*
  cultural 9, 24, 29, 30, 46, 50
  imperial 46, 49–50
  linguistic 11, 20, 49, 50
  literary 10, 20
  political 20, 25, 29
authorship 31, 106, 112, 165, 167–8
  theory of 11

behaviour 51, 109–11, 139: *see also under* translation
  codes of 13, 21, 23, 74, 112, 165
  conceptions of 9–10
  courtly 45, 73, 84, 98–9, 103, 112, 165
  gendered 23, 43, 124, 143–50
  social 29, 44, 73, 78, 106
Baldwin, John W. 44
Barnes, Geraldine 92
Bassnett, Susan 5 n.10
Bennett, Michael 15 n.42
Bergen 28
Bevers saga 22
Blaisdell, Foster W. 83
Blois, House of 128
Blois (place) 147 n.82
Boeve de Haumtone 22
Bödtker, A. Trampe 116–18, 120, 140
Brennu-Njáls saga 64–5, 66 n.34, 69–70
  Gunnarr 64–5
  Kári Sölmundarson 69
  Kolskeggr 65
  Njáll 69
  Otkell 64, 65
  Runólfr 65
  Skammkell 64
Britain 3, 4, 22, 46, 99: *see also* England
Brittany 50
Bruckner, Matilda Tomaryn 79
Busby, Keith 94, 108
Byzantium 128 n.42, 131, 149

Caluwé-Dor, Juliette de 101 n.66
Camille, Michael 145 n.80
Cannon, Christopher 11 n.28, 167
Canute, king of Denmark, Norway and England 17
Charlemagne (historical) 56, 90
capital, cultural 44 n.60, 52 n.79
Cerquiglini, Bernard 7 n.13
chansons de geste 14, 18 n.50, 20, 52 n.79, 70, 72, 166: *see also* Chanson de Roland
    as a genre 56–7, 61–2, 165
    form and language of 59–60, 73
La Chanson de Roland 3, 20, 57, 73–5, 79
    analysis of 58–64, 65–72
    and emotion 65–70
    dating of 56
    Norse version of: *see Rúnzivals þáttr*
    Archbishop 67–8
    Bramimonde 61
    Charlemagne 59, 68
    Oliver 62, 65–6
    Roland 61, 62, 64, 65–6, 67–8, 71
Chaucer, Geoffrey 8 n.16, 38 n.46, 167
Chef d'Oire 147 n.82
Chestre, Thomas, *Sir Launfal* 5, 20, 21, 49, 50–51, 165
    analysis of 39–45
    and audience 41, 51
    dating of 19, 38–9
    historical context of 39
    Arthur, King 41, 42
    Guinevere (Gwenore/Gwennere), Queen 42–3
    Huwe, Sir 45
    Jon, Sir 45
    Launfal, Sir 41, 42–3, 44–5
    Mayor 44–5
    Tryamour, Dame 41
Le Chevalier au Lion: *see* Yvain *under* Chrétien de Troyes
Chrétien de Troyes 21, 87, 92–3, 96, 101
    and *matière* 89, 100, 112
    and *sens* 89, 99, 100
    Erec et Enide 80, 84 n.23
    Le Chevalier de la Charrette 91
    Li Contes del Graal 84 n.23
    works of 80, 83–4, 118 n.16
    Yvain 3, 97, 110, 124, 145 n.79
        analysis of 85–93, 99–101, 104–8
        and audience 85
        and love 84–9, 91–3, 99, 104–8, 111
        and narrative structure 85–9, 92, 103
        dating of 81
        Middle English version of: *see Ywain and Gawain*
        Norse version of: *see Ívens saga*
        translation of 21, 78, 80, 83, 95, 165
        Arthur, King 87, 91
        Calogrenant 87
        Esclados 89, 92
        Gauvain 88–9
        Kex (Kay) 87
        Laudine 85, 88–9, 104, 111
        Laudine and grief 106–8
        Laudine and love 92, 145 n.79
        lion 88, 88–9 n.36, 101
        Lunete 88
        Yvain and character development 85, 88–9, 101, 104–5
        Yvain and love 84, 92, 105, 145 n.79
Clover, Carol 62 n.26
codicology 6
Constantinople 128
Cook, Robert 32 n.31
Cooper, Helen 76 n.1
Copeland, Rita 2, 10, 48
Cotton, Sir Robert 81
Crane, Susan 36 n.40
Crapelet, G.-A. 115
crusade, ideology of 62
culture
    and language 73–5
    and imperialism 24–6, 35–8, 46, 166
    and literature 7–9, 13, 53–4, 122–5
    and translation 1–3, 5, 55, 63–4, 116, 166–8
    as semiotic system 13–14, 21, 51–2, 54–5, 74–5, 78–9
Cupid and Psyche myth 113, 114 n.4, 116 n.9, 128 n.44, 148: *see also* Apuleius

Dunclaw 49
Danes 17
Denmark 4, 17
discourse: *see also under* translation
    cultural 13–14, 61–4, 74–5, 78–9

Index

contestatory 45, 52
definition of 13–14
dominant 35–8
dominance 38, 50
cultural 9, 14 n.38, 20, 24, 29
Doyle, Michael 29

Edwards, Robert R. 100
Eleanor of Aquitaine 14
Eley, Penny 118 n.16, 128
Elís saga 28
encounter, cultural 2–3, 23, 63 n.26, 76, 166, 168
Enders, Jody 18 n.51
England 3, 6
and transmission of texts 18–20, 22, 57, 118–19
history of 25–6, 49–50
language and culture in 14–17, 36–8, 48–50, 164, 166–7
literature in 44, 76, 110, 112, 127 n.40
relations with Norway 17–18
English
co-existence with French 14–15, 20, 36–8, 49–52
definition of 4
as literary language 15–17, 37–8, 50
Erex saga 84 n.23
Eufemia, Queen 18, 82 n.17
Eufemiavisor 117 n.12
Europe 60 n.19
transmission in 24, 116
movement in 24, 49 n.74, 76, 113, 166, 168
Eysteinn I Magnússon, king of Norway 17 n.47

Faroe Islands 4
Ferrante, Joan M. 142
Finlayson, John 109 n.74, 110 n.77
Floire et Blancheflor 117 n.12
Flóres saga ok Blankiflúr 117 n.12
Foote, Peter G. 72 n.44
formation, cultural 2, 166
fornaldarsögur (legendary sagas) 22, 52 n.79
Fourrier, Anthime 117 n.9
France 3, 14, 61, 76 n.1, 112
and transmission of texts 18–20, 118–19, 166–7
literature in 83

French 19, 20, 29, 48: *see also* Anglo-Norman
definition of 4
in England 14–15, 36–8, 49, 51
as literary language 14–15, 167
Friedman, Albert B. 94

Gaelic 38
Gaunt, Simon 14
gender 9, 143, 150, 165: *see also under Partalopa saga*; *Partonope of Blois*; *Partonopeu de Blois*
as construct 10 n.24
Geertz, Clifford 63
Gilbert, Jane 56
Gildea, Joseph 115
Greimas, A. J. 10 n.23
Guddat-Figge, Gisela 95 n.54, 140 n.65
Guillaume de Dole 45, 83
Guillaume de Palerne 45 n.62
Gvímars saga 52 n.79, 62 n.24, 93 n.46: *see also* Guiamars lioð under *Strengleikar*; Guigemar under Marie de France

Haidu, Peter 46
Hákon Hákonarson, king of Norway 17–18, 19, 82 n.17, 103: *see also* Norway
and literary activity 18, 26–9, 57, 82–4, 117–19, 167
Hákon V Magnússon, king of Norway 18, 82 n.17
Hákonar saga Hákonarsonar 19 n.52, 30 n.26
Halliday, M. A. K. 55
Halvorsen, E. F. 5, 59, 70–2
Hamilton, Gayle K. 99
Hanna, Ralph 8
Harðacnut, king of Denmark 17
Haraldr harðráði (the Ruthless), king of Norway 17
Harold Harefoot, king of England 17 n.45
Harrington, Norman T. 94, 107 n.71
Harris, Julian 88
Hasan, Ruqaiya 51
Hastings, battle of 17 n.46
Hazell, Dinah 42
Hebrides 17 n.47
Heimskringla 30 n.26
Helga þáttr Þórissonar 52 n.79

193

Heng, Geraldine 76 n.1
Henry II, king of England 14
Henry III, king of England 15 n.40, 18, 28
Henry VI, king of England 15 n.40
Herr Ivan 82 n.17
Hindman, Sandra 84
Hosington, Brenda B. 96
Hundred Years War 15, 50
Hunt, Tony 89 n.36

Iceland 4, 57, 61
   and transmission of texts 18, 82, 84 n.23, 118–19, 166–7
   history of 19–20
   literature in 21–2, 30 n.26, 118, 167
Icelandic saga: see *Íslendingasögur*
identity 4, 29 n.24, 46 n.64, 54, 56, 145
   and language 38, 48
   cultural 2, 3, 20, 61, 165, 167
   masculine 64–65, 109, 146
ideology 25, 62: *see also under* translation
   and texts 29, 78, 79–80, 84,
   and imperialism 25, 29–30, 83
   courtly 50–1, 76, 78, 93, 112
      and French literature 15, 83–4
      and largesse 44–5
imperialism 9, 20: *see also under* culture; *under* ideology; *under* Norway; post-colonial criticism; *under* translation
   and language 35–8
   cultural 25–6, 29–30, 46, 164–5, 167
   theory of 24–5
Ingham, Patricia Clare 24
Ingham, Richard 37
intent 18, 58, 70, 103, 104
   authorial 11, 19, 21, 99, 136, 167
intentionality 18 n.51
interlacing 88, 100
Íslendingasögur (sagas of Icelanders) 30, 60, 62 n.26, 77, 91, 124
Ívens saga 19, 21, 28, 78, 117 n.12
   analysis of 97–8, 100–1, 103–6, 110–12
   analysis of narrative structure 87, 89–93, 112
   as translation 79–80, 165
   dating of 82–3
   Íven(t) 92, 100, 103
   Lady (Laudine) 92, 110–11, 112
   Lancelot 90

Jackson, Claire M. 146
Jaeger, Stephen C. 78, 84
Jauss, Hans Robert 79 n.7
Jón Vigfússon 83

Kabir, Ananya Jahanara 166 [166 n.1]
Kalinke, Marianne E. 2, 28, 62 n.24, 92–3, 100
Karl Jónsson 30 n.26
Karlamagnús saga 18 n.50, 56–7, 60, 72, 74
Kay, Sarah 8 n.14, 83 n.22, 135, 138, 144, 147 n.82
Kelly, Douglas 100
Ketill Jörundsson, síra 56 n.10
Kjær, Joanna 72 n.44
Knútr 17
Kölbing, Eugen 116 n.9
konungasögur (sagas of kings) 30, 59–60, 72
Konungs skuggsjá 29, 30 n.26
Krueger, Roberta J. 143

Lacy, Norris J. 84, 88, 89 n.36
Lai of Graelent 39 n.47, 43 n.55
lais 14, 42 n.52, 44, 72: *see also* Lais *under* Marie de France
Laskaya, Anne 38 n.46
Lay le Freine 20, 21, 44 n.60, 50, 51–2, 165: *see also* Lai le Fresne *under* Marie de France
   analysis of 45–9
   and audience 45
   dating of 38
   Ash 47
   Hazel 47
lays, Breton 131
Latin 2, 10, 19–20, 36, 38, 48, 56
Latinity 101 n.65
Lawton, David 13, 54, 167 n.2
Leach, Henry Goddard 28

Magnús berfætí (Barelegs), king of Norway 17 n.47
Magnús the Good, king of Norway 17
Magnús saga lagabætis 30 n.26
Mals, Mats 60 n.20
manuscripts (general) 8, 12–13
   English 6–7, 20
   French 84–5, 95 n.55, 116 n.9, 150 n.87
   Icelandic 52 n.79, 62 n.24, 93 n.46

Index

Icelandic and Norse translations 7, 18–20, 56–7, 82, 84 n.23, 117 n.12
Norwegian 7, 18
transmission of 7, 18, 119, 121, 139–41, 165, 168
manuscripts
Ormsbók (lost MS) 83, 93 n.45, 118 n.14, 120 n.23
ARNAMAGNÆAN INSTITUTE, COPENHAGEN:
  AM 533 4to 119–20, 130
  AM 666b 4to 27
  Paper MS no. 180d fol. 56–7
  Paper MS 531 4to 56–7
  Vellum MS no. 180a fol. 56–7
  Vellum MS no. 180c fol. 56–7
BIBLIOTHÈQUE DE L'ARSENAL, PARIS:
  Arsenal 2986 150 n.87
BIBLIOTHÈQUE NATIONALE, PARIS:
  Fr. 368 116 n.9
  Guiot MS (f.fr. 794) 81, 85
BODLEIAN LIBRARY, OXFORD:
  Digby 23 56, 57, 58, 67
  Douce Fragments e. 40 (early printed book) 38–9 n.47
  Eng. Poet. C.3 120
  Lat. Misc. B.17 120
  Malone 541 (early printed book) 38 n.47
  Rawl. C.86 38 n.47
  Rawl. Poet. 14 120, 140
  University College 188 120, 127 n.40, 139–40, 147 n.82
BRITISH LIBRARY, LONDON:
  Add. 4857 83 n.20
  Add. 27897 38 n.47
  Add. 35288 120, 127 n.40, 139–41, 167
  Cotton Caligula A.ii 38
  Cotton Galba E.ix 81, 94–5
  Harley 978 26, 31 n.29, 33 n.32, 42 n.52
  Lansdowne 388 20 n.54
CAMBRIDGE UNIVERSITY LIBRARY, CAMBRIDGE:
  Kk v.30 38 n.47
LANDSBÓKASAFN-HÁSKÓLA-BÓKASAFN, REYKJAVÍK:
  JS 27 fol. 119

NATIONAL LIBRARY OF SCOTLAND, EDINBURGH:
  Auchinleck MS (Adv. 19.2.1) 38
PRIVATE COLLECTION (TOSHIYUKI TAKAMIYA):
  Takamiya 32 (*olim* Penrose 10, *olim* Vale Royal, *olim* Delamere) 120
ROYAL LIBRARY, STOCKHOLM:
  Holm 6 4to 82–3, 93 n.45, 112
  Holm 46 fol. 82–3, 93 n.45, 112
  Papp. fol. nr. 46 119–20, 130
STOFNUN ÁRNA MAGNÚSSONAR, REYKJAVÍK:
  AM 489 4to 82–3, 93 n.45, 112
UPPSALA UNIVERSITY LIBRARY, UPPSALA:
  Codex De la Gardie 4–7 27, 33 n.32, 93
Marches 50
Marie de France 3, 31 n.29, 32, 46
  Bisclavret 35, 52 n.79
  Eliduc 26–7
  Guigemar 30–3, 41, 42 n.52, 52 n.79, 62 n.24
  Lai le Fresne 38, 46–8
  Lais 3, 20–1, 24, 38, 79, 83, 165–7
    analysis of 30–5, 46, 73–4
    and audience 44, 42 n.79, 39
    dating of 26
    Middle English versions of: *see Lay le Freine*; *Sir Launfal* under Thomas Chestre
    Old Norse version of: *see Strengleikar*
  Lanval 38–45, 49, 50, 51–2
    Arthur, King 42, 42 n.52
    Lanval 41–3, 42 n.52
    Maiden 42–3
  Laüstic 33–4
Mehl, Dieter 5, 44, 94
memory 8, 62, 94
  cultural 52
Middle English: *see* English
Middleton, Anne 12, 94 n.52
Midlands 94, 95
Minnis, A. J. 11
modification: *see* transformation
Möttuls saga 28
mouvance 7, 23, 141, 164–6, 168

narrative grammar 10 n.23, 80

195

narrative structures 77–80, 165: *see also Yvain under* Chrétien de Troyes; *under Ívens saga*; *under Ywain and Gawain*
narrative theory 10
New Medievalism 7–8, 9
New Philology 8 n.14
Nichols, Stephen G. 9
Njal's saga: *see Brennu-Njáls saga*
Norman Conquest 17, 166
  colonial implications of 36
  effects of 14, 25–6
Norse 19, 33, 37–8
  definition of 4
Norsemen 17
Norway 21–2, 25 n.6, 44, 49, 117–9: *see also* Hákon Hákonarson, king of Norway
  and imperialism 29–30, 50, 167
  and transmission of texts 14, 18–20, 55, 57, 84 n.23, 166–7
  history of 17, 27
  language and culture in 4, 38–9
  literary activity in 27–30, 72, 82
  relations with England 17–18

Óláfr Magnússon, king of Norway 17 n.47
Óláfr the Peaceful, king of Norway 17 n.47
Old Norse: *see* Norse
Orkneys 17 n.47

Parcevals saga 84 n.23
Partalopa saga 18, 22, 116, 135, 138, 141: *see also Partonopeu de Blois*
  analysis of 121–30, 143, 147 nn.82, 84, 149–51
  and audience 122, 124–5
  and authority 126, 135
  and gender 121–6
  and maiden-king lore 121–3
  and concept of masculinity 123–5
  and female power 125–6, 135
  dating of 117–20
  summary of 121
  Barbarus 150–1 n.87
  Marmoria (Melior) 121, 122–6, 127, 129–30, 135, 142, 150
  Partalopi (Partonope) 121, 123–6, 130, 135, 147 n.84, 150
  Urækia 150–1 n.87

Partonope of Blois 116: *see also Partonopeu de Blois*
  short version (fragment)
    analysis of 121–2, 126–32, 143, 150–1
    and audience 127, 130
    and gender 131–3
    dating of 120–1
    Melior 120–1, 127, 129, 131–2
    Partonope 121, 127, 131–2
  long version
    analysis of 123–4, 125, 128–9, 135–51
    and audience 138
    and authority 141, 144–9, 151
    and gender 136–9, 144–50
    and female sexuality 136–9, 141–3
    and manuscript transmission 139–41
    dating of 120
    king of France 136
    Melior 128, 129, 137–42, 144–7, 149
    Partonope 123, 129–30, 135, 136–40, 142, 144–7, 149
    Partonope's mother 138, 144, 147
Partonopeu de Blois (French text and general references) 3, 21–2, 165
  analysis of 123–6, 128–39, 141–4, 146–51
  and audience 115, 118, 128, 132, 135–7, 150
  and gender 131–5, 138
  and readership (all versions) 113, 115, 124, 128–30, 138, 150
  critical history of 115–16
  dating of 118
  Middle English version of: *see Partonope of Blois*
  Norse version of: *see Partalopa saga*
  summary of 113–5
  versions of 21, 23, 113–19, 141, 143, 150–1, 167
  Armans 114
  Bishop 114
  Gaudin 114, 150 n.87
  king of France 113, 133, 150 n.87
  Melior 113–15, 126, 129, 131, 144, 146

seduction of 132–5, 138–9, 141
Partonopeu 113–15, 129–31, 141,
144, 146, 150 n.87
and concept of manhood 123–
6, 132–9
Partonopeu's mother 114, 138
Persewis 114
Sornegur 114
Urrake 114, 150 n.87
perspective 63
Piers Plowman 109
Plantagenet dynasty 128
post-colonial criticism 9, 20, 24–5, 166:
see also imperialism
application of 46
Pseudo-Turpin 20 n.54, 72 n.44
public 59, 60, 72, 95, 128, 150, 168:
see also audience; reader; reading
community
theory of 12–13, 94 n.52
Powers, Rosemary 52 n.79

reader 8, 84–5, 98, 107: *see also* audience; public; reading community;
under translation
Francophone 33, 42 n.52, 103, 128,
144 n.75
implicit 11, 42, 87, 105, 110, 136
Middle English 15–16, 20, 88
modern 13, 38, 54, 88
Nordic 51, 56, 61, 90–1
theory of 11–13, 94 n.52
Reader-Response Criticism 11 n.26
reading community 21, 29, 118, 128–9,
143: *see also* audience, reader; *under*
translation
and cultural evidence 6–7, 55, 77,
116, 164, 167–8
definition of 11–13
Middle English 14–17, 44, 48–51,
94, 131, 141
Old Norse 49, 61, 83, 104, 111, 122
Renart, Jean 45
L'escoufle 45 n.62
*Romance of the Rose or Guillaume
de Dole* 45, 83
Reynolds, Suzanne 11
Rezeptionsästhetik (Reception Aesthetics) 11 n.26
riddarasögur: *see* Icelandic *under*
romance
Robert, A. C. M. 115

Robert, Brother 28
Roðbert, ábóti (Abbot) 28
Röder, Gabriele 59, 71
romance 20, 41, 84, 124, 143
and narrative material 78–9, 88–9,
147
as genre 14, 76–9, 83, 113, 143–5
French 14–15, 21, 83 n.22, 135, 144
n.75, 166–7
Icelandic 2, 19, 21–2, 70, 83, 122,
167
Middle English 39, 44, 98, 108, 110,
112, 138
Norse translations of 18, 27, 92–3,
100–1, 118
romanz (as language) 4 n.5
Rothwell, W. 48 n.68
Rowe, Elizabeth Ashman 51 n.79
Rúnzivals þáttr 5, 21, 55–6, 79, 91: *see
also Karlamagnús saga*
analysis of 57–64, 66–74
analysis of emotion 66–70
analysis of form and style 57–61
and audience 59, 62, 69, 71–5
dating of 56–7
Archbishop (erkibyskup) 66–7
Charlemagne (Karlamagnús) 69
Roland (Rollant) 66–7

Saga af Tristram og Ísodd 117
Saga af Tristram og Ísönd: *see Tristrams saga ok Ísöndar*
Sagas of Icelanders: *see Íslendingasögur*
Salisbury, Eve 38 n.46
Sanders, Christopher 22
Saunders, Corinne 76 n.1
Saxo Grammaticus, *Gesta Danorum* 74
n.49
Scandinavia 3, 58, 69, 71, 74, 76,
165–166
Schleich, Gustav 95 n.55, 107 n.71
semiotics 47, 101, 104, 164–5: *see also
under* culture
Sigurðr Jórsalafari (the Crusader), king
of Norway 17 n.47
Simons, Penny 118 n.16, 128
Sir Gawain and the Green Knight 110
Sir Landevale 38 n.47, 39, 41 n.51, 44
n.60: *see also Sir Launfal under*
Chestre, Thomas
Sir Launfal: *see under* Chestre, Thomas
Snell-Hornby, Mary 55, 63

197

Snorri Sturluson 19 n. 52, 30 n.26
Song of Roland (Middle English) 20 n.54
space 50, 79, 145–9
Spearing, A. C. 5, 49, 145–6
Speculum Regale 29, 30 n.26
Stahuljak, Zrinka 54
Stamford Bridge, battle of 17
Stock, Brian 12, 79 n.7
Strengleikar 44 n.60, 46–9, 79, 165
    analysis of 30–5, 72–5
    and audience 30, 33, 52 n.79, 73
    Bisclarets lioð 35, 52 n.79
    dating of 19, 26–8
    Eskia 47
    Guiamars lioð 30–3, 93 n.46
    Janual 52 n.79
    Laustiks lioð 33–4, 51
Sturla Þórðarson 19 n.52, 30 n.26
subversion 9, 79, 103, 128, 164–165, 168
Sverrir Sigurðsson, king of Norway 17, 27
Sverris saga 30 n.26
Sweden 4
Sweyn II, king of Denmark 17 n.46

text 6
    as cultural evidence 13
    as object 11 n.28
    as product 7–8
    concept of in Middle Ages 8
textual community 12, 79 n.7, 151: *see also* reading community
textuality 8, 21
Thomas of Brittany 18 n.50
    Tristan 18 n.50, 101 n.65
Tiodielis saga 52 n.79
transformation 1, 23, 49, 72
    and language 50–2, 71, 166–7
    cultural 2–3, 7, 10, 50–2, 112, 116
    narrative 77–8, 93, 119, 168
    textual 7, 72, 116, 136
translatio 8, 164
translatability 55
translation: *see also under* culture
    and audience 5, 9, 54–5, 63–4, 77–80, 150–1
    and cultural exchange 1–3, 5–10, 14–20, 22–3, 164–8
    and ideology 99, 132, 142–3, 150, 165
    and imperialism 24, 29–30, 35
    and reader 10, 35, 63, 79–80

    and reading community 3, 52, 79, 132, 141–3
    and rhetoric 2, 48
    as discourse 14
    as interpretation 2, 55, 164–5
    as concept 164–5
    medieval concept of 5, 48, 72, 116, 164
    Middle English (general) 5, 9, 15–17, 95, 166, 168
    Old Norse (general) 9, 12, 70, 76–77, 90, 166–8
    of behaviour 54–6, 63–70, 143, 168
    theory of 53–5
    vernacular 2, 10–11
transmission 132, 143, 168: *see also under* England; Iceland; manuscript
    and cultural dominance 20, 29–30, 35
    and ideological structures 63–4, 77
    and modifications 95, 112
    cultural 19, 21–3, 150, 165
    textual 20–3, 24, 82, 116, 121, 142, 165–6
Tristan 18 n.50, 101 n.65
Tristan (legend of) 117, 124
Tristrams saga ok Ísöndar 18 n.50, 27, 28, 73 n.48, 101 n.65, 117
Turpin, *Vita Caroli Magni* 20 n.54, 72 n.44
troubadours 14
Tveitane, Mattias 32 n.31

Uri, S. P. 115

Vance, Eugene 14, 61, 89 n.36
variance 7 n. 13
vernacular 24, 30, 166–8: *see also under* translation
    in England 6, 14–15, 76, 103
    writing in 7, 37–9, 58–9, 61, 116, 130
Vinaver, Eugène 88
voice 31–3, 40–3, 46, 59, 103, 167

Wales 87
Warren, Michelle R. 46 n.65, 54
Watson, Nicholas 38
Welsh 38
Western Isles 17 n.47
William the Conqueror, king of England 17 nn.46, 47
Williams, Deanne 166 [166 n.1]

Index

Wogan-Browne, Jocelyn 11 [11 n.29], 12 n.30

Yvain: *see under* Chrétien de Troyes
Ywain and Gawain 5, 21, 78, 79, 80, 87, 165
   analysis of 95–110
   and audience 88 n.36, 93–5, 98, 106, 108–10, 112
   and narrative structure 101–10, 112
   and 'throwth' 99, 103, 105–6, 112
   dating of 19, 81–2
   Alundyne 99, 102, 106–9
   Arthur, King 98–9
   Gawain 99, 102
   lion 101–2
   Lunete 102
   Ywain 99, 101–2, 105–9

Zumthor, Paul 7

www.ingramcontent.com/pod-product-compliance
Lightning Source LLC
Chambersburg PA
CBHW070805230426
43665CB00017B/2495